Rental Housing
in the 1980s

ANTHONY DOWNS

Rental Housing in the 1980s

THE BROOKINGS INSTITUTION
Washington, D.C.

Copyright 1983 by
THE BROOKINGS INSTITUTION
1775 Massachusetts Avenue, N.W., Washington, D.C. 20036

Library of Congress Cataloging in Publication data:

Downs, Anthony.
  Rental housing in the 1980s.
  Includes bibliographical references and index.
  1. Rental housing—United States.   I. Title.
HD7288.85.U6D68   1983   333.33'8   83-10124
ISBN 0-8157-1922-1
ISBN 0-8157-1921-3 (pbk.)

9 8 7 6 5 4 3 2 1

Board of Trustees
Robert V. Roosa
Chairman
Andrew Heiskell
Vice Chairman;
Chairman, Executive Committee
Louis W. Cabot
Vice Chairman
Vincent M. Barnett, Jr.
Barton M. Biggs
Frank T. Cary
A. W. Clausen
William T. Coleman, Jr.
Lloyd N. Cutler
Thomas Donahue
Charles W. Duncan, Jr.
George M. Elsey
Robert F. Erburu
Hanna H. Gray
Robert D. Haas
Philip M. Hawley
Roger W. Heyns
James T. Lynn
Donald F. McHenry
Bruce K. MacLaury
Robert S. McNamara
Arjay Miller
Herbert P. Patterson
Donald S. Perkins
J. Woodward Redmond
Charles W. Robinson
James D. Robinson III
Ralph S. Saul
Henry B. Schacht
Roger D. Semerad
Gerard C. Smith
Howard R. Swearer
Morris Tanenbaum
Phyllis A. Wallace

Honorary Trustees
Eugene R. Black
Robert D. Calkins
Edward W. Carter
Bruce B. Dayton
Douglas Dillon
Huntington Harris
John E. Lockwood
William McC. Martin, Jr.
H. Chapman Rose
Robert Brookings Smith
Sydney Stein, Jr.

THE BROOKINGS INSTITUTION is an independent organization devoted to nonpartisan research, education, and publication in economics, government, foreign policy, and the social sciences generally. Its principal purposes are to aid in the development of sound public policies and to promote public understanding of issues of national importance.

The Institution was founded on December 8, 1927, to merge the activities of the Institute for Government Research, founded in 1916, the Institute of Economics, founded in 1922, and the Robert Brookings Graduate School of Economics and Government, founded in 1924.

The Board of Trustees is responsible for the general administration of the Institution, while the immediate direction of the policies, program, and staff is vested in the President, assisted by an advisory committee of the officers and staff. The by-laws of the Institution state: "It is the function of the Trustees to make possible the conduct of scientific research, and publication, under the most favorable conditions, and to safeguard the independence of the research staff in the pursuit of their studies and in the publication of the results of such studies. It is not a part of their function to determine, control, or influence the conduct of particular investigations or the conclusions reached."

The President bears final responsibility for the decision to publish a manuscript as a Brookings book. In reaching his judgment on the competence, accuracy, and objectivity of each study, the President is advised by the director of the appropriate research program and weighs the views of a panel of expert outside readers who report to him in confidence on the quality of the work. Publication of a work signifies that it is deemed a competent treatment worthy of public consideration but does not imply endorsement of conclusions or recommendations.

The Institution maintains its position of neutrality on issues of public policy in order to safeguard the intellectual freedom of the staff. Hence interpretations or conclusions in Brookings publications should be understood to be solely those of the authors and should not be attributed to the Institution, to its trustees, officers, or other staff members, or to the organizations that support its research.

Foreword

THE IMPORTANCE of rental housing in the United States has long been eclipsed by the value Americans place on homeownership, even though over one-third of all households are renters. In the 1980s, however, rental housing will become more significant, as the number and proportion of renters rise. These increases will not occur because more people will really prefer renting, but because they will find they cannot afford to own their homes.

The resulting increase in demand for rental housing will not at first be matched by a corresponding increase in the construction of new rental units. Development of such units reached record levels in the housing boom of the early 1970s, but fell by about half in the late 1970s and dropped even lower in the housing depression of the early 1980s. These declines occurred because both construction and operation of rental units were not profitable enough to justify creating new ones without substantial government subsidies. New rental construction will not become adequately profitable until rents rise far above their current levels.

Greater demand for rental housing combined with little new construction will soon push rents up rapidly wherever they are free from political constraints. But the impact of such rent escalation on low- and moderate-income renters—and on middle- and upper-income renters, who are better organized to resist—will create strong pressures on many local governments to control rents. Controls protect renters from higher costs in the short run, but experience shows they are detrimental to the rental supply—and thus harmful to renters—in the long run.

The prospect of intensifying political struggles over rental housing makes it important for policymakers to have a clear understanding of housing markets and the range of alternative policy responses to the impending shortage. Yet most analyses of housing have neglected rental markets and have not taken account of the changes in real estate finance that occurred in 1980. In that year the financial community shifted its expectations about inflation and radically increased the nominal and real rates of interest it demanded from real estate borrowers. Although inflation has abated considerably since then, high interest rates are likely to dampen housing demand for many years to come.

In this book Anthony Downs summarizes the current state of rental housing markets and analyzes past trends in rents, occupancy, and construction. He also describes the recent shift in real estate finance and considers its implications for rental housing and homeownership. Drawing on the most current data available, he projects the demand for and the likely production of both rental and owner-occupied housing to the year 2000. He then develops a financial model of rental housing profitability. In the final chapter and appendixes, he evaluates policy alternatives for coping with possible shortages of rental housing.

This book began as part of a study of urban decline carried out at Brookings by Katharine L. Bradbury, Anthony Downs, and Kenneth A. Small which produced two earlier Brookings books: *Neighborhoods and Urban Development* (1981) and *Urban Decline and the Future of American Cities* (1982). Downs's analysis evolved into a third book over a three-year period. The project received support from the Ford Foundation and the Departments of Transportation and Housing and Urban Development, as well as the Brookings Institution.

Anthony Downs is a senior fellow in the Brookings Economic Studies program. He is especially grateful to Katharine L. Bradbury for her cogent critiques; to John Yinger and Robert Sheehan for their reviews of the manuscript; to Jacquelyn G. Sanks for typing it; to Penelope Harpold and Judith Kleinman for verifying the facts; to Carol Cole Rosen for editing it; and to Ward and Silvan Indexing for making the index.

The views expressed in this book are those of the author and should not be ascribed to the persons or organizations whose assistance is acknowledged above, or to the trustees, officers, or other staff members of the Brookings Institution.

BRUCE K. MAC LAURY
President

June 1983
Washington, D.C.

Contents

Introduction and Summary ... 1
  Current Trends in Rental Housing *2*
  The Importance of Profitability *3*
  Housing Values and the Rent Gap *3*
  Future Demand for Rental Housing *7*
  Future Supply of Rental Housing *7*
  A Framework for Public Policies *8*
  Further Adjustments for Households *12*

1. Some Basic Facts about Rental Housing ... 13
  The Characteristics of Rental Housing *13*
  Some Important Traits of Renters *21*

2. Recent Trends in Rents ... 27
  Who Is Being Injured? *31*
  Why Haven't Rents Increased Faster? *32*
  How Has Inflation Affected Rental Housing? *38*
  How Has the Rent Gap Affected Rental Housing? *40*

3. Future Availability of Capital ... 43
  Capital Flows into Housing during the 1970s *43*
  The Failure of Lenders to Anticipate Inflation *45*
  Favorable Borrowing Terms in the 1970s *45*
  Advantages of Housing over Alternative Investments *48*
  Rental Property's Relative Disadvantage in Attracting Capital *49*
  Household Savings in the 1970s *51*
  The Revolution in Real Estate Finance *54*
  Future Effects of Higher Real Capital Costs *58*

4. Future Demand for Rental Housing   62
Need versus Demand 63
Rental Demand to Accommodate Population Growth 64
Rental Demand Overall 69

5. Recent Changes in Housing Supply   73
Changes in the Inventory of Rental Housing 73
Changes in the Inventory of Ownership Housing 80
Net Replacement Rates 84

6. Future Profitability of Rental Housing   92
Influences on Market Value 92
Influences on Profitability 95
The Refinancing Problem 97
A Model for Profitability and Market Value 100
Why Rental Housing Has Been Profitable despite Lagging Rents 109
Why Profitability Is Changing 113
Future Profitability and Market Value 114

7. Future Housing Construction and Potential Shortfalls   117
Projected New Housing Construction 117
Projected Demand for New Housing Construction 119
Comparing Future Construction and Demand 121
Avoiding Shortfalls through Other Means 126
Market Adjustments to Potential Shortfalls 127

8. Future Rental Housing Policies   131
The Tension between Supply and Demand Objectives 133
The Importance of Federal Policies 135
The Limitations of Federal Policies 141
Desirable Federal Policies 142
Desirable Local Policies 147
The Future of Rental Housing 149

Appendixes   153
A. Projecting Number, Type, and Tenure of Households 153
B. Possible Federal Policies on Rental Housing 165
C. Possible Local Policies on Rental Housing 181

Index   197

Tables

1-1. Housing Inventory, 1970 and 1980	15
1-2. Occupied Housing Units, by Type of Tenure, Selected Years, 1970–80	16
1-3. Housing Starts, by Type of Unit, Selected Periods, 1970–80	17
1-4. Housing Tenure, by Type of Household, 1970 and 1980	24
2-1. Indexes of Residential Rents, Selected Years, 1960–80	30
2-2. Income and Rent Increases, 1973–79	32
2-3. Annual Increase in Renter-Occupied Units, Selected Years, 1970–79	41
3-1. Mortgage Interest Rates on Loans Made in 1951–75	47
4-1. Projections of the Number of Households, Selected Years, 1980–2000	65
4-2. Projections of the Increase in Households, Selected Periods, 1980–2000	65
4-3. High-Growth Projections of the Number of Households, by Type of Tenure, Selected Years, 1980–2000	66
4-4. Low-Growth Projections of the Number of Households, by Type of Tenure, Selected Years, 1980–2000	67
4-5. High-Growth Projections of the Increase in Households, by Type of Tenure, Selected Periods, 1980–2000	68
4-6. Low-Growth Projections of the Increase in Households, by Type of Tenure, Selected Periods, 1980–2000	69
4-7. Vacancy Rates, Selected Years, 1970–80	70
4-8. High-Growth Projections of the Housing Inventory, Selected Years, 1980–2000	71
4-9. Low-Growth Projections of the Housing Inventory, Selected Years, 1980–2000	72
5-1. Housing Inventory, by Type of Unit, Selected Years, 1970–79	74
5-2. Multifamily Housing Starts, by Type of Unit, Selected Years, 1970–79	75
5-3. New Construction of Rental Housing, 1970–80	77
5-4. Average Annual Change in the Rental Housing Inventory, 1974–79	81
5-5. New Construction of Ownership Housing, 1970–80	82
5-6. Average Annual Change in the Ownership Housing Inventory, 1974–79	83
5-7. Net Replacement of Housing Units, Selected Periods, 1950–78	86
5-8. Annual Net Replacement Rates, by Type of Unit, Selected Periods, 1950–78	87
5-9. Annual Net Replacement as a Percentage of the Housing Inventory	89
5-10. Projections of New Housing Construction Needed for Replacement with Low Net Replacement Rates, Selected Periods, 1980–2000	89

5-11.	Projections of New Housing Construction Needed for Replacement with High Net Replacement Rates, Selected Periods, 1980–2000	90
6-1.	Estimated Market Values for Rental Units, Based on Current-Year Interest Rates, 1960–80	104
6-2.	Estimated Market Values for Rental Units, Based on Weighted-Average Interest Rates, 1960–80	105
6-3.	Estimated Monthly Rent, Selected Years, 1960–80	106
7-1.	Projections of Annual New Housing Construction, 1980–90	119
7-2.	Projections of Demand for New Housing Construction with Low Net Replacement Rates, Selected Periods, 1980–2000	120
7-3.	Projections of Potential Shortfalls in Rental Housing, 1980–90	122
7-4.	Projections of Potential Shortfalls in Ownership Housing, 1980–90	124
8-1.	Ownership of Rental Housing Units, 1979	134
A-1.	Original and Adjusted Series B Projections of Households, Selected Years, 1980–95	154
A-2.	High-Growth and Low-Growth Projections of Households, Selected Years, 1980–2000	158
A-3.	High-Growth and Low-Growth Projections of the Increase in Households, Selected Periods, 1980–2000	158
A-4.	Series B Projections and Actual Percentage of Households, by Type, Selected Years, 1970–95	159
A-5.	Series B Projections and Actual Change in Households, by Type, Selected Periods, 1970–2000	160
A-6.	Low-Growth Projections of Percentage Change in Households, by Type, Selected Periods, 1980–2000	160
A-7.	High-Growth Projections of the Increase in Households, by Type, Selected Periods, 1980–2000	161
A-8.	Low-Growth Projections of the Increase in Households, by Type, Selected Periods, 1980–2000	161
A-9.	High-Growth Projections of Households, by Type, Selected Years, 1980–2000	162
A-10.	Low-Growth Projections of Households, by Type, Selected Years, 1980–2000	162
A-11.	Renting among Husband-and-Wife Households, Selected Years, 1970–80	163
B-1.	Evaluation of Possible Federal Policies on Rental Housing	166
C-1.	Evaluation of Possible Local Policies on Rental Housing	182

CONTENTS

Figures

1-1. Occupied Rental Units, by Size of Structure, 1980 — 14
1-2. Growth of the Housing Inventory, by Type of Tenure, 1970–80 — 15
1-3. Homeowners as a Percentage of All Households, Selected Years, 1920–80 — 16
1-4. Sources of Net Additions to the Housing Inventory, Selected Periods, 1950–80 — 18
1-5. Age of Housing Units, by Type of Tenure, 1980 — 20
1-6. Household Size, by Type of Tenure, 1980 — 23
1-7. Percentage Change in Housing Units and Occupants, 1970–80 — 24
1-8. Renters, by Type of Household, 1970 and 1980 — 25
1-9. Changes in the Composition of Renting Households, 1970–80 — 26

Introduction and Summary

WHAT IS the future of rental housing in the United States? Most people in the housing industry believe there is a worsening shortage of such housing, soon to become a crisis. They point to the low vacancy rates, especially in certain near-downtown markets such as Manhattan's East Side and Chicago's Near North Side, and to the drastic decline in the building of new unsubsidized multifamily rental housing in the last half of the 1970s and the early 1980s. Moreover, they argue, conversion to condominium ownership has removed thousands of units from the rental supply. Many communities have adopted rent controls to protect low-income tenants from rising rents.

Some housing experts believe the rental housing shortage is so severe the federal government should subsidize the construction of new rental units for middle-income households.[1] Otherwise, they claim, the private, unsubsidized rental housing market in the United States will rapidly fade away, as it has in Great Britain. And millions of existing rental units will deteriorate because of overcrowding and neglect.

Other housing experts, including most academics and President Reagan's top appointees to the Department of Housing and Urban Development,[2] say there is no shortage of rental housing. They see no justification for subsidizing new rental units for people who are not poor. If a rental housing shortage really existed, they argue, rents would be

    1. Lawrence Simon, assistant secretary of housing and urban development for housing in the Carter administration, strongly promoted this idea.
    2. See John C. Weicher, Kevin E. Villani, and Elizabeth A. Roistacher, eds., *Rental Housing: Is There a Crisis?* (Urban Institute, 1981).

soaring. But residential rents have gone up much more slowly than prices in general since the early 1960s. Few unsubsidized rental units are being built because there is no real demand for them. Rather, almost everyone who can afford new housing prefers to own instead of rent because of the overwhelming tax advantages and other benefits of homeownership. Hence, if public policies on housing need to be changed, those changes should reduce the relative advantages of homeownership, not subsidize the building of more rental units.

Which of these views is correct?[3] Or is another perspective superior to both? And what does the "true" perspective reveal about the role of rental housing in sheltering the nation? The answers are vital to private behavior and public policies concerning housing.

This volume tries to answer those questions, based on the data and analysis available in early 1983. Although I talked to many rental housing developers and academic experts, the study relies on empirical work done by others, rather than on original surveys or other data collection.

Current Trends in Rental Housing

Rental housing sheltered about 28.6 million U.S. households in 1980—over one-third of all households.[4] Eight out of nine occupied rental units are provided by private owners for profit; the ninth is publicly subsidized. Private rental markets are dominated by small-scale operators. About 60 percent of all rental units are in structures with fewer than five units, and a third of these are single-family homes. The rental housing inventory increased 21 percent from 1970 to 1980, but the owner-occupied inventory increased 30 percent.

Most American households believe that buying their own home is the best use of their wealth and the most effective easily available hedge against future inflation. Therefore, more and more households with economic means have become homeowners. The number of husband-

---

3. This dichotomy in prevailing attitudes toward rental housing was formulated by Kevin Villani in a paper presented in December 1980 at a conference on rental housing in Washington, D.C., sponsored by the U.S. Department of Housing and Urban Development.

4. This is the total number of renter-occupied units counted in the decennial census of 1980. It is somewhat larger than the number derived from the Annual Housing Surveys for 1973 through 1979 conducted by the Department of Housing and Urban Development and the Bureau of the Census. This book relies mainly on Annual Housing Survey data because far more complete tabulations of that information were available when it was written.

INTRODUCTION AND SUMMARY

and-wife households that rent, for example, declined 21.1 percent from 1970 to 1979, though the total number of such households rose 8.2 percent. Their shift out of renting has left the overall renting population with a higher fraction of households that have low earnings. Among these are households headed by women, which now constitute over 40 percent of all renters, the largest single group. The average income of female-headed renting households is less than half that of husband-and-wife renting households. Thus the future rental housing market will be increasingly constrained by the low purchasing power of tenants. However, higher real borrowing costs will probably slow the shift to homeownership. Rental housing will continue to perform a major role in U.S. housing markets for decades.

The Importance of Profitability

The quality and quantity of future housing services provided by private owners will depend on the profitability of such housing. If existing units are profitable enough for owners to afford adequate maintenance, the average quality of those units may rise, as it has since the early 1950s. Potential profitability will also stimulate the building of new rental units to help replace the older ones removed from the market each year. But if profitability is inadequate, owners will be unable to earn reasonable rates of return on any added capital they spend on maintenance. Hence many will not make such investments, and the rental inventory will deteriorate. Similarly, developers and investors will not create new rental units if they cannot get competitive rates of return on the required capital.

Profitability is not evenly distributed through the rental inventory. It is least adequate in low-income neighborhoods within large cities; future deterioration is most likely there. Profitability is much greater in high-income neighborhoods, such as those in many newer suburbs.

Housing Values and the Rent Gap

From the early 1960s until 1982, residential rents did not increase as fast as consumer income, operating costs, or construction costs. This was true even after correcting for substantial underestimation of rental costs by the consumer price index. The best available estimate is that real rent levels *fell* about 8.4 percent from 1960 to 1980, or roughly 4.2 percent each decade.[5]

As a result of this gap between costs and rental income, rents would have to be much higher than they are now to make creation of new rental properties economically feasible. Construction costs will surely not fall in the future, though interest rates might come down. Hence rents must rise faster than prices in general for some time before construction of new unsubsidized rental units takes place.

In fact, rents would have to rise tremendously just to support the past real values of rental properties—*if* their real market values depended solely on the earnings derived from their rents. In 1980 rents would have had to be 77 percent higher than they actually were to support real market values equivalent to those in 1960 or 30 percent higher to support such values equivalent to those in 1970.

Putting that conclusion another way, the real value of rental housing properties in the United States *sustainable from rents alone* appears to have fallen substantially since 1960—perhaps by 50 percent or more. This enormous drop results from much faster increases in operating costs and interest rates than rents. How closely actual market prices have followed this pattern cannot be determined, since no accurate data exist covering rental housing prices for the entire nation. However, recent data from the Seattle area tend to validate the model used to derive these conclusions. Nevertheless, equity investments in rental housing seem to have been very profitable until 1980, judging from investors' experiences.

This paradox results from four factors other than current net operating income (rents less operating expenses).

1. Tax shelter helped offset low net operating income because deductible losses benefit high-bracket investors.

2. Leverage, the advantage gained by borrowing most of the cost of each investment, magnified the positive effects of depreciation deductions and increases in property values during the inflationary 1970s.

3. Low real rates of interest occurred in the late 1960s and throughout the 1970s because lenders failed to foresee rising inflation.

---

5. Ira S. Lowry, "Inflation Indexes for Rental Housing," working draft WD-1081-HUD (Rand Corporation, May 1981). Unlike the rent component of the consumer price index, Lowry's index measures gross rent, including fuel and utility bills, and it takes account of the declining quality of rental units.

INTRODUCTION AND SUMMARY

4. Anticipated appreciation resulted in many cases from the possibility of converting rental units to condominiums. It was also stimulated by a rising belief among most investors that real estate was a good hedge against inflation.

All four factors helped raise yields on equity investments in rental units far above their current earnings from rents. That persuaded investors to pay higher prices for such units than could be justified solely from their rent-based earnings.

Moreover, in the late 1970s, apartment syndicators were skimming the cream off the rental market. They built small units with high annual turnover rates, mainly in fast-growing areas. Hence they were able to raise rents rapidly and to pass most operating cost increases through to their tenants. Consequently, market values of their units rose faster than the average for the nation's rental inventory, which includes millions of much older units.

In 1980 and 1981 high interest rates changed three of these four factors in ways adverse to the ownership of rental housing. These changes are likely to persist for several years and perhaps throughout the 1980s. They reduce the past beneficial effects on equity yields and market prices of leverage, low real interest rates, and anticipated future appreciation. Therefore, future yields and prices of rental housing will depend more on profits from current operations, thus on rents.

The real cost of capital for housing and other real estate will be much higher in the 1980s than in the 1970s. Fearing more inflation, lenders are demanding higher nominal rates. Many have also shifted to flexible financial instruments that transfer most of the risk of inflation onto borrowers. Hence the low real rates caused by unanticipated inflation will no longer be available to aid real estate investors, no matter what inflation rates actually occur.

Higher real capital costs will also make homeownership harder to attain. Higher interest rates can no longer be offset by stretching out loan terms or increasing the borrower's share of income devoted to housing, because such tactics have gone nearly as far as they can. Therefore, many households that, on a purely demographic basis, would have become homeowners in the past will be forced to rent instead. This is especially likely among potential first-time home buyers. As a result, the demand for more rental housing will form a larger share of total demand for additional housing in the 1980s than in the 1970s.

At the same time, home prices will rise more slowly in relation to the overall price level. They will increase at about the same pace as consumer prices generally, except in high-demand areas with stringent restrictions on new housing construction. Hence it will be less profitable to invest in homeownership, though still worthwhile for those who can afford it. This will reduce investors' anticipation of appreciation in the market price of rental units, too.

Moreover, lenders will not supply the capital that equity investors in rental housing need except in forms that greatly reduce the benefit-multiplying power of leveraging. These forms include joint ventures, variable-rate loans, and renegotiable-rate loans. In fact, many capital suppliers are so disenchanted with rental housing they will not invest in it at all. Consequently, many small-scale investors will be unable to get any long-term funds. So the supply of rental housing will not grow very rapidly from new construction in the near future. This will remain true until rents have risen greatly, both absolutely and relative to construction and interest costs.

Higher real capital costs will also create pressure to economize on all uses of space. This will result in more widespread occupancy of smaller housing units, through both the construction of small units and the subdivision of many existing large units into smaller ones.

Because nonrent factors that aided yields and increased market prices in the past are weakening, rents will be a stronger determinant of market prices. The current gap between existing rent levels and those needed to sustain market prices is likely, therefore, to prompt owners to try to raise rents rapidly. Fortunately for owners in most areas, they will be able to raise rents quickly as the demand for rental housing rises faster than supply. Exceptions will exist in markets where many units are created through means other than new construction, where demand is stagnant because of out-migration, or where rent controls are adopted. Nonetheless, in the next few years, residential rents will rise faster than prices generally—a reversal of the experience of the past two decades. In fact, this reversal had already appeared by 1982.

Future Demand for Rental Housing

The net number of households formed in the 1980s will be held down by high housing costs. Hence it will not average 1.7 million a year as in the 1970s, but about 1.5 million a year or less.

INTRODUCTION AND SUMMARY

Estimates of the number of *renting* households added over the whole decade range from 2.9 million to 5.8 million, depending partly on how fast husband-and-wife households switch from renting to homeownership. The most probable estimate is based on relatively low overall household growth and relatively slow switching to homeownership among husband-and-wife households. It indicates a gain of 4.2 million renting households in the 1980s, or 424,000 a year.

Converting projections of household growth to projections of the demand for new housing requires forecasting the number of new units necessary for replacing older ones withdrawn from the inventory. If the net replacement rate is low, the number of all types of new units demanded from 1980 to 1990 under the most probable household projection is 1,881,000 a year, including 612,500 new rental units.

Future Supply of Rental Housing

In the late 1970s annual construction of new housing units from all sources averaged about 470,000 rental units and 1,400,000 ownership units.[6] The ownership units include most new mobile homes. Creation of "non-new" units also plays an important role in meeting housing demand. This includes conversion of nonresidential structures to residential use, retrieval of units temporarily removed from use, and subdivision of large older units into more smaller ones. Such non-new creation exceeded new construction as a source of added rental units in the late 1970s. It was less important for ownership units, relative to total demand.

Construction of new unsubsidized rental housing will fall short of demand in the next few years because of high interest rates and the continuing gap between current rents and the levels needed for economic feasibility. If slower inflation or a relaxation of tight monetary policy brings interest rates down, as began to happen in late 1982, new building will rise once rents have increased enough to close the rent gap. When

---

6. The term "ownership housing" is not the technically correct opposite of "rental housing," since all housing is owned by someone. "Owner-occupied housing and vacant housing for sale" is proper, but I will often use the more convenient "ownership housing" to mean the same thing.

that might happen depends on how fast rents go up in relation to construction costs and interest rates. It will occur first in fast-growing areas and for small, high-turnover rental units.

Meanwhile, making better use of the existing inventory will be vital to expanding the rental supply. The creation of additional non-new units will greatly reduce the shortfall in supply, particularly in areas containing large older inventories of housing and nonresidential properties. But refinancing and selling existing rental properties will be difficult as long as interest rates remain high. This will reduce owners' abilities to take funds out of their equities to pay for renovating or maintaining their properties. The overall result will be a decline in the quality of existing rental housing and a shortfall in total supply compared with potential demand. The biggest housing shortages will be in fast-growing areas, especially where rent controls have been adopted and nearly all new rental construction has ceased.

Where large potential shortfalls seem likely, key actors in the housing market will adjust their behavior in ways that balance supply and demand. Landlords will increase rents rapidly, if no rent controls are adopted. Eventually rents will become high enough to make new building of unsubsidized rental properties feasible again. In addition, many people who would have established separate households in the 1970s, when housing costs were low, will double up—or "unsingle"—reversing the recent tendency toward relatively lavish consumption of housing space. From 1970 to 1980 the number of rental units rose 21.4 percent, but the number of persons living in them rose only 1.2 percent. Another balancing factor will be more intensive use of the existing inventory by both landlords and tenants. This includes using older units longer, creating more non-new units, and increasing the average number of persons in each unit.

A Framework for Public Policies

Public policies concerning rental housing should aim at three goals: stimulating construction of rental units, making more intensive use of existing structures, and helping poor renters meet rising rental costs. Achieving the first two goals requires increasing the profitability of rental housing by raising rents considerably. But that adds to the cost of aiding

INTRODUCTION AND SUMMARY

poor households, thereby making achievement of the third goal more difficult.

Why adopt any public policies requiring more federal subsidies when direct federal income maintenance for the poor is being cut back? Such new policies should provide benefits comparable to the ones being reduced, or they represent lower-priority actions than restoring those cuts.

Policies to Stimulate Construction of New Rental Housing

The best way to generate more new rental housing construction would be to create conditions under which interest rates generally would decline. This began to occur in late 1982 when the Federal Reserve shifted to a less stringent monetary policy. But interest rates might rise again after 1983 if future federal deficits are not reduced.

Direct subsidies for housing are not desirable because other uses of federal funds are more urgent. Indirect subsidies, such as extending more tax advantages to rental housing, would have a relatively small impact on new building and would unduly distort the allocation of capital among alternative investments.

Other potentially effective ways to stimulate the construction of new rental housing are the following.

—Congress should prohibit rent controls or create strong financial incentives for local governments to eschew such controls. A national prohibition would allow rents to rise rapidly in areas of high demand and would thus encourage lenders to risk capital in creating new rental housing. However, this policy should be linked to a housing allowance or voucher program (which would give poor renters aid redeemable for rent only) to protect poor renters from soaring rents.

—State housing agencies should be permitted to continue using tax-exempt bonds to finance construction of certain types of new rental apartments under restricted conditions, even though this subsidy is not very efficient economically.

—Limited numbers of new public housing units should be built for very large families and for the elderly in communities where they could be induced to move out of large single-family homes.

—Local governments should raise allowable densities in areas already zoned for multifamily housing.

Several other proposed policies for stimulating new rental housing production should *not* be adopted. These include a direct interest-rate subsidy for middle-income rental units and expansion of the federal construction program for low-income units.

Policies to Use the Existing Inventory More Intensively

This goal should probably have priority over stimulating construction as long as interest rates are high. Specific means of attaining it include the following.

—Grants or low-interest loans should be made available for rehabilitation of rental housing, both from the federal government directly and from local governments using federal community development block grants.

—Local governments should postpone property tax increases on rehabilitated properties for an initial period to reduce the disincentive of such taxes.

—Local governments should change zoning laws and housing codes to encourage division of large, older single-family homes into multiple dwellings.

—Local governments should selectively enforce housing codes to accommodate different levels of quality in differing neighborhoods. All code enforcement should aim at encouraging owners to maintain their properties rather than at punishing violators.

—Local governments should develop property tax credits, rebates, or other specific incentives to encourage owners to reside on the premises of their rental properties.

Policies to Help Poor Renters Meet Rising Costs

Rapid rent increases in the near future will make renters worse off, especially poor ones for whom rent is already their greatest expense. In fact, higher rents will offset much of the net positive impact on poor people's real living standards of many federal programs, including food stamps, welfare, and social security. The best way to help poor renters meet rising housing costs would be to expand existing federal housing subsidies into a comprehensive housing voucher entitlement program for households with very low incomes (below 50 percent of their area's median). Implementing this program should have equal priority with restoring funds cut from the food stamp program, since most of the money in both cases is used for general income maintenance.

Such a housing voucher entitlement program for poor renters could be fully funded without raising net federal spending. This would be possible using savings achievable by modifying present homeownership tax benefits. The current practice of deducting mortgage interest and property taxes from taxable income produces huge benefits received mainly by high-bracket households. If such deductibility were replaced by a tax credit and the credit were reduced by about 14 percent, three desirable goals would be attained. First, the tax system would still encourage homeownership. Homeowners as a group would receive net tax benefits 86 percent as large as those they get now. Second, those benefits would be distributed much more fairly. Each dollar of interest or property taxes paid would produce the same tax savings for every household, regardless of its income, instead of aiding wealthy households disproportionately. Third, the federal funds saved by reducing these overall benefits about 14 percent would pay for a nationwide housing allowance entitlement program covering all renting households with income below 50 percent of their areawide medians. This would greatly improve the overall fairness of present housing subsidies and tax benefits.

In the absence of federal action, many renters will respond to rising housing costs by pressuring local governments to adopt rent controls. Such controls would undoubtedly benefit most renters in the short run. But widespread rent controls would choke off additions to the rental housing supply, thus increasing shortages as the number of potential renters rises in the 1980s. Furthermore, the gap between controlled rents and market rents rises over time, especially during inflationary periods. Therefore, the longer rent controls are in effect, the harder it is to get rid of them. Yet prolonged controls accompanied by rising demand for rental housing will lead to crowding, shortages, and deterioration of the existing inventory. These conditions would affect middle-income renters as well as poor ones.

As housing conditions declined under rent controls, the federal government would increasingly be pressured to respond, even in a time of conservative political dominance. Other Western democracies have found it politically difficult to end rent controls and let rents rise high enough to make construction of new rental housing and maintenance of existing units feasible again. Controls can be ended if the federal government cushions the impact on the poor by rapidly expanding its income subsidies to them, as West Germany has done. But a politically easier course is retaining rent controls and expanding publicly subsidized housing, as Great Britain has done. This causes the private rental sector to shrink, dramatically reducing its role in housing markets in the long run.

This analysis implies that refusal to expand federal aid to the poor to help offset soaring rents may have unexpected and undesirable long-run results. It may lead to the eventual decline of private rental housing and to its partial replacement by publicly subsidized housing. This conclusion is by no means certain. But it emphasizes the need for decisionmakers to consider rent controls and federal aids to the poor simultaneously, since they are both potential policy responses to the coming market pressure for higher rents.

Further Adjustments for Households

Whichever policies are adopted, some further adjustments will have to be made by many households, including behavior changes they will regard as undesirable. These adjustments include the following.

—Most households will be paying higher fractions of their income for housing than in the past.

—Many households that would like to own their own homes will be renting because they cannot afford the higher costs of homeownership.

—Many persons who would like to form additional households will be living with others because they cannot afford separate units.

—Owners of rental property will be keeping it in use longer than they might otherwise; hence the inventory will be older, on the average. Therefore it will probably be more deteriorated, although higher rents will enable many owners to maintain their properties better.

—Persons who buy or rent new accommodations will be living in smaller units, on the average, than if they had done so in the 1970s.

—The total share of capital flowing into home mortgages will be smaller than in the 1970s because of the greater attraction of other forms of investment compared with homeownership and rental housing.

1

Some Basic Facts about Rental Housing

BECAUSE rental housing is a major component of the U.S. housing inventory and will remain so for many years, some basic information about the characteristics of rental housing and renters is essential to any discussion of public policies on housing.

The Characteristics of Rental Housing

In 1980 the rental housing supply topped 28.5 million units.[1] About 60 percent of all renter-occupied units were in structures containing fewer than five units (see figure 1-1). Over 31 percent were single-family dwellings, either detached (26.3 percent) or attached (5.1 percent). Another 23.3 percent were in buildings containing between two and four units. Only 16.5 percent were in structures containing twenty or more units. Even in central cities, this fraction was only 25.0 percent.[2] Thus it is crucial to analyze the entire rental housing market, not just structures containing five or more units.

---

1. U.S. Bureau of the Census, *1980 Census of Population and Housing: Provisional Estimates of Social, Economic, and Housing Characteristics*, PHC80-S1-1 (U.S. Government Printing Office, 1982), p. 70.
2. U.S. Department of Housing and Urban Development and Bureau of the Census, *Annual Housing Survey, 1980, Part A* (GPO, 1982), pp. 1, 4. This document will hereafter be referred to as *Annual Housing Survey, 1980, Part A*. Other parts and volumes of the Annual Housing Survey will be given similar short titles.

Figure 1-1. *Occupied Rental Units, by Size of Structure, 1980*

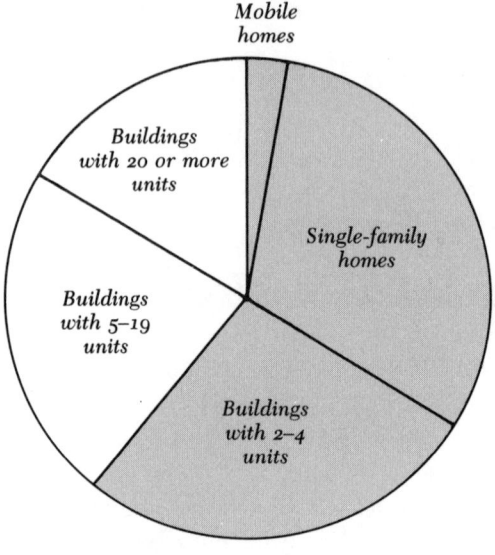

Units in small structures

Source: U.S. Department of Housing and Urban Development and U.S. Bureau of the Census, *Annual Housing Survey, 1980* (U.S. Government Printing Office, 1982).

Changes in the Inventory

The supply of rental housing increased about 21 percent over the 1970s (see table 1-1 and figure 1-2). The owner-occupied supply expanded even faster, however, resulting in a slight decline in the proportion of all housing occupied by renters (see table 1-2 and figure 1-3).

These changes occurred partly because new construction in the 1970s was increasingly dominated by single-family homes. From 1970 to 1973, 9.9 million new private housing units were started. Of these, 6.4 million (65 percent) were single-family homes, including mobile homes. The other 3.6 million were in structures containing more than one unit, most of which became renter-occupied. From 1974 to 1980, 12.9 million more new private housing units were started, including 9.7 million single-family units (75 percent). Only 3.2 million multifamily units were started in this longer period, and a higher fraction of those were for the ownership market.[3] Annual average starts in these two periods are shown in table

3. Bureau of the Census, *Housing Starts*, construction report C-20, August 1981, p. 8.

FACTS ABOUT RENTAL HOUSING

Table 1-1. *Housing Inventory, 1970 and 1980*

Type of unit	Total units (thousands)		Additions, 1970–80	
	April 1970	April 1980	Number (thousands)	Percent
Owner-occupied	39,886	51,794	11,908	29.9
Renter-occupied	23,560	28,595	5,035	21.4
Total occupied	63,445	80,389	16,944	26.7
Vacant and other	4,254	6,380	2,126	50.0
Total[a]	67,699	86,769	19,070	28.2

Source: U.S. Bureau of the Census, *1970 Census of Population and Housing* (U.S. Government Printing Office, 1972) and *1980* (GPO, 1982).
a. Units for year-round occupancy only.

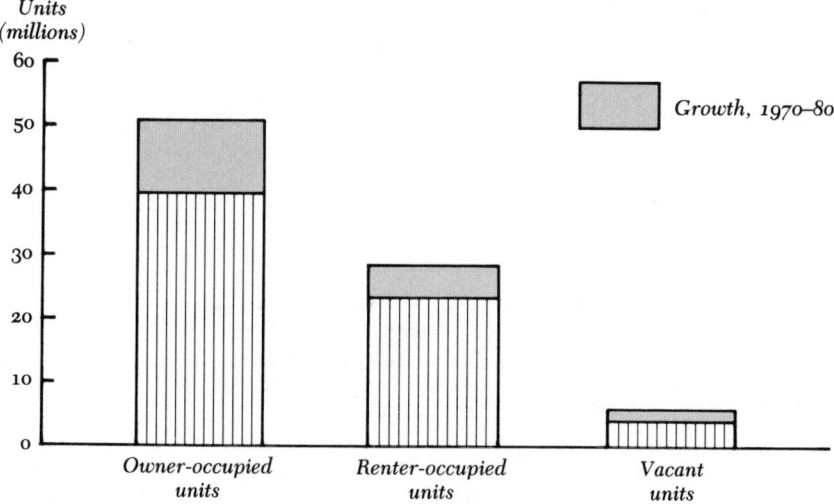

Figure 1-2. *Growth of the Housing Inventory, by Type of Tenure, 1970–80*

1-3. The average number of units started each year was the same in both periods for conventionally built single-family units, but only half as large in the later period for multifamily units and mobile homes.[4]

Each year, thousands of housing units are removed from the available inventory either temporarily or permanently, and thousands more are

---

4. This statement does not imply that the high production levels of the early 1970s should be considered normal and the lower levels of the late 1970s considered abnormally

Table 1-2. *Occupied Housing Units, by Type of Tenure, Selected Years, 1970–80*
Percent

Year and source of data	Renter-occupied units	Owner-occupied units
1970 census	37.1	62.9
1975 housing survey	35.4	64.6
1980 census	35.6	64.4
1980 housing survey	34.4	65.6

Source: U.S. Department of Housing and Urban Development and Bureau of the Census, *Annual Housing Survey, 1975* (GPO, 1977) and *1980* (GPO, 1982); Bureau of the Census, *1970 Census of Population and Housing* and *1980*.

Figure 1-3. *Homeowners as a Percentage of All Households, Selected Years, 1920–80*

Source: Bureau of the Census, *1980 Census of Population and Housing: Provisional Estimates of Social, Economic, and Housing Characteristics*, PHC80-S1-1 (GPO, 1982); and Bureau of the Census, *Statistical Abstract of the United States*, various years.

added through actions other than new construction. These changes, which fall into the following categories, substantially affect the supply of available units, particularly in the short run.[5]

Temporary removals include units that are withdrawn from use as

---

low. On the contrary, the high levels attained in the early 1970s were abnormally high in comparison with levels achieved either before or after. Data from Council of Economic Advisers, *Economic Indicators*, May 1979, p. 19; and Bureau of the Census, *Statistical Abstract of the United States, 1978* (GPO, 1978), p. 788. This publication will henceforth be referred to as *Statistical Abstract, 1978* or other relevant year.

5. This discussion is largely based on Duane T. McGough, "Housing Inventory Losses as a Requirement for New Construction," paper prepared for an Economic Commission for Europe seminar on housing forecasting and programming, January 1981, Washington, D.C.

Table 1-3. *Housing Starts, by Type of Unit, Selected Periods, 1970–80*

Type	Average annual number started (millions) 1970–73	Average annual number started (millions) 1974–80	Change (percent)
Single-family units	1.6	1.4	−13
Conventionally built homes	1.1	1.1	0
Mobile homes	0.5	0.3	−40
Multifamily units	0.9	0.5	−44
Total	2.5	1.9	−24

Source: Bureau of the Census, *Housing Starts*, construction reports C-20, June 1981, p. 8.

housing but that could be returned to it. These include merged units that could be separated again, units converted to nonresidential use, structures damaged so as to be temporarily uninhabitable, units condemned because they do not meet building codes, and units converted to use as hotels. *Permanent losses* include units merged with others in such a way as to lose their individual character, units demolished, units destroyed by disasters like fires or floods, and units removed from their sites (though the last type can become additions to the inventory at their new sites). *Non-new additions* include units temporarily removed but returned to housing use, such as those restored from uninhabitable or condemned condition, those converted from large units into various smaller ones, and those in structures converted from nonresidential to residential use.

Housing analysts have long recognized that permanent losses from the inventory generate demands for new construction to replace them. It is not as widely known, however, that some of those demands can be met through non-new additions, especially in the short run. Whenever new housing construction falls sharply, net non-new additions tend to rise. In 1974, 1978, and 1979, for example, over 2 million newly constructed units were completed annually, while net non-new additions to the inventory averaged 475,000 units, or 23 percent of new construction. In 1975, 1976, and 1977, new construction averaged 1,646,000 units, but net non-new additions averaged 644,000, or 39 percent of new construction.[6]

An analysis of all units in the 1973 inventory that had been removed by 1979 showed a six-year loss of 5.7 percent for all housing units, but 8.6 percent for renter-occupied units. Among the latter, the fraction lost

6. Ibid., p. 17.

Figure 1-4. *Sources of Net Additions to the Housing Inventory, Selected Periods, 1950–80*

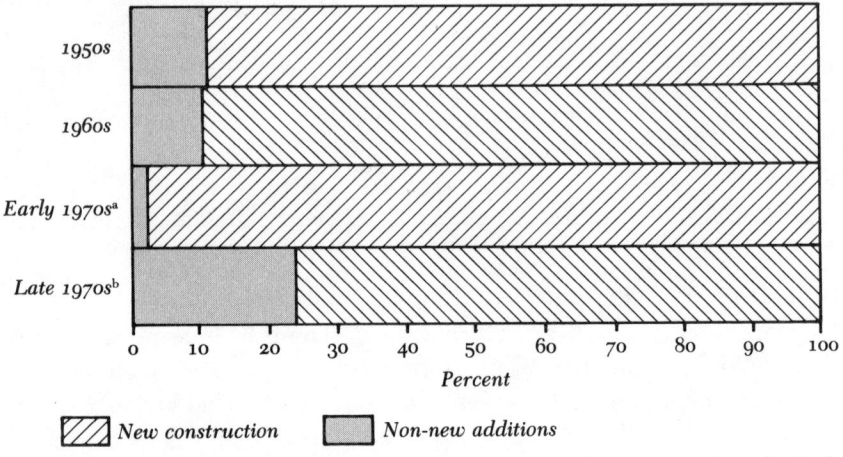

Source: Bureau of the Census, *Housing Starts*, construction reports C-20, January 1983; and author's calculations.
a. April 1970–October 1973.
b. October 1973–October 1979.

was highest for mobile homes (40.4 percent), next highest for single-family units (9.5 percent), and lowest for units in structures with twenty or more units (5.8 percent).[7] Loss rates for all types of units were much higher for rural areas than for metropolitan areas and almost twice as high within central cities as within suburbs.

In the 1950s, 11.1 percent of the net growth in the housing inventory came from non-new additions (see figure 1-4). This fraction was 10.5 percent in the 1960s and only 2.4 percent from April 1970 through October 1973. But it soared to 23.9 percent from October 1973 to October 1979.[8] The relatively high share in the last period probably reflected both very low new housing construction in 1974 and 1975 and high housing prices in later years, which make non-new additions profitable.

The Condition of the Inventory

In 1977 about one out of every six renter-occupied units could be considered physically inadequate, compared with one out of every sixteen

7. Ibid., p. 23.
8. Ibid., p. 15.

FACTS ABOUT RENTAL HOUSING

owner-occupied units. This finding comes from a recent study that considered a unit physically inadequate if it exhibited any of eight major flaws in physical condition.[9] Poor maintenance accounted for almost half of all major flaws in rental units. Physical inadequacy was slightly above average in the West and slightly below average in the North Central region.

Old age contributes to the physical problems of many rental units (see figure 1-5). In the suburban population explosion of the 1950s, new construction focused on single-family homes.[10] Consequently, by 1980, 29.1 percent of all renter-occupied units had been built before 1940, compared with 24.3 percent of all owner-occupied units. The fraction of units built since April 1970 was 23.5 percent for rental units and 26.1 percent for owner-occupied units.

The Scope of the Subsidized Inventory

Eight out of every nine rental units have no direct government subsidies; private markets provide the vast majority of rental housing. But about one of every three poor renting households lives in a subsidized unit. As of September 30, 1980, programs of the Department of Housing

---

9. Anthony M. Yezer, "The Physical Adequacy and Affordability of Housing in America: Measurements Using the Annual Housing Survey for 1975 and 1977," Department of Housing and Urban Development, Office of Policy Development and Research, draft report (GPO, June 1981), pp. 7, 12. The eight areas to which Yezer looks for flaws are plumbing, kitchen facilities, maintenance, public halls, heating, electricity, sewerage, and access to bath.

This definition of "physical inadequacy" is more stringent than the usual definition of "substandardness" as lacking adequate plumbing. Hence the resulting percentages of physically inadequate units are much higher than in many past studies.

A household's probability of occupying a physically inadequate unit (irrespective of tenure type) is most powerfully affected by its total income. Households with an adjusted income below $2,500 in 1977 had close to a 25 percent chance of occupying a physically inadequate unit; those with an adjusted income of $2,500 to $3,000 had about a 17 percent probability. (Income was adjusted so that $3,000 was equivalent to a poverty-level income regardless of household size.) Corresponding percentages declined sharply with higher income, falling to less than 5 percent for all households with an adjusted income of $6,000 or more, and 1 percent or less for all those with an adjusted income of $12,000 or more.

The conclusion that many very low-income households live in physically inadequate units is consistent with findings from the experimental housing allowance program. See Katharine L. Bradbury and Anthony Downs, eds., *Do Housing Allowances Work?* (Brookings Institution, 1981), p. 69.

10. In the 1950s, 84.4 percent of all new units were single-family homes. *Statistical Abstract, 1956*, p. 773, and *1960*, p. 762.

Figure 1-5. *Age of Housing Units, by Type of Tenure, 1980*

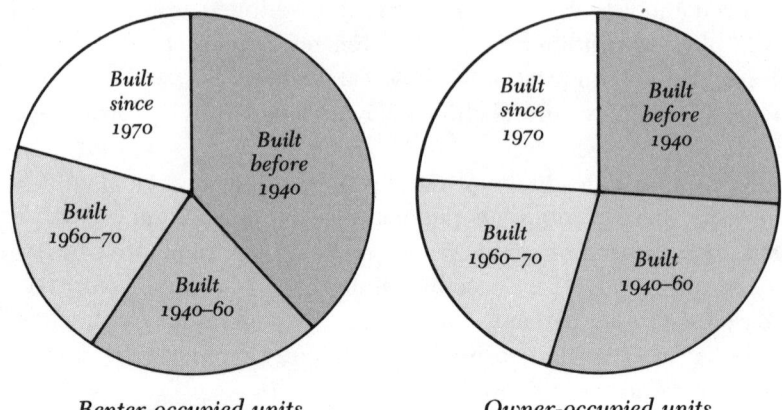

Renter-occupied units   Owner-occupied units

Source: *Annual Housing Survey, 1980*, Part A, pp. 1–2.

and Urban Development (HUD) supported 3,049,000 rental units, or about 11.1 percent of all renter-occupied units.[11] These subsidized units included 1,192,000 public housing units, 1,153,000 Section 8 units, 538,000 Section 236 units, and 165,000 rent supplement units. These three programs all subsidized construction of new units and their occupancy by low- and moderate-income households. The Section 8 and rent supplement programs help such households pay rents; the Section 236 program also contains an interest rate subsidy. Altogether, these programs subsidize the housing of about 8.4 million persons, or 13 percent of all renters.

However, the fraction of very poor renters living in subsidized units is much higher. Very poor households are defined as those having income under 50 percent of their area's median income. Including Section 8 units likely to be occupied sometime in 1982, there were 3.5 million subsidized rental units in 1981, of which 2.7 million served very poor households. Thus 29.7 percent of the nation's 9.1 million very poor households lived in subsidized units.[12]

---

11. This computation assumes there were 27,460,000 renter-occupied units at that time, because 300,000 units were added to the inventory according to the 1979 Annual Housing Survey. Data on the number of units subsidized by HUD and the populations living in them were obtained from Helmuth R. Wiemann of HUD in August 1981.

12. Data from Jill Khadduri and Raymond J. Struyk, *Housing Vouchers: From Here to Entitlement?* (Urban Institute, 1980), p. 4.

Some Important Traits of Renters

The 28.6 million households that rented their homes in 1980 differed markedly from those that owned their homes in their income, the size of their households and housing units, their types of households, and their tendency to move from one place to another.

Income

Renters typically have much lower income than homeowners, partly because so many households switch from renting to owning as their income rises. In 1980 median annual income among renting households was $10,500, or 53 percent of the $19,800 median among homeowning households. Renters composed 56.0 percent of all households with an annual income below $3,000, 34.5 percent of those with an income of $15,000 to $19,999, and only 9.5 percent of those with an income of $35,000 or more. Almost 48 percent of all renters had an income below $10,000, compared with 23 percent of all owner-occupants.[13]

Furthermore, the income of renting households has been rising more slowly than that of homeowning households. From 1970 to 1980, median income rose 66.7 percent among renters but 104.1 percent among owner-occupants, as compared with a 112.2 percent rise in the consumer price index.[14] These data must be interpreted cautiously because the particular households renting in 1980 are not the same ones that were renting in 1970. Moreover, many of those renting in 1970 whose income rose the most shifted to homeownership, thus exaggerating the apparent stagnation of renters' income. The 71 percent rise in the reported median income of all renters from $6,300 in 1970 to $10,787 in 1980 was a result of both a change in the mixture of types of households and a change in average income for each type. Correcting for the change in mixture of households shows that the average income for all types rose about 105 percent.[15]

---

13. *Annual Housing Survey, 1980, Part A.*
14. *Statistical Abstract, 1980,* p. 487.
15. The 1970–80 increase in the percentage of renters who were not in husband-and-wife households caused a drop in the median income of renters as a whole, apart from any changes in the income of each household type. If income for each type of renting household had remained unchanged from 1970 to 1980, but the composition of household types had

Therefore, the capacity of renting households to pay more for housing rose about the same as that for homeowning households and was in line with the rise in prices overall.

The median percentage of income paid for gross rent among all renting households increased from 20 percent in 1970 to 27 percent in 1980. Moreover, the proportion of such households paying 35 percent or more of their income for gross rent rose from 25.3 percent in 1970 to 33.5 percent in 1980. Both of these seemingly adverse changes were also caused partly by the shift in household types among all renters.[16]

The Size of Households and Housing Units

Average household size is smaller among renters than among owner-occupants (see figure 1-6). In 1980 over one-third of all renting households consisted of one person, and almost two-thirds were one or two persons. Among homeowning households less than a sixth were one person, and about half contained one or two persons. Whereas 9.1 percent of renting households contained five or more persons, 15.5 percent of homeowning households did so. Median household size was 2.0 among renters and 2.6 among owner-occupants.[17]

Moreover, the average size of renting households has been falling. In 1970, 23.6 million renter-occupied units contained 64.3 million persons,

---

shifted as actually happened, the average income among renters would have declined from $6,300 to about $5,270. But the average income among renters actually rose to $10,787 in 1980, or 105 percent above what the same household composition would have produced with 1970 income. The estimate of $5,270 assumes that the average income of all renting households in 1970 was $6,300 and that the three types of renting households had the following ratio of average incomes in that year: husband and wife, 100; female head, 33.4; and other male head, 43.6. These 1970 relative sizes were derived by comparing 1975 relative sizes with those for 1980 and extrapolating the 1975–80 change to 1970. The estimating procedure also treats the median incomes reported by the Annual Housing Surveys as averages for purposes of computation; hence it is probably conservative. Data were taken from *Annual Housing Survey, 1975, Part F*, p. 2, and *1980, Part C*, p. 6.

16. The median household income among female-headed households in 1980 was about $7,160, and the majority of households with that income paid approximately 40 percent of their income for rent. The median shares of income paid for rent were about 23 percent for husband-and-wife households and 29 percent for other male-headed households. Thus the rise of ten percentage points from 1970 to 1980 in the proportion of female-headed households among all renters undoubtedly accounted for much of the rise in the proportion of all renters paying over 35 percent of their income for rent. This could have occurred even if no particular type of household increased the share of income it paid for rent from 1970 to 1980. Data from *Annual Housing Survey, 1980, Part C*, pp. 7, 12, 14.

17. Ibid., pp. 2, 6.

FACTS ABOUT RENTAL HOUSING

Figure 1-6. *Household Size, by Type of Tenure, 1980*

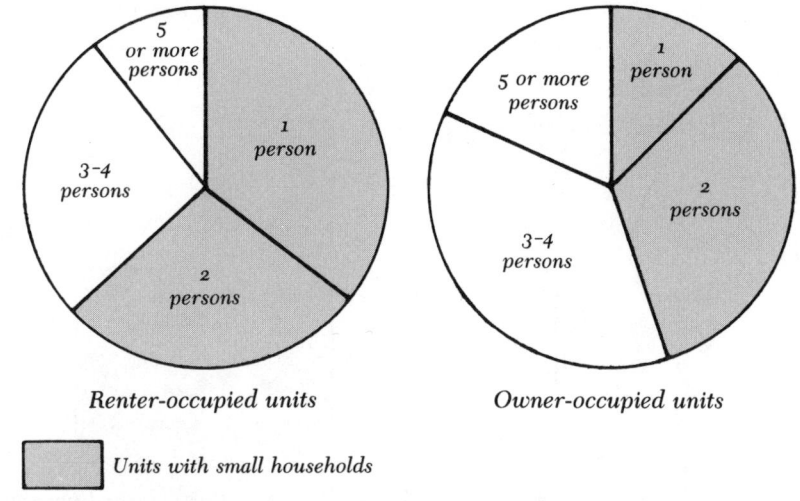

Source: *Annual Housing Survey, 1980, Part A,* p. 5.

or 2.73 persons a unit. From 1970 to 1980 the number of renter-occupied units increased by 21.4 percent, but the total number of persons living in them rose only 1.2 percent. Hence, in 1980, 28.6 million such units held only 65.1 million persons, or an average of 2.28 in each unit. During that period, the average number of rooms in each rental unit remained about 4.0; thus the number of rooms per person rose from 1.47 to 1.75, or 19 percent—a marked improvement in the average quality of housing services received by renters (see figure 1-7).

Similar spreading out occurred during the 1970s among owner-occupants. The number of owner-occupied units rose 29.9 percent from 1970 to 1980, whereas the number of persons living in such units increased only 19.4 percent. The average number of persons in each unit dropped from 3.27 in 1970 to 3.00 in 1980, while the average number of rooms rose from 5.62 to 5.86. Thus the number of rooms per person increased from 1.72 to 1.95, or 13 percent. Renters thus experienced a slightly greater improvement in rooms per person than owner-occupants during the 1970s.[18]

18. Data for 1970 are from *Annual Housing Survey, 1974, Part A* and for 1980 from *Annual Housing Survey, 1980, Part C*. See also Ira S. Lowry, "Rental Housing in the 1970s: Searching for the Crisis," working draft WD-820-HUD (Rand Corporation, June 1981), p. 20.

Figure 1-7. *Percentage Change in Housing Units and Occupants, 1970–80*

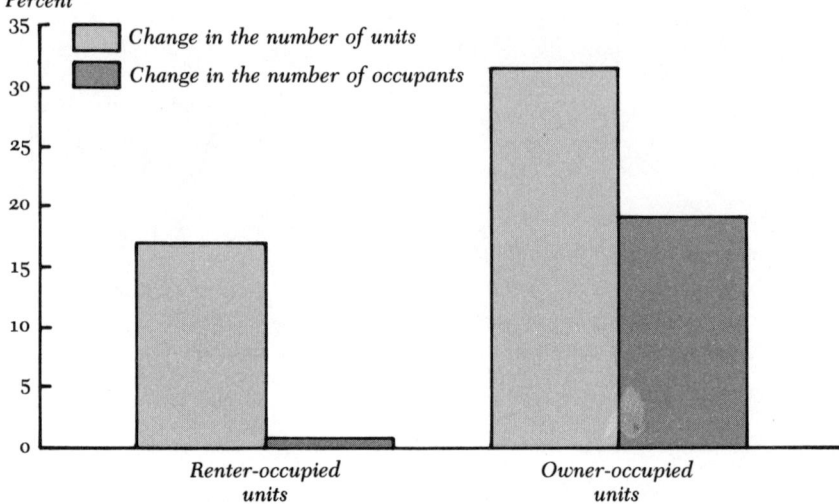

Source: *Annual Housing Survey, 1980,* Part A, p. 5.

Table 1-4. *Housing Tenure, by Type of Household, 1970 and 1980*

Type	Husband-and-wife households[a]	Other male-headed households	Female-headed households	All households
All households				
1970 (thousands)	43,565	6,374	13,507	63,446
1980 (thousands)	47,327	11,238	21,507	80,072
Change, 1970–80 (percent)	8.6	76.3	59.2	26.2
Renting households				
1970 (thousands)	12,759	3,747	7,055	23,560
1980 (thousands)	9,818	6,520	11,218	27,556
Change, 1970–80 (percent)	−23.1	74.0	59.0	17.0
Renting households as a percentage of each household type				
1970	29.3	58.8	52.2	37.1
1980	20.7	58.0	52.2	34.4
Household type as a percentage of renting households				
1970	54.2	15.9	29.9	100.0
1980	35.6	23.7	40.7	100.0

Source: *Annual Housing Survey, 1980,* Part A, pp. 5, 6.
a. Both present.

FACTS ABOUT RENTAL HOUSING

Figure 1-8. *Renters, by Type of Household, 1970 and 1980*

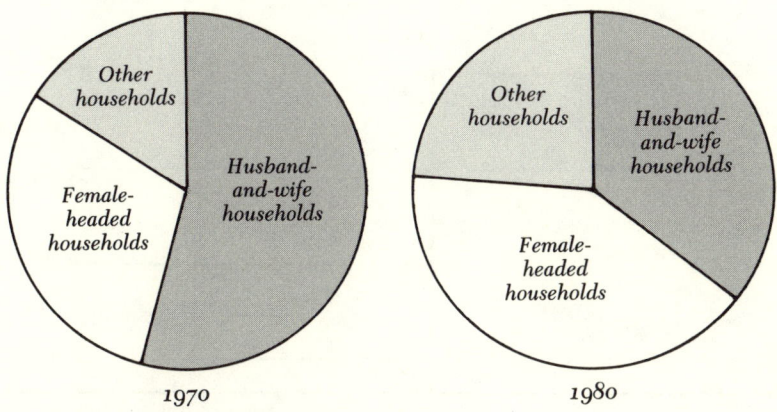

Source: *Annual Housing Survey, 1980,* Part A, p. 6.

The Types of Households

As husband-and-wife households have moved rapidly into homeownership, the ranks of renters have been increasingly dominated by households headed by women and single men. They are now almost two-thirds of all renting households, compared with less than half in 1970 (see figure 1-8).

From 1970 to 1980 the total number of households rose 16.9 million, or 26.7 percent, but husband-and-wife households rose only 8.6 percent while other male-headed households soared 76.3 percent and female-headed households increased 59.2 percent (table 1-4). Nonetheless, the proportions of other male-headed and female-headed households that rent were remarkably constant from 1970 to 1980. In contrast, the proportion of husband-and-wife households that rent declined (see figure 1-9). By 1980 female-headed households were 40.7 percent of all renters, though only 26.9 percent of all households.[19] One reason so many female-headed households rent is that they have much lower incomes than male-headed ones, on the average, and renting is generally less costly than homeownership.

Turnover Rates

Annual moving rates for renters are 4.6 times as high as those for owner-occupants. Hence rental housing is difficult to manage, and renter-

---

19. Data are from *Annual Housing Survey, 1980,* Part C, pp. 2, 6.

Figure 1-9. *Changes in the Composition of Renting Households, 1970–80*

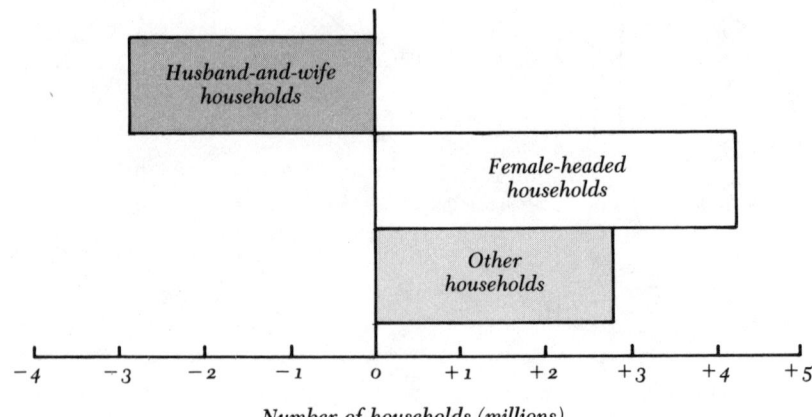

Source: *Annual Housing Survey, 1980,* Part A, p. 6.

dominated neighborhoods are relatively less stable than owner-occupied neighborhoods. In 1980, 36.7 percent of all renting households had moved into their dwellings within the previous year, compared with 7.9 percent of all owner-occupants. This situation does not result from the smaller size of renting households. In fact, annual turnover rates are three to four times greater among renters than among owner-occupants for every household size.[20] The rental mobility rate varied with regions: it was 24.9 percent in the Northeast, 37.8 percent in the North Central states, 41.6 percent in the South, and 41.9 percent in the West. About 71 percent of all household moves made each year involve renters, even though almost twice as many households own rather than rent their homes.[21]

20. In fact, in 1980, two-person, three-person, four-person, and five-person households all had higher turnover rates than one-person households among both renters and owner-occupants. *Annual Housing Survey, 1980,* Part D, p. 1.

21. *Annual Housing Survey, 1980,* Part D, pp. 1, 33, 56, 79, 102.

2
Recent Trends in Rents

FOR MANY YEARS residential rents have not risen as rapidly as other housing costs, consumer prices, or consumer incomes. However, determining exactly how much rents have lagged is difficult because of uncertainty about how best to measure them. I will describe two measures, then indicate the conclusions I draw from them.

The first measure is the consumer price index (CPI) for residential rent. It is based on semiannual surveys of a rotating panel of urban rental housing units by the Bureau of Labor Statistics (BLS). The panel currently contains about 21,000 units in eighty-five cities.[1]

From 1960 to 1970 the CPI for all items increased 31.1 percent, but the CPI residential rent component rose only 20.1 percent, or two-thirds as fast. This component supposedly measures rental changes in housing units of constant quality. If the rent component is adjusted by using the entire CPI as a deflator, the real level of residential rents declined 8.4 percent over the 1960s. In the same period per capita disposable personal income rose 73.1 percent, or about 3.6 times as rapidly as nominal rents.[2]

From 1970 to 1980 the overall CPI soared 112.2 percent, but its rent component went up 74.0 percent—again about two-thirds as fast. By this measure real residential rents fell 18.2 percent in this eleven-year period. Per capita disposable personal income rose 136.0 percent, or about 1.8

---

1. This analysis draws heavily on Ira S. Lowry, "Inflation Indexes for Rental Housing," working draft WD-1081-HUD (Rand Corporation, May 1981). As usual, Lowry has made a major contribution in this excellent paper.

2. U.S. Bureau of the Census, *Statistical Abstract of the United States, 1981* (U.S. Government Printing Office, 1981), pp. 423, 467–68.

times as rapidly as rents.[3] Operating costs also increased much faster than rents. From 1970 to 1980 the CPI for housing fuel and utilities rose 158.9 percent and that for household furnishings and operations increased 84.2 percent.[4]

CPI rents have also increased much more slowly than the cost of constructing new rental units. The E. H. Boeckh building cost index for apartments, hotels, and small office buildings rose 84.8 percent from 1970 to 1978, but residential rents increased only 49.0 percent.[5] This index understates total construction costs because it does not include land costs, which rose even faster. Contract interest rates on loans for apartment properties rose from 8.5 percent in 1970 to 13.7 percent by the end of 1979, a gain of 61.2 percent.[6] Even though real, after-tax interest rates were much lower than contract rates in the 1970s, the former rose during the credit crunches of 1980 and 1981. In fact, because interest rates were at historically high levels in 1980–81, money costs inhibited both the building of new rental units and the renovation of older ones.

The CPI rent index probably understates true rent increases for two reasons. First, its assumption of constant-quality units is incorrect.[7] The

3. Ibid.
4. These disparities between increases in rents as measured by the consumer price index and in other key variables were not confined to the early 1970s; they persisted throughout the decade. Thus gains from 1978 to 1980 were 16.8 percent for rents, but 29.0 percent for fuel and utilities, 15.6 percent for household furnishings and operations, 26.3 percent for the overall CPI, and 21.8 percent for per capita disposable personal income; ibid. Rental data from the Annual Housing Surveys (AHS) show more rapid increases in rent. Thus, median gross rent for all rental units increased by 23.1 percent from 1970 to 1973, by 19.8 percent from 1976 to 1978, and by 50.4 percent from 1973 to 1978 overall. The CPI for all items rose by 14.4 percent, 14.6 percent, and 46.8 percent in the same periods, respectively, thus increasing more slowly than rents by this measure. However, CPI rental data are standardized for "constant-quality" units, whereas AHS data are not. Hence the AHS data include rent changes resulting from improvements in the average quality of units over time. Therefore, this study relies much more heavily on CPI rental data than AHS rental data, though studies of the latter are also discussed in the text. See U.S. Department of Housing and Urban Development and Bureau of the Census, *Annual Housing Survey, 1973, Part A* (GPO, 1973), p. 71; *1976, Part F*, p. 96; and *1978, Part F*, p. 56.
5. Ibid., and *Statistical Abstract, 1981*, p. 754.
6. Federal Home Loan Mortgage Corporation, *Primary Market Survey*, week ending April 2, 1971, and week ending December 28, 1979.
7. See Larry Ozanne, "Expanding and Improving the CPI Rent Component," working paper 1090-1 (Urban Institute, May 1981), chap. 3; and Ira S. Lowry, "Rental Housing in the 1970s: Searching for the Crisis," working draft WD-820-1-HUD (Rand Corporation, June 1981).

BLS collects rental data from the same sample of units repeatedly, excluding those with major decay or renovations. But the quality of housing services provided by most units declines over time because of normal wear and tear and functional obsolescence, even without major decay or renovation. The BLS does not take such depreciation into account; rent increases for units of truly constant quality would be higher than those BLS reports.

Furthermore, the BLS index measures "contract rent" excluding fuel and utility bills paid by tenants. But such bills are normally part of gross rent and should be included in measuring true consumer housing costs. Leaving them out further underestimates increases in true rents, especially since fuel and utility costs have risen so rapidly.

How large are these underestimates? Larry Ozanne and Thomas Thibodeau of the Urban Institute recently constructed several residential rent indexes from Annual Housing Survey data and compared them with the CPI rent index to measure its reliability.[8] Their index for all urban areas for 1974–77 was remarkably similar to the CPI rent index. Their index increased 19.30 percent, compared with 18.28 percent for CPI rents. They concluded that not taking depreciation into account led the BLS to underestimate rents by about 0.6 to 0.7 percent a year.[9] This bias is far too small to account for the difference between increases in general prices and rents in both the 1960s and the 1970s.[10]

---

8. Thomas Thibodeau and Larry Ozanne, "Constructing a Rent Index from the Annual Housing Survey" (Urban Institute, March 1981).

9. Thibodeau and Ozanne used a hedonic index, which uses multiple regression analysis, to estimate the contribution of each of a number of specific structural and other components of rental units to their total rent, based on a large sample. By deriving such indexes in different years, it is possible to estimate the size of rent increases from year to year, holding the specific qualities of a housing unit constant. See Ozanne, "Improving the CPI Rent Component," pp. 11–17.

10. Another study by Anthony M. Yezer also used AHS data to estimate constant-quality-unit rent increases, but diverged much more from the CPI rent index. See Anthony M. Yezer, "The Physical Adequacy and Affordability of Housing in America: Measurements Using the Annual Housing Survey for 1975 and 1977," draft report (George Washington University, Department of Economics, June 1981), pp. 24–30. Yezer's sample of housing units differed from the Bureau of Labor Statistics' sample in two ways. He included utility costs as part of rent. Also, his calculations focused on physically adequate units that did not contain any of eight major flaws, whereas the BLS sample does not necessarily contain only such units. Both these differences would tend to cause Yezer's rent increase estimates to be higher than the BLS estimates even if both were based on the same "true" data. For the period 1975–77, Yezer estimates that rent for a constant-quality, physically adequate unit for a four-person household within a metropolitan area increased from 17.5 to 23.5 percent, depending on the population of the area. In contrast, the CPI rent index rose

Table 2-1. *Indexes of Residential Rents, Selected Years, 1960–80*
1967 = 100

Year	All items (consumer price index)	Contract rent (CPI rent component)[a]	Adjusted gross rent (Lowry index)[b]
1960	88.7	91.7	89.2
1965	94.5	96.9	96.2
1970	116.3	110.1	112.1
1975	161.2	137.3	150.6
1980[c]	247.6	190.8	227.2

Source: Ira S. Lowry, "Inflation Indexes for Rental Housing," working draft WD-1081-HUD (Rand Corporation, May 1981), table A.10, p. 30.
a. Contract rent is the tenant's payment to his landlord.
b. Adjusted gross rent incorporates the tenant's direct payments for fuel and utilities as well as rent.
c. Data for 1980 are for the month of June; all other data are annual averages.

Ira S. Lowry of the Rand Corporation recently combined several data sources on rents, operating costs, and other relevant information in trying to correct for both the omissions in the BLS index mentioned above.[11] His index measures gross rent, including fuel and utility bills; it also takes account of declining quality. I believe Lowry's index is the most accurate available measure of rent changes from 1960 to 1980. This index is compared with the CPI contract rent measure in table 2-1. Lowry's index indicates a much greater increase in rents during the twenty years than that shown by the CPI. Thus from 1960 to 1970 rents increased 20.1 percent according to the CPI, but 25.7 percent according to Lowry. From 1970 to 1980 rents rose 73.3 percent by the CPI measure, but 102.7 percent by Lowry's measure. This larger disparity reflects soaring fuel and utility bills in the 1970s, which the CPI excludes but Lowry includes. Lowry's measure also implies that real rents declined only 8.8 percent over these twenty years—not 25.5 percent, as the CPI suggests. From 1960 to 1970, Lowry calculates, real rents fell 4.2 percent; from 1970 to 1980 they dropped another 4.8 percent. I conclude that residential

---

11.8 percent in that period; the AHS index constructed by Ozanne and Thibodeau rose 12.4 percent; and the overall CPI rose 12.6 percent. Thus Yezer's estimate is roughly 70 percent higher than the other two estimates and implies that rents increased 70 percent faster than the overall cost of living in these two years. It is plausible that rents for physically adequate units would have increased faster than rents for the entire inventory. Nonetheless, I find an estimate this large hard to accept in the absence of any other evidence supporting such a remarkable discontinuity of conditions in rental housing markets.
   11. Lowry, "Inflation Indexes for Rental Housing."

rents in real terms have indeed fallen in the past two decades, but much less than the CPI indicates.

Who Is Being Injured?

Recent rent trends are injuring both owners of rental units and their poorest tenants, but not all tenants. The median income among all renters increased 58.7 percent from 1970 to 1979.[12] Although the CPI rent component went up almost the same percentage (59.9), Lowry's adjusted gross rent index rose 81.4 percent. However, the income of individual renting households actually also went up by about 85 percent, because the median for all renters was shifted downward by a change in household composition among renters, as noted in chapter 1. Thus most of the apparently greater rise in median income among owner-occupants than among renters from 1970 to 1979 is a statistical illusion.

Nevertheless, the income of the poorest families rose more slowly than family income generally; it might be supposed that the income of many very poor families rose more slowly than their rents. From 1970 to 1979 the median income among the lowest income quintile (the lowest 20 percent) of families rose 92.2 percent, compared with 101.8 percent for all families and over 102 percent for all other quintiles of families. However, among unrelated individuals, the lowest quintile had the highest increase in median income (142.9 percent), with smaller rises among higher quintiles.[13] The CPI rent index rose only 58.7 percent in that period, but Lowry's index increased 81.4 percent. Thus, even using Lowry's index as a measure of rent, the median income of every type of household increased faster than rents from 1970 to 1979.

This conclusion does not apply throughout the period 1970–79, however. From 1973 to 1979, for example, the median income of two-or-more-person households headed by women or unmarried men rose much less than their rents regardless of the rent index used; thus their rent burdens increased. In contrast, median incomes of the other two household types increased almost as much as or more than their rents (see table 2-2).

12. Data from *Annual Housing Survey, 1973* through *1979*.
13. Data from *Statistical Abstract, 1981*, p. 438. This conclusion must be qualified by the observation that the specific persons in the lowest income quintile in 1978 or 1979 are not necessarily the same ones who were in that group in 1970.

Table 2-2. *Income and Rent Increases, 1973–79*
Percent

Type of increase	Increase
Median income of renters	
Husband-and-wife households[a]	49.5
Other male-headed households[a]	25.6
Female-headed households[a]	20.7
One-person households	66.7
Rent	
Lowry index	56.3
CPI rent index	40.5

Source: U.S. Department of Housing and Urban Development and U.S. Bureau of the Census, *Annual Housing Survey, 1973, Part C* (U.S. Government Printing Office, 1976), p. 3, and *1979, Part C*, p. 6; and Lowry, "Inflation Indexes for Rental Housing," p. 30.
a. Households containing two or more persons.

The impact of recent rent trends on rental property owners seems clear. For almost all owners, rents have risen more slowly than either operating costs or the costs of new construction and renovation. This has reduced yields on investments received by owners who refinanced recently. Moreover, higher operating costs were offset by fixed debt-service costs for owners who did not refinance or buy recently.

Thus many owners can legitimately describe recent rent increases as being too small because rents have risen too slowly to provide an adequate return on their investments. Yet most owners who did not refinance or buy recently gained because their fixed debt-service costs allowed them to increase profits even though rents went up more slowly than operating costs. Furthermore, some owners who refinanced took large sums of money out of their properties tax-free, though they subsequently had to pay higher debt-service costs.

Why Haven't Rents Increased Faster?

Rents have not risen very rapidly compared with other living costs for six main reasons: the eagerness of some tenants to own their homes; the poverty of those who remain tenants; the perceived self-interest of many owners to avoid rapid turnover of their tenants; the owners' fear of rent controls; the ability of vacancies to absorb rising demand; and the tendency of owners to invest in rental housing as a tax shelter.

The Lure of Homeownership

Homeownership became so attractive in the 1970s it undermined the market for rental housing. Investing in housing—particularly owner-occupied units—was extremely profitable during the 1970s, as will be discussed in chapter 3. Moreover, many local governments taxed owner-occupied housing less than rental housing. For example, when Cook County, Illinois (which contains Chicago and many suburbs) adopted explicitly different assessment ratios for various types of property in the 1970s, it initially assessed single-family homes at 22 percent of market value but rental apartments at 30 percent.[14] Many other jurisdictions in practice assessed single-family homes at much lower percentages of actual market value than large apartment complexes, even when legally required to treat all properties identically.

As a result, more and more households began viewing housing primarily as an investment rather than as necessary shelter. As George Sternlieb puts it, they moved into the "post-shelter society," in which their attitudes toward housing were dictated mainly by financial motives.[15] Hence many people who once considered renting living space as a reasonable transaction came to view it as "throwing their money away for nothing but a bunch of rent receipts." That attitude was encouraged by home builders, brokers, and others with vested interests in promoting owner occupancy. So a large proportion of all households that could afford relatively high rents decided instead to buy housing. From 1970 to 1979 the increase in homeowning households composed 76 percent of the total increase in households, even though the proportion of all households that occupied their own homes increased modestly from 62.9 to 65.4 percent.[16]

This shift in demand tremendously undermined the market for rental housing—particularly high-rent units. Because newly built apartments have relatively high rents, such erosion especially weakened the market for new units. In the past, a steady stream of newly built, relatively high-rent units at one end of the inventory replaced the older, lower-rent

---

14. Data from studies, which the author supervised, by Real Estate Research Corporation for the Cook County assessor.
15. See George Sternlieb and James W. Hughes, "The Post-Shelter Society," in Sternlieb and Hughes, eds., *America's Housing: Prospects and Problems* (Rutgers University, Center for Urban Policy Research, 1980), pp. 93-102.
16. *Annual Housing Survey, 1979, Part A*, pp. 5-6.

units being abandoned or demolished at the other end. This continually upgraded the overall rental inventory. Removal of relatively obsolete older units seems to have been continuing apace at least through 1977, based on Annual Housing Survey data. But much lower production of new unsubsidized rental units will eventually create pressure for more intensive use of older existing units, unless total rental demand falls even faster than total supply.

The Poverty of Tenants

The movement of most high-income households out of the rental market increases the proportion of renters that are poor. Because the income of many poor households that cannot afford, or do not want, homeownership has not risen as rapidly as the cost of building or operating housing, landlords often cannot raise rents much without facing increased collection problems and hostility. These landlords cannot maintain a competitive or even a stable rate of return on invested capital unless they allow their properties to deteriorate badly or refuse to pay local property taxes. But those tactics eventually cause a complete loss of the properties.

The Dominance of Small-Scale Owners

Reliable data on who owns the nation's rental housing are not available, but my impression is that ownership is scattered among many small-scale landlords. This impression is based on the high percentage of rental housing containing fewer than five units, as noted in chapter 1, and on my experience in talking to realtors and investors across the nation over the past fifteen years. Many large-scale real estate investors avoid residential properties, partly because the high tenant turnover described earlier raises management costs of residential properties compared with other rental real estate. But small-scale investors who manage their own properties rarely take full account of the cost of their time. So they have lower management costs—both apparent and real—than large-scale operators who employ professional management and maintenance personnel. That often leads small-scale operators to charge lower rents than those needed by large-scale operators to earn yields competitive with alternative investments.

Moreover, vacancy is much more threatening to small-scale than large-scale operators. Every rental owner has a strong incentive to avoid raising rents so fast that vacancy increases, because each vacancy usually involves a loss of income, an investment in redecoration, and considerable effort to find a suitable new tenant. But this incentive affects small-scale operators differently from large-scale ones. If a hundred units are operated by a hundred different owners, every vacancy represents a 100 percent loss of rental income to some operator. Such owners try to avoid that outcome by raising rents cautiously. But if a hundred units are all run by one owner, the same vacancy is only a 1 percent loss of income. That owner can afford to raise rents more boldly without risking as serious a loss of net income as the small-scale owners would. This situation, plus the high rate of normal turnover among renters, makes most small-scale landlords *turnover minimizers* rather than *rent maximizers*.

One way to minimize turnover is to find good tenants who will stay a long while, pay on time, and not damage the property. Most small owners give such tenants an incentive to remain by keeping their rents relatively low. As a result, long-term tenants typically have lower rents than short-term ones. The experimental housing allowance program showed that each year of occupancy tends to reduce monthly gross rent below its true market level by an average of 3.8 percent, up to a maximum of 11 percent.[17] In 1976, 19.7 percent of all tenants had occupied their units more than six years.[18]

When a market is dominated by small-scale operators, most of whom restrain rent increases to avoid turnover, even large-scale operators may not realize they could charge more than the prevailing rents, based on the actual balance of supply and demand. This would not happen if everyone were perfectly informed, but information in housing markets is often quite imperfect. Rental owners set their prices either by adding "reasonable" increments on existing rents or by surveying rents in nearby competitive properties. The latter method is likely to generate a mutual underestimation of the price needed to "clear the market" at the margins. However, as Lowry points out, this factor alone cannot explain why rents have lagged so far below the general cost of living.[19]

17. Taken from Lowry, "Rental Housing in the 1970s," p. 42. See also C. Peter Rydell, *Vacancy Duration and Housing Market Condition*, N-1135-HUD (Rand Corporation, October 1979).

18. *Annual Housing Survey, 1976, Part D*, p. 4.

19. Lowry, "Rental Housing in the 1970s," p. 42. He estimates the overall discount due to longevity at about 6.5 percent as of the mid-1970s.

The Fear of Rent Controls

During rapid inflation, actual rent controls or fear of them keeps many landlords, especially large-scale ones, from raising rents as fast as the market would permit—or fast enough to keep up with operating costs.[20] Tenants with relatively fixed incomes, especially elderly persons, become angry and frustrated when the prices of many necessities rise faster than their income. They cannot retaliate against distant farmers or Arab oil sheiks who raise prices, but they can against their landlords. Immobile rental properties are easily made hostages of a local government sensitive to the desires of renting constituents. In many communities strong political protests will lead to rent controls if landlords try to raise rents fast enough to maintain their return on capital. Such protests are especially likely against owners of large rental projects with high visibility. Many nations with prolonged inflation have adopted residential rent controls for this reason.

In theory, all rent control systems let owners "pass through" major expense increases to their tenants, allowing owners to maintain competitive returns on equity. But political pressures from tenants—who vastly outnumber landlords—usually persuade rent control administrators to prevent rents from rising as fast as expenses. An analysis by the Rand Corporation concluded that New York City rent controls from 1943 to 1969 had constrained rents to 36 percent below their true market level as of 1968.[21] Because few other U.S. cities have had rent controls for that long, it is not clear what impact such controls would have on rent levels elsewhere. The fear of rent controls probably has not caused landlords to restrict rents by very much. Yet new unsubsidized rental housing is rarely built wherever rent controls exist, even where all new units are "permanently free" from controls. Once a legislature has passed any form of rent controls, builders, developers, and investors have no confidence that such exemptions will not be arbitrarily changed in the future, as they have been so often in the past. Because rent controls both cut off the building of new private rental units and undermine the

---

20. Owners who do not raise rents as fast as operating costs can still increase their profits if their debt-service charges remain fixed as rents rise, since debt-service charges are a high fraction of total costs. Whether particular landlords made profits during this period depends in part on whether they refinanced their properties, and—if so—exactly when they did and what specific changes in interest rates and other terms were involved.

21. See Ira S. Lowry, Joseph S. deSalvo, and Barbara M. Woodfill, *Rental Housing in New York City*, vol. 2: *The Demand for Shelter*, R-649-NYC (Rand Corporation, June 1971), pp. 87–92.

profitability of existing ones, they tend to reduce the inventory of such units over time. In Great Britain, for example, long-term rent controls have contributed to a striking decline in privately owned rental units. In 1945 over 50 percent of the total housing inventory was rented from private landlords. By 1966 this share had fallen by half; by 1977 it was less than 15 percent.[22] Rent controls were not the only cause of this withering away, but they contributed significantly. A recent study of rent controls in Ontario from 1975 through 1980 concluded that they had "substantially inhibited new rental construction, generated rental shortages, . . . [and] encouraged deterioration in the quality of the existing housing stock." These ill effects occurred even though newly built dwellings were exempt from controls.[23]

The Absorption of Demand by Reduced Vacancy

Increased rental demand can often be accommodated by a fall in the number of vacant units or the average duration of vacancy or both. Until the vacancy rate falls very low, such absorption of higher demand does not increase rents much because it does not noticeably intensify competition for each occupied unit. Yet lower vacancy increases the average unit's profitability by raising the amount of time it earns income without proportionally increasing its operating costs. That increases the unit's market value. In many U.S. metropolitan areas, the market value of rental housing has risen significantly even though average rents have not gone up much—they may even have fallen in real terms. Vacancies rose in the mid-1970s because of massive new multifamily construction in the early 1970s plus a weakening of demand in the 1974–75 recession. From 1976 to 1981 rental demand rose, vacancies declined, and the market values of rental properties went up substantially—all without any rapid increases in rents. Only in submarkets where vacancies fell extremely low have rents begun to escalate rapidly. Even there, such escalation is often constrained by the other factors described in this chapter.[24]

22. See J. B. Cullingworth, *Essays on Housing Policy: The British Scene* (London: Allen and Unwin, 1979), p. 37.
23. Lawrence B. Smith and Peter Tomlinson, "Rent Controls in Ontario: Roofs or Ceilings?" *Journal of the American Real Estate and Urban Economics Association*, vol. 9 (Summer 1981), pp. 93-114.
24. This analysis was developed from the experimental housing allowance program. See Rydell, *Vacancy Duration and Housing Market Condition;* and C. Peter Rydell, *Shortrun Response of Housing Markets to Demand Shifts,* R-2453-HUD (Rand Corporation, September 1979), p. 3.

The Advantages of Tax Shelter

Much of the economic reward of owning rental housing derives from the tax shelter it provides for other income. *Builder,* the National Association of Home Builders magazine, recently published the projected benefits to investors of a subsidized Section 8 rental project. The investor was to contribute $30,000 in cash over five years and receive $12,234 in rental income over twenty years, after which the building was to be sold. The investor would benefit from tax reductions of $51,463 during those twenty years, assuming a 60 percent tax bracket, less capital gains taxes of $19,041 at the time of sale.[25] In fact, the first-year tax benefit of $10,047 would exceed the first-year investment of $9,750, and combined rental and tax benefits in every subsequent year would also exceed cash inputs. Thus the investor essentially has no equity in the deal. Nearly all the benefits from this hypothetical investment spring from sheltering other income from taxes. This greatly reduces the owner's incentive to maximize rents. Small-scale investors are more strongly motivated to seek tax shelter than large institutional investors, many of which are tax exempt. Hence the importance of tax shelter combines with the dominance of small-scale investors to reduce pressure to increase rents as fast as would be necessary if operating profits were the sole economic benefit to ownership.

How Has Inflation Affected Rental Housing?

These causes of lagging rents were connected with the inflation of the late 1970s, which most capital suppliers—and many borrowers—did not anticipate. It greatly stimulated the demand for homeownership, thereby reducing rental demand. It also cut the real income of many poor households, making it difficult for them to pay higher rents.

Although inflation reduced the current profitability of rental properties by raising operating expenses and interest rates faster than rents, it stimulated the demand for owning rental units for several reasons.[26]

—Investors could leverage small equity investments with large amounts borrowed on long-term, fixed-rate mortgages. The debt service on such

---

25. "Oxford Group Finds Room for Rentals," *Builder,* June 1, 1980, p. 85.
26. These reasons are related to four factors discussed in chapter 6.

mortgages declines in real terms during periods of inflation. Lenders made such loans in the 1960s and the early 1970s at interest rates too low to compensate for subsequent inflation because they failed to anticipate it.

—Purchasers were often able to shift units bought in the rental market into the ownership market by converting them to condominiums. This generated large capital gains because ownership units sold at much higher prices.

—Inflation reduced total returns on other forms of investment like stocks and bonds for reasons discussed in chapter 3. Consequently, more and more investors shifted into real estate, driving down capitalization rates on net income from real properties.[27] This raised the price of many real properties, including those that did not have rising net income streams. It also tended to reinforce expectations that real estate values would continue rising.

—By pushing people into higher income tax brackets, inflation made tax shelter more important to them. Rental properties provided considerable tax shelter because of accelerated depreciation and the deductibility of both mortgage interest and property taxes.

The resulting increase in demand raised the price of rental properties so high they often produced very low or negative cash-on-cash yields. (Cash-on-cash yield is the percentage of return formed by gross current revenues minus operating costs and total debt service, measured against the total initial cash investment. It does not take tax shelter or proceeds from possible future sale into account, nor does it count amortization as income.) These low yields caused most large-scale investors to avoid rental housing; the rising demand was concentrated among small-scale investors. Their pursuit of tax shelter and avoidance of vacancies kept rents lower than they might otherwise have been. Hence it became more and more infeasible for large-scale investors to construct and operate new unsubsidized rental housing. Rapid inflation also helped generate enough general frustration among consumers to create a favorable political climate for rent controls in many communities. Thus unanticipated inflation plus prevailing tax laws strongly inhibited the creation of new private rental housing in 1974–80. Thereafter the situation changed, as discussed in chapter 3.

27. Those capitalization rates are the percentages of market price formed by current net income. Strong demand for ownership drives up prices relative to income, thus reducing capitalization rates.

How Has the Rent Gap Affected Rental Housing?

Because rents have lagged behind construction and operating costs, it has not been economically feasible to build new rental apartments for several years. Lenders have usually appraised proposed apartment projects at market values well below actual construction costs and, when they have offered mortgages for such projects, loans have been much smaller than developers needed for attractive profitability. Some equity investors have been willing to enter apartment projects at very low initial cash-on-cash rates of return because they believed that future appreciation and current tax shelter would provide sufficient total return to compensate for low initial cash flow. However, only small-scale investors have been willing to put up money so completely "on the come." Most large institutional investors have been reluctant to take such risks, especially because of the high cost of management and the potential of rent controls.

The marked slowdown in the development of new unsubsidized rental housing projects can be seen from changes in new multifamily housing construction, even though not all multifamily units are destined for private rental and some new rental units are single-family homes. The average annual rate of new multifamily housing starts was 871,000 from 1970 to 1973, but fell 47 percent to 458,000 from 1974 to 1980.[28] Furthermore, a much greater share of new multifamily units was destined for condominium ownership in the second period.

This slower building of new rental units has been accompanied by faster removal of existing ones from the inventory. Between 1970 and 1976, 1.5 million rental units built before 1965 were removed from the inventory, or about 250,000 each year. Between 1973 and 1978, 1.6 million rental units built before 1960 were removed from the inventory, or 315,000 each year.[29]

In addition, thousands of rental units are being converted each year to condominium occupancy. From 1970 through 1979, 366,000 rental units were converted to either condominiums (95 percent) or cooperatives (5 percent).[30] By the end of 1979, about 1.3 percent of the nation's

---

28. *Statistical Abstract, 1981*, p. 757.
29. *Annual Housing Survey, 1976, Part A*, p. 27, and *1978, Part A*, p. 29.
30. Department of Housing and Urban Development, *The Conversion of Rental Housing to Condominiums and Cooperatives* (GPO, 1980), pp. i-ix. All data in this paragraph are taken from this document.

Table 2-3. *Annual Increase in Renter-Occupied Units, Selected Years, 1970–79*
Thousands of units

Year	Renter-occupied units	Annual increase
1970	23,560	...
1973	24,684	375[a]
1974	25,046	362
1975	25,656	610
1976	26,101	445
1977	26,515	414
1978	26,884	369
1979	27,160	276

Source: *Annual Housing Survey, 1973* through *1979.*
a. Average 1970–73.

occupied rental inventory had been converted. Over 70 percent occurred from 1977 to 1979, at an annual rate of 86,700 units. The Department of Housing and Urban Development (HUD) expects an increase to about 183,000 units a year in the first half of the 1980s.

Conversion, however, does not produce a large decline in rental availability relative to demand. Many buyers of converted units are former renters who no longer need or desire rental units. Moreover, many converted units are rented out by their new owners. And many persons displaced by conversion buy units elsewhere, removing themselves from the rental market. Taking all these factors into account, HUD estimated that conversion of 366,000 rental units from 1970 to 1979 reduced the number of available rental units only 18,000 more than it reduced the number of renting households.[31]

In spite of these removals, the total number of rental units available is still rising (see table 2-3). The average annual increase in renter-occupied units was 374,000 in 1970–73, 472,000 in 1973–76, 392,000 in 1977–78, but only 276,000 in 1979. Nevertheless, rental demand has risen faster than the number of rental units. The overall rental vacancy rate fell from 6.2 percent in 1974 to 4.8 percent in the first quarter of 1979.[32] It then rose to 5.7 percent in the third quarter of 1980, but

31. Ibid., p. iii.
32. Council of Economic Advisers, *Economic Indicators,* June 1981, p. 19.

dropped to 5.2 percent in the first quarter of 1981.[33] Acute shortages of rental housing have developed in some urban neighborhoods, such as Chicago's Near North Side and Manhattan's Upper East Side.[34] Rents have been rising faster there than in the nation as a whole—sometimes 10 to 20 percent a year (unless constrained by rent controls). Even so, in most of the nation, rents were still far too low in 1982 to stimulate much construction of unsubsidized rental housing.

33. Ibid. The data in this paragraph are from various Annual Housing Surveys, but they are not consistent with preliminary data from the 1980 census. The actual count in April 1980 revealed 28.591 million renter-occupied units and 51.787 million owner-occupied units, plus 8.018 million unoccupied units in various categories, according to information obtained by telephone in March 1982 from the Census Bureau. This count indicates that the number of renter-occupied units rose by 1.4 million from October 1979 to April 1980—a clear impossibility. Either the actual count was too high or the Annual Housing Survey estimates were too low—probably the latter. However, if the 1980 count was correct, then the average annual increase in renter-occupied units from April 1970 to April 1980 was 503,000. That is 4 percent higher than the average new construction of rental units from 1974 to 1979 estimated later in chapter 5. Hence the 1980 census data do not seriously invalidate the basis of the projections made in chapters 5 and 7. Furthermore, the 1980 census showed a rental vacancy rate of 7.1 percent, significantly above that derived from Current Population Surveys in 1980. Reconciliation of these actual counts with the numbers shown in the text derived from Annual Housing Surveys was not possible at the time this book was completed, since the Census Bureau had not yet released detailed information about housing from the 1980 count.

34. The shortage on Chicago's Near North Side was partly alleviated by a surplus of condominium units, many converted from rental apartments. Purchasers of such units for speculation often offered them for rent in 1980–82, when high interest rates weakened the ability of consumers to buy these units for owner occupancy.

3
Future Availability of Capital

IN 1980 a revolution occurred in real estate finance when most suppliers of financial capital changed their expectations about inflation. As a result, the share of total capital flowing into housing will probably be lower in the 1980s than in the 1970s, and its real cost to borrowers will be much higher. This chapter considers the future implications of this revolution for rental housing.[1]

Capital Flows into Housing during the 1970s

The relative importance of housing compared with other uses of financial capital is shown by the fractions of total credit raised that went into different activities. From 1970 through 1979 financial and nonfinancial sectors combined raised $2,847.3 billion in current dollars. Home mortgages absorbed 21.3 percent of that total and 24.5 percent of the $2,453.3 billion raised by nonfinancial sectors—more than any other use. U.S. government borrowing by the Treasury and other agencies accounted for the second largest fraction of funds raised by nonfinancial sectors—15.3 percent. The next largest shares went into consumer credit (9.9 percent), bank loans not elsewhere classified (8.5 percent), corporate bonds (7.9 percent), state and local government obligations (7.7 percent), and commercial and industrial mortgages (6.3 percent).[2]

---

[1]. Some of the chapter deals with owner-occupied housing because of its central influence on all residential finance, but rental housing is emphasized as much as possible.

[2]. Board of Governors of the Federal Reserve System, *Flow of Funds Accounts*, 2d Quarter 1982 (The Board, 1982), p. 3.

Housing's share of total financial capital flows was larger in the 1970s than in the late 1960s but smaller than in the 1950s or early 1960s. The annual fraction of all capital raised by both financial and nonfinancial sectors going into home mortgages averaged 15.1 percent between 1966 and 1969. It started at 12.5 percent in 1970 but rose to 25.2 percent in 1977, 23.6 percent in 1978, and 24.5 percent in 1979.[3] In 1950–65 this fraction had averaged 25.0 percent.[4] But then the nation was catching up after twenty years of depressed new home construction in the 1930s and the 1940s. Similar pressures of long-deferred demand did not exist in the 1970s because by then both the quantity and quality of our housing were vastly superior to what they had been in 1950.[5]

During the 1970s housing finance also shifted emphasis from constructing new units to refinancing or selling existing ones. The ratio of all residential mortgage lending to the total cost of new housing is a rough measure of how closely mortgage finance is related to new building. In the 1950s that ratio was 50.7 percent, that is, total mortgage finance was half the cost of building new homes. It rose to 70.0 percent in the 1960s, 79.0 percent in the first half of the 1970s, and 110.6 percent in 1976–78.[6] The total share of home mortgages used to finance existing homes rose from 55.9 percent in 1970 and 59.3 percent in 1974 to an average of 68.2 percent from 1975 through 1979.[7]

Some observers argue that housing received a smaller share of total resources in the 1970s than in the past because the fraction of gross national product (GNP) formed by residential construction declined. That fraction averaged 4.5 percent in 1970–79, compared with 5.3 percent in

3. Ibid., pp. 2–3, 36–37.
4. Board of Governors of the Federal Reserve System, *Flow of Funds Accounts, 1946–75* (The Board, 1976), pp. 4–5, 57–58.
5. See John Weicher, Lorene Yap, and Mary S. Jones, *Metropolitan Housing Needs for the 1980s* (Urban Institute, 1982).
6. Data are taken from the table on mortgage finance in *Flow of Funds Accounts, 2d quarter*, pp. 36–37; from the table on gross national product components in the U.S. Bureau of the Census, *Statistical Abstract of the United States* (U.S. Government Printing Office), various years; and from Bureau of the Census, *Historical Statistics of the United States: Colonial Times to 1970* (GPO, 1975), p. 229. This ratio should be interpreted with caution. Two data sources are involved with different statistical inputs. Some of the ratio's increase reflects lower down payments for new homes in later years. Moreover, many homes are sold without mortgages. During the 1970s about 15 percent of new single-family homes were not initially financed with mortgages. The fraction of existing owner-occupied homes without mortgages declined from about 50 percent in the 1950s to about 36 percent in the last half of the 1970s. Data are from *Statistical Abstract, 1980*, pp. 788, 801.
7. *Statistical Abstract, 1980*, p. 801, and *1981*, p. 771.

AVAILABILITY OF CAPITAL 45

1950–59.[8] Thus the share of real resource flows into new housing production and rehabilitation fell slightly, although the share of financial flows increased sharply, as noted above. This is possible because not all financial capital flowing into housing is translated into real resources and not all of that so translated is spent improving housing.

The Failure of Lenders to Anticipate Inflation

Most U.S. capital suppliers did not anticipate the accelerating inflation of the 1970s. The general price level had been quite stable throughout the 1950s and the early 1960s and rose only moderately in the late 1960s. Each time the rate of price increase rose noticeably, it soon fell back down again. Its acceleration in the mid and late 1970s was largely due to unforeseeable events, including the war in the Middle East and worldwide crop failures in 1973 and the explosion of world oil prices in 1974 and 1979. Hence lenders thought they were reasonably prudent in making long-term loans in the 1960s and early 1970s at fixed, relatively low nominal interest rates. These rates turned out to be far too low in real terms from the viewpoint of the lenders and the savers who supplied the money. Even if a few lenders had correctly anticipated rising future inflation, they could not have obtained high rates because of competition from others willing to make long-term, fixed-rate loans at low rates. This inability of lenders to anticipate future inflation, even more than the inflation itself, created an immensely favorable climate for borrowing.

Favorable Borrowing Terms in the 1970s

A primary cause of large financial capital flows into housing in the 1970s was the favorable credit terms available to home buyers and developers. These consisted of high loan-to-value ratios and low real after-tax interest rates.

Households could borrow 80–95 percent of the cost of acquiring homes with fixed-rate mortgages, and apartment developers up to and sometimes over 100 percent of project costs. Such leveraging produces extremely high yields on initial equity investments whenever market values rise

---

8. *Statistical Abstract, 1976,* p. 394, and *1980,* p. 439; *Historical Statistics of the United States,* p. 229.

swiftly. Between September 1976 and September 1980, for example, the median selling price of existing single-family homes increased at a compound annual rate of 13.5 percent.[9] The average home purchased with a 20 percent down payment thus experienced a 67.5 percent increase in initial equity each year. Even after deducting associated costs, the profits resulting from leveraged homeownership were remarkable—and tax free. Similar profits were made on rental apartment investments during the first part of the 1970s.

Unanticipated inflation also cut the real carrying costs of fixed-payment mortgages during the 1970s. Debt service usually accounted for well over half the gross costs of occupying a home or operating rental apartments. But, even when operating costs rose rapidly, mortgage payments were fixed. Thus, as household income increased with inflation, homeowners typically paid declining real amounts and falling percentages of their income for housing each month. So did owners of rental apartments initially financed at relatively low nominal rates, as long as they did not refinance at higher rates.

This favorable situation was obscured by the escalating costs of first-year occupancy in the late 1970s. Many analysts who looked only at first-year costs drew gloomy conclusions about how few Americans could afford to buy homes. Home buyers themselves knew better; they recognized that multiyear occupancy costs were falling in real terms throughout the 1970s.[10]

Another effect of unanticipated inflation was reduction of the real after-tax rate of interest paid by borrowers. A simple example will make this clear. If a borrower pays 12 percent interest on a fixed-rate mortgage when prices in general are rising 10 percent a year, the real rate of interest is 1.8 percent before taxes for the first year (1.12 divided by 1.10). That rate falls to minus 2.5 percent after taxes for people in the 40 percent bracket. Similar computations apply to apartment owners with

9. National Association of Realtors, *Monthly Report: Existing Single-Family Homes Sales*, October 1980, p. 1. Some of this rise reflects improved quality because the overall inventory was upgraded by the addition of new units and the removal of old ones. But such quality improvements are relatively small in a four-year period; most of the gain was a true price increase.

10. For some calculations about how fast those costs fell, see Douglas B. Diamond, Jr., "Taxes, Inflation, Speculation, and the Cost of Homeownership," paper presented at the American Real Estate and Urban Economics Association meetings in Washington, D.C., May 1979, revised October 1979. See also Patric H. Hendershott, "Real User Costs and the Demand for Single-Family Housing," *Brookings Papers on Economic Activity*, 2:1980, pp. 401–52 (hereafter cited as *BPEA*).

Table 3-1. *Mortgage Interest Rates on Loans Made in 1951–75*[a]

Mortgage type and period	Nominal interest rate	Real interest rate	Ratio	Real after-tax rate
Single-family residential[b]				
1951–59	5.25	3.43	0.625	2.22
1960–69	6.29	1.39	0.348	0.09
1970–75	8.13	−1.37	...	−2.87
Industrial and commercial[c]				
1951–59	5.02	3.23	0.643	0.83
1960–69	6.58	1.59	0.242	−1.11
1970–75	9.34	−0.58	...	−3.84

Source: Anthony Downs and S. Michael Giliberto, "How Inflation Erodes the Income of Fixed-Rate Lenders," *Real Estate Review* (Spring 1981), p. 46.
a. Each loan amortized for twenty-five years but held for ten years, then paid off. (Loans made after 1970 are held only until 1980.) Interest rates shown are annual averages for the periods indicated.
b. Tax rate used is 25 percent.
c. Tax rate used is actual corporate tax rate for each year.

mortgages, as long as the market prices of their units keep rising. These calculations are based on a one-year loan. The results are even more dramatic when compounded over longer-term loans as long as inflation is escalating.

Michael Giliberto and I examined real interest rates actually received by lenders and paid by borrowers on both single-family home mortgages and commercial and industrial mortgages made each year from 1951 through 1975. We assumed each loan was made at the average nominal mortgage interest rate for that year, amortized for twenty-five years, held for ten years, and then fully paid off.[11] Using the consumer price index, we deflated annual payments of interest and principal and final payment of the outstanding balance into dollars with purchasing power equal to that in the year when each loan was made. We then computed the effective real interest rate for loans made in each year. We also computed the after-tax rate paid by the borrower, assuming a 25 percent tax bracket for home mortgagors and the corporate tax rate for industrial and commercial mortgagors. The average results for three periods are shown in table 3-1. *Real* interest rates fell sharply in the 1960s and early 1970s, at the same time that *nominal* rates were rising to record levels. The

11. Computations concerning most loans made in the 1970s assume they were held only until 1980. See Anthony Downs and S. Michael Giliberto, "How Inflation Erodes the Income of Fixed-Rate Lenders," *Real Estate Review* (Spring 1981), pp. 43–51.

same conclusions apply to the real after-tax interest costs of apartment developers, who obtained funds at similar rates.

Advantages of Housing over Alternative Investments

Inflation in the 1970s gradually pushed millions of households into higher marginal income tax brackets, even though Congress reduced tax rates occasionally. The higher the marginal tax bracket, other things equal, the more any given amount deductible from taxable income is worth in tax savings and the less any given amount of interest or dividend is worth after taxes. So this "bracket creep" made housing (and other tax-sheltering investments) more attractive to investors, while rendering stocks, bonds, and savings accounts that paid fully taxable returns less attractive.

Inflation also penalized investments in stocks and business in other ways. Until the Economic Recovery Tax Act of 1981, corporations and other businesses computing their taxable income could only deduct depreciation calculated on the basis of historical costs. Yet true replacement costs of depreciating assets were constantly rising because of inflation. This systematic underestimation of replacement costs overstated profits, thereby raising income taxes above what would have been owed if accounting were done in real terms. Owners of rental housing also suffered from this handicap, but they were allowed to use faster-than-straight-line depreciation. Similar overstatements of real profits earned by businesses occurred because of inventory price increases. Hence many businesses paid federal and state income taxes far too large in relation to their "real" profitability.[12] Some estimates placed this overpayment as high as 25 percent on the average, though no comprehensive data are available.[13] The greater the rate of inflation, the worse this bias against business became. It helps explain why the real value of the 500 stocks

12. See Martin Feldstein and Lawrence Summers, "Inflation, Tax Rules, and the Long-Term Interest Rate," *BPEA*, 2:1978, pp. 62–109.

13. In a recent undated speech entitled "Inflation and Its Impact on Financial Executives," Duane R. Kullberg, chairman of the accounting firm of Arthur Anderson and Company, cited a 1974 study of eighty corporations concerning the impact of constant-dollar accounting. He stated that inflation had raised the average corporate tax rate by about 25 percent to an effective rate of 55 to 65 percent. This reference was supplied to me by Stanley S. Surrey of the Harvard Law School. Professor Surrey also pointed out that inflation aids companies that have borrowed heavily with fixed-rate loans; hence it may raise their profits over what they would be in a noninflationary situation or at least offset exaggerations in their taxable income because of factors described in the text.

AVAILABILITY OF CAPITAL

listed in the Standard and Poor's index fell 48 percent from 1965 to 1980.[14]

Inflation also reduced the purchasing power of investments in bonds, savings accounts, and other instruments with values fixed in nominal dollars. For example, if an investor had bought $100,000 in bonds in 1970 and received interest only until 1980, when the entire $100,000 was repaid, the 1980 purchasing power of that amount in 1970 dollars would have been only $47,270. If the investor had used the same $100,000 to buy a home for all cash and that home rose in price at the national average rate, it would have been worth $278,200 in 1980! The 1980 purchasing power of that amount in 1970 dollars would have been $131,506—or 2.8 times as great as that resulting from investing the same initial amount in bonds. Instead of losing 53 percent of its initial real value, the original investment would have gained 32 percent.

These calculations do not take into account the bondholder's receipt of interest or the fact that the home buyer would have benefited from living in the house for ten years. Nevertheless, they illustrate the striking difference between fixed-value instruments and homeownership as hedges against inflation in the 1970s. Moreover, homeowner equities leveraged with mortgages increased at much faster rates than the all-cash equity in this example.

Rental Property's Relative Disadvantage in Attracting Capital

Though housing attracted immense financial capital flows during the 1970s, the share financing rental properties declined after 1973, partly because of a drop in construction of new multifamily units (see chapter 1). The dollar value of all mortgages for structures containing five or more units—mostly built for private rental—composed less than 6.0 percent of all residential mortgage lending from 1975 to 1979, compared with 22.8 percent from 1970 to 1974.[15]

14. In 1965 the Standard and Poor's index of 500 stocks stood at 88.2; in December 1980 it was 118.8. That was an increase of 34.7 percent in fifteen years during which the consumer price index rose 161 percent. Hence the real value of stocks measured by this index fell by 48 percent, or 4.2 percent a year compounded. This calculation does not take dividends into account. See *Statistical Abstract, 1981*, pp. 467, 542.

15. *Flow of Funds Accounts, 2d Quarter 1982*, pp. 36–37. The average number of units built each year in structures containing two to four units was 106,560 from 1970 through 1974 and 103,720 from 1975 through 1979. Hence it declined only 2.7 percent in the second period. Such units composed 5.7 percent of all conventionally built housing units in the first half of the decade and 6.1 percent in the second half. Council of Economic Advisers, *Economic Indicators*, January 1977, p. 19, and April 1980, p. 19. Thus there was probably no significant decline in the number of such units destined for the rental market.

Why did this happen? The superior attractions of homeownership weakened the demand for renting, especially at the high-priced end of the market. Developers are most strongly motivated to build new rental units when they can "mortgage out," that is, borrow over 100 percent of project costs. They had done so previously when prospective rents were high enough to justify appraising new units at values much greater than the costs of building them. Then a loan at 90 percent or even 80 percent of appraised value often exceeded out-of-pocket costs of project development. But in the late 1970s developers could not set prospective rents on new projects high enough to do this, especially with rapidly rising costs of development. Accelerating inflation magnified the relative advantages of homeownership even more, further reducing the ability of large rental projects to attract capital.

Patric Hendershott has measured the real user costs of owner-occupied and rental housing and the real user costs of capital invested in both types.[16] His definition of real user costs includes allowances for capital appreciation in user-owned assets, inflation, and tax deductibility of mortgage interest and other items. He concluded that:

> The real user cost of capital for owner-occupied housing of households in the 15 percent tax bracket declined from just under 8 percent in the early 1960s to 4 percent in 1978. This drop follows directly from a sharp fall in real after-tax interest rates. . . . In contrast, the real user cost for rental housing . . . fell by only about 1.5 percentage points during the same period. The use of historical cost depreciation in an inflationary period and the passage of legislation that increased taxation of investments in rental housing have acted to offset, in large measure, the decline in real after-tax financing rates. As a result, homeownership has been encouraged.[17]

His analysis indicated that about 4.5 million households were induced to shift from renting to homeowning from 1964 to 1979 because of the "sharp decline in the implicit rent of owner-occupied housing relative to that of rental housing."[18]

True, many small-scale investors purchased single-family homes, townhouses, or multifamily condominium units as investments, renting them out while waiting for their value to appreciate on the ownership market. Yet from 1975 to 1978 the number of renter-occupied units increased 6.0 percent in structures containing five or more units and 9.7 percent in structures containing two to four units, but only 1.6 percent

16. Hendershott, "Real User Costs," pp. 402–44.
17. Ibid., p. 440.
18. Ibid., pp. 443–44.

AVAILABILITY OF CAPITAL 51

in single-family detached structures.[19] Equity from small-scale investors and loans made to them as owners of single-family units were relatively small sources of capital for new rental units. The main profits on these investments came from appreciation and tax shelter, rather than the excess of current income over current costs (including debt service). In fact, small-scale rental investments often yielded negative current cash flows.

Another source of "interim rentals" consisted of rental units converted to condominium ownership and then rented out again. A study by the Department of Housing and Urban Development revealed that 37 percent of converted units were being rented. Half were rented from the converters; presumably they would eventually be purchased by their occupants. About 20 percent were rented by purchasers who hoped to sell them later.[20] Assuming 100,000 units are being converted from rentals to condominiums each year, that process adds 20,000 units back to the rental supply, for a net loss of 80,000 units.[21]

Thus, even before the severe credit crunches of 1979–81, very little capital was being invested in new large-scale, unsubsidized residential projects to be permanently for rent. This was true even though capital was readily available at low real after-tax interest rates for financing ownership of housing.

Household Savings in the 1970s

Future availability of capital for building rental housing will depend partly on the rate of household savings. It is particularly crucial for thrift institutions (savings and loan associations and mutual savings banks), which have traditionally financed a lot of new rental housing. Ironically, one apparent result of homeownership's great profitability in the 1970s was a reduction in the rate of consumer savings out of current income. This occurred because many households came to regard rising equities in their own homes as a key form of savings. Until high yields on short-term instruments appeared in 1980, households could earn far greater

---

19. U.S. Department of Housing and Urban Development and Bureau of the Census, *Annual Housing Survey, 1975, Part A* (GPO, 1975), p. 1, and *1978, Part C*, pp. 1, 4.

20. Department of Housing and Urban Development, *The Conversion of Rental Housing to Condominiums and Cooperatives* (GPO, 1980), p. VI-14.

21. However, it is a smaller net loss relative to the number of renting households, since many of them become owners by buying converted units; ibid.

real yields from investing in their own homes—if they borrowed most of the purchase price—than from savings accounts. Hence many came to look upon *borrowing* to buy housing as the best way to *save*. They believed, as my father used to say, What you owe today, you will be worth tomorrow.

This behavior was encouraged by inflationary expectations among households during the 1970s. People who believed prices generally would keep rising looked for ways to protect their wealth against currency depreciation. Housing had a good recent record in that regard, whereas savings accounts, stocks, and bonds were failing to hold anything like their original real values.

Possibly for this reason, consumer savings out of current income during the late 1970s fell below its former levels.[22] During 1979 households saved only 5.9 percent of disposable personal income. Savings rates hit lows of 5.1 percent and 5.5 percent in the last quarter of 1979 and the first quarter of 1980, respectively. These low rates came between two downturns in real GNP growth in the second quarters of 1979 and 1980. Their position in the business cycle was thus comparable to all of 1974 and 1975, when the savings rate averaged 8.5 percent and 8.6 percent, respectively.[23] Thus the rate of consumer savings out of current income dropped almost in half compared with the previous business cycle.

However, these figures do not include increases in homeowners' equity. In 1979 total personal savings out of current income equaled $86.2 billion, but total homeowners' equity rose about $119.3 billion, or 40 percent more than personal savings.[24] Because the number of housing

22. It is impossible to prove unequivocally that the decline in the household savings rate was caused by rising home equities. Nevertheless, I am persuaded that the latter clearly helped bring about the former.

23. The savings figures for 1979–80 are revised numbers issued by the Bureau of Economic Analysis of the Department of Commerce in July 1982. See BEA, *Survey of Current Business: Revised National Income and Product Account Estimates* (GPO, 1982), pp. 37–38. Figures for 1974–75 are found in BEA, *The National Income and Product Accounts of the United States, 1929–76: Statistical Tables* (GPO, 1981), p. 75.

24. In 1978 the median value of owner-occupied housing units was $41,500, according to self-reporting by respondents to the Annual Housing Survey. See *Annual Housing Survey, 1978, Part C*, p. 3. In the same year the median value of single-family homes sold was $48,700, according to annualized data of the National Association of Realtors. Hence use of the Annual Housing Survey median value should result in relatively conservative estimates of total housing equity. There were 50.28 million owner-occupied units in 1978 so their total market value was about $2,086.6 billion (treating the median as an average). From December 1978 to December 1979 the median price of existing single-family homes sold rose by 11.0 percent, according to the National Association of Realtors, *Monthly Report*, December 1978 and December 1979. If the total market value of owner-occupied

units sold each year is only 4–8 percent of the total inventory, most of this equity gain is unrealized. Therefore its value as perceived by homeowners should be discounted. If discounted by 50 percent, it would equal $59.7 billion. That would still be equivalent to 69.3 percent of total 1979 personal savings out of current income. Clearly, home equity increases in the late 1970s represented major unmeasured increments to consumers' savings from personal disposable income.

Moreover, the ratio of annual gains in unrealized home equities to personal savings out of current income rose during the late 1970s. Total undiscounted net home equity gains were 38 percent larger than consumer savings out of disposable personal income in 1979, compared with 20 percent larger in 1974.[25] Discounting these equity gains 50 percent, then adding them to personal savings, produces estimated total household savings of $136.2 billion in 1974 and $145.9 billion in 1979. Those amounts equal 13.6 percent and 8.9 percent of total personal disposable income, respectively.[26] Thus, when increases in home equities are taken into account, personal savings in the 1970s were considerably greater in relation to total personal disposable income than has usually been reported.

Other factors have influenced recent savings rates, too. A demographic shift toward younger households probably lowered the overall savings

---

units rose by the same percentage in 1979, it increased $229.5 billion. From the end of 1978 to the end of 1979, total mortgage debt outstanding on one-to-four-family homes rose $110.3 billion. This mortgage debt total was taken from Board of Governors of the Federal Reserve System, *Annual Statistical Digest, 1970–79* (GPO, 1981), p. 281. Subtracting mortgage debt for all one-to-four-family units from the market value of one-family units is necessary because mortgage debt for the latter is not broken out from the former in available data. The resulting error tends to understate the actual net increase in homeowners' equity, rather than exaggerate it. Subtracting this amount from the estimated gross equity gain of $229.5 billion yields a net increase in homeowners' equity of $119.3 billion.

25. In 1974 there were 45.784 million owner-occupied housing units, with a median value of $27,200, as reported by the Annual Housing Survey. From December 1973 to December 1974 the median price of existing single-family homes sold in the United States rose 10.85 percent, according to the National Association of Realtors. Therefore, the total gross value of all homes was $1,245.3 billion in 1974, and it rose approximately $135.1 billion in that year. Total mortgage debt outstanding on one-to-four-unit residences rose by $33.2 billion during 1974, according to *Annual Statistical Digest, 1970–79*, p. 281. Subtracting that amount from the gross gain cited above yields a net gain of $101.9 billion as the undiscounted, unrealized increase in home equities in 1974.

Total personal savings out of current income equaled $85.2 billion in 1974 and $86.2 billion in 1979; *Statistical Abstract, 1981*, p. 427.

26. Disposable personal income equaled $998 billion in 1974 and $1,642 billion in 1979; *Statistical Abstract, 1981*, p. 427.

rate in the 1970s, since young households typically spend more of their income than older ones. The rising share of transfer payments in total personal income had a similar effect. Transfer recipients probably spend higher percentages of their payments on consumption than wage earners do of their wages. In addition, the rise in nominal interest rates as a result of inflation increased personal income flows from interest but decreased the market value of fixed-rate assets. Because government data measured only the former, they overstated savings by exaggerating net improvements in consumers' actual assets.[27]

Because of all these factors, it is hard to tell how much of the decline in savings rates in the late 1970s was due to the increased attraction of investing in housing. Yet the latter surely contributed at least somewhat to that decline, which in turn cut the funds received by the thrift institutions that typically financed rental housing.

The Revolution in Real Estate Finance

In 1980 a dramatic change occurred in the expectations of most capital suppliers concerning future inflation. As gradually increasing inflation rates culminated in consecutive double-digit years in 1979 and 1980, institutional lenders decided they would have to protect themselves from the possibility of continued high inflation rates. This required (1) charging very high nominal interest rates initially and (2) adopting flexible investment forms that would vary nominal payments in response to future changes in inflation.

This change of perspective and behavior was widespread enough to constitute a virtual revolution in real estate finance, especially for income properties funded by big insurance companies. It caused major structural changes in the institutions that finance housing and other real estate and shifted the savings behavior of millions of households.

As noted above, consumers reduced their rate of savings from current income in the late 1970s, partly because they were receiving low real interest rates from savings accounts.[28] In fact, savers' desires to obtain higher real yields during inflation generated a major restructuring of financial institutions. Until 1978 banks, savings and loan associations, and

27. I am indebted to Owen Evans for pointing out these diverse influences on savings.

28. It is necessary to qualify this conclusion because there is no conclusive statistical evidence proving that lower consumer savings rates from current income were caused by lower interest rates received by savers. Nevertheless, this is a reasonable inference that I will continue to use in the analysis, suitably qualified.

AVAILABILITY OF CAPITAL 55

other thrift institutions that supplied most home mortgage funds were limited by federal regulations to paying relatively low interest rates on savings. Accelerating inflation transformed those low nominal rates into even lower real ones, while raising nominal rates on other short-term instruments to record levels. This disparity created an arbitraging opportunity seized by the Wall Street entrepreneurs who invented money market funds. To lure savings from thrift institutions, those funds offered savers floating short-term rates just below the high yields available from such other short-term instruments as Treasury bills and bank certificates of deposit. Fund operators invested their deposits in these other instruments, passed the interest through to their savers, and collected a management fee as their reward. These funds were accessible to small-scale depositors, whereas high-rate instruments offered by banks and thrifts had been available only to large-scale depositors. This innovation began drawing money out of thrift institutions as nominal interest rates increased in 1978.

In response, federal regulators devised a new instrument to prevent massive loss of deposits from thrifts. It was a "money market certificate" offering savers a floating rate just above the current Treasury bill rate, available with a minimum deposit of $10,000. Short-term rates have remained much higher than the previous ceilings on savings accounts almost continuously since then. Hence savers have gradually shifted most of their deposits out of low-rate thrift accounts into either money market certificates or money market funds. The latter contained $206.6 billion at the end of 1982—a remarkable growth from their inception about four years earlier.[29]

Equally important, most savers have learned to demand higher real interest rates than they received in the 1970s. If they do not obtain higher real after-tax yields on savings from current income in the 1980s, they are likely to keep such savings relatively low, as they did in 1979. Then the sheer scarcity of savings will force mortgage rates up. In 1979 and 1980 traditional home mortgage lenders experienced such small net savings in-flows they had to seek other sources of money—especially the secondary mortgage market.[30] In 1981 and early 1982 they had net losses of savings, further restricting their lending capacity.

29. Investment Company Institute, *Monthly Reports*. Total deposits in these funds dropped sharply in early 1983 after banks and thrift institutions were permitted to offer competitive accounts with federal insurance and no rate ceilings.
30. This is a market in which financial institutions seeking secure investments (for example, pension funds) buy mortgage loans from the original lenders.

Mortgage fund suppliers have also altered their investment instruments in response to uncertainty. The best-known characteristic of inflation is a rising general price level. But inflation also involves inherent uncertainty about how fast prices will rise in the future. This uncertainty prevents lenders from protecting themselves against inflation by establishing interest rates that are high initially or that rise over time according to a predetermined schedule. If the initial rate or schedule is set too high in relation to how much inflation most people expect, no one will accept the lender's terms. But if it turns out to have been too low, it will have failed to protect the lender against devaluation of assets, as in the 1970s.

The only way to cope with such uncertainty is to structure investments so that their interest payments vary as future conditions unfold, thereby offsetting unpredictable changes in the general price level. That can be done by linking the contract interest rate to some other rate that varies with the price level (as in variable-rate mortgages), by shortening the time until the initial rate can be revised (as in renegotiable or roll-over mortgages), or by capturing a share of those revenues likely to rise with prices generally (as in shared equity and shared-appreciation mortgages or in straight equity investments). By early 1981 most major sources of capital for large rental housing projects had shifted from making long-term, fixed-rate mortgages to using one or more of these instruments or hybrids of them. Most thrift institutions providing mortgage funds for households made similar shifts.

Furthermore, in 1981 and 1982 lenders began charging extraordinarily high real interest rates for long-term loans. When inflation rates were low, long-term nominal interest rates had been two to four percentage points above the inflation rate. But in early 1982 long-term nominal rates rose as high as ten percentage points above the inflation rate, averaging seven to eight points above it. Lenders were apparently including a large premium for the volatility of interest rates as a component of their interest rates. They were trying to compensate for possible wide swings in future interest rates similar to the unprecedented variations experienced in 1981. They were adding this premium to (1) the "riskless" base interest rate, (2) a premium for the riskiness of each particular property, and (3) a basic anti-inflation premium offsetting future inflation expected on the basis of recent inflation rates.

As inflation declined in 1981 and 1982 compared with 1979 and 1980, the basic inflation premium was expected to fall. But the new interest-rate volatility premium more than offset any decline in the basic inflation

AVAILABILITY OF CAPITAL

premium, at least in late 1981 and early 1982. The combined size of these two premiums will probably remain large until (1) the rate of increase in general prices falls relatively low (perhaps under 5 percent a year), (2) it remains low for several years in a row, and (3) interest rates stop surging up and down rapidly and unpredictably. It took the financial community about six years from the time a high inflation rate first appeared in 1974 to decide that continuing inflation should affect its basic approach to lending. Hence it will take at least several years without serious inflation to convince that community it no longer needs to charge special premiums to protect itself from uncertainty about future inflation.

This adoption of both inflation-sensitive instruments and an inflation-uncertainty premium will reduce the future profitability of leveraged equity investments in real estate, compared with the 1970s. It will do so by raising the real interest rates charged by capital suppliers and shifting the risk of unanticipated inflation from lenders to borrowers.

Moreover, the once-sheltered position of housing in the competition for financing has ended. Thrift institutions have lost their interest-rate differential (they could formerly pay slightly higher interest rates on savings than commercial banks). More important, both thrift institutions and banks are no longer shielded by federal rate ceilings from having to pay market interest rates to savers. Small-scale savers now have alternative places to put their money without rate ceilings, and as a result the share of total savings in low-ceiling accounts has fallen drastically. Thrifts have to pay higher rates for the funds they lend, thereby raising the rates they must charge developers and home buyers. These changes weaken the relative advantages of investing in housing compared with stocks, bonds, and small businesses. The Economic Recovery Tax Act of 1981 further reduced that advantage by increasing the tax benefits of investing in plant and equipment, reducing marginal income and capital gains tax rates, and liberalizing other tax-sheltering investments, such as individual retirement accounts and Keogh accounts.[31]

Sharp declines in capital flows into housing by early 1982 are shown by precipitous drops in investment in both new and existing homes. About 2.2 million new housing units were started in 1978 (including mobile home shipments), but starts plunged to 1.5 million in 1980 and 1.0 million in 1982.[32] About 3.9 million existing single-family homes were

---

31. See *An Analysis: 1981 Tax Legislation* (New York: Coopers and Lybrand, 1981).
32. Bureau of the Census, *Housing Starts*, construction report C-20, October 1982, p. 8.

sold in 1978; by 1982 sales had dropped to 1.9 million—down 51 percent.[33] These steep declines were aggravated by very high real interest rates; they are not solely due to housing's loss of a sheltered position on credit markets. But that loss increased the vulnerability of housing markets to suffering sharp declines during periods of high interest rates. Thus the share of total financial capital flows going into housing in the 1980s is likely to be below the share in the 1970s, although it will be higher over the whole decade than in 1980, 1981, and 1982.

Future Effects of Higher Real Capital Costs

The real after-tax cost of capital for investment in housing will surely be much higher in the 1980s than in the 1970s, regardless of the level of inflation or the nominal rate of interest (which declined sharply from 1982 to 1983). In the late 1960s and the 1970s accelerating inflation magnified the advantages of owning housing over alternative investments. But, if inflation occurs in the 1980s, it will penalize further investments in housing by generating very high real interest rates instead of the very low ones it created in the 1970s. This difference results from the shift in capital suppliers' expectations from failing to anticipate inflation to strongly anticipating it.

Higher real capital costs will not completely eliminate the profitability of homeownership. Buying will remain attractive to most households as long as (1) most of the funds can be borrowed, (2) the general price level continues rising, and (3) housing prices increase at least as fast as the general price level. These conditions preserve the multiplier effect of leveraging on profitability. For example, assume general inflation is 12 percent, the mortgage interest rate is 14.7 percent (producing a real before-tax interest rate of 2.7 percent), and a buyer borrows 80 percent of a home's $67,500 purchase price. This buyer has a household income of $30,000 and a marginal tax rate of 30 percent. The annual profit on the buyer's down payment investment is defined as the home's appreciation, plus the tax savings from deductibility of mortgage interest payments, minus the mortgage interest payments. The home buyer can make a first-year profit of 18 percent on the down payment if the home's price rises 12 percent—the same as consumer prices generally. That profit is large enough to offset inflation's impact in depreciating the initial

33. National Association of Realtors, *Annual Report: Existing Home Sales* (NAR, 1982), p. 32.

AVAILABILITY OF CAPITAL

down payment and still provide a rate of return on that down payment equal to the mortgage interest rate.

If the mortgage interest rate rises to five percentage points higher than the inflation rate, first-year profit on the down payment drops to 12.4 percent, assuming the home's value still increases at the general inflation rate. Thus high real interest rates can greatly reduce the profitability of leveraged homeownership. If the interest rate remains 14.7 percent but the home appreciates more slowly than prices generally, first-year profit falls notably. It drops from 18 to 12 percent if home value rises 90 percent as fast as prices generally, but it plummets to 6 percent if home value rises only 80 percent as fast as prices generally.[34]

The profitability of homeownership is therefore highly sensitive to changes in both real interest rates and the real rate of home appreciation. Home prices have risen faster than prices generally nearly every year since 1968, except during severe credit crunches. However, from December 1980 to December 1981, the median sales price of existing single-family homes rose 5.7 percent, or less than the 8.9 percent rise in the consumer price index.[35] Moreover, in some markets, home prices in current dollars did not rise at all during that year. Furthermore, the stated median price increase of 5.7 percent exaggerated the true price increase, even before correction for inflation, because many sellers were providing buyers with secondary financing at below-market interest rates. Such financing amounted to a discount on the true market price. I estimate this discount caused the true nominal price to rise only about 3.4 percent from December 1980 to December 1981. The real price *fell* about 5.0 percent. Thus tight credit conditions and high interest rates can slow or even reverse home appreciation. This drastically reduces the profitability of homeownership, at least in the short run.

Furthermore, the higher nominal interest rates become, the fewer households can qualify for mortgage loans. If the share of income they must devote to monthly housing payments rises, it may exceed prudent guidelines established by lenders, even though those guidelines have been greatly liberalized. Twenty years ago most lenders would not permit the borrowing household to devote over 25 percent of the main earner's income to housing. Today some lenders will make mortgage loans even

---

34. These calculations are based on a model of housing investment profitability designed by the author.

35. National Association of Realtors, *Monthly Report*, December 1981, p. 1; and Council of Economic Advisers, *Economic Indicators*, January 1982, p. 23.

if 40–45 percent of the *combined* income of two earners is needed to cover housing expenses, if the household has no other debts. Most lenders, however, will not go beyond 28–36 percent. This greater liberality helps explain why households could afford costlier homes out of any given income in the 1970s than earlier, in spite of higher nominal interest rates. But when mortgage rates exceed 16 percent, millions of potential home buyers are unable to qualify even under liberalized guidelines. Therefore, continued very high interest rates will restrict the flow of capital into housing.

Another impact of higher real capital costs in the 1980s will be smaller housing units. Reducing unit size cuts the cost of each unit, thereby helping compensate for higher real costs of capital. So a higher percentage of new units will consist of townhouses, condominiums, and attached single-family homes. Also, the average size of each structural type will decline. Even renovated and rehabilitated units will be small on the average, as many large homes are divided into two or more units.

Shifting to smaller units does not necessarily imply shifting to more rental units, since the lure of homeownership will continue to undermine the rental market. Though homeownership's profitability will decline, it will remain high enough to restrict the demand for high-rent housing. Most households that can afford to pay enough to make new construction profitable would rather own than rent. Moreover, the additional cost of building units for ownership instead of rental will be small. Even if the percentage of new multifamily units in all starts rises, many of those units will be aimed at the ownership market. These will include projects that developers initially rent but intend to sell as condominiums within a few years. Moreover, any increase in the real cost of mortgage capital will reduce still further the low profitability that has already caused a fall in construction of new unsubsidized rental housing. Therefore, financing new unsubsidized rental housing will remain difficult in the 1980s.

Nonetheless, two positive factors will increase the likelihood that such housing will be built. Many households that want to buy homes but cannot afford the monthly payments will reluctantly become renters of existing units, forming a strong source of rental demand. Therefore, rents will rise rapidly in the middle of the market, although much of this demand will evaporate if homeownership financing terms become more favorable. Astute investors will put capital into new rental units serving this market only if those units can quickly be shifted to ownership.

The second positive factor is the larger depreciation allowances included

AVAILABILITY OF CAPITAL

in the Economic Recovery Tax Act of 1981. It allows writing off rental property in fifteen years instead of the much longer periods formerly required. It also permits accelerating depreciation with a 175 percent declining-balance method on rental housing (200 percent on units for low-income households), without full recapture of the depreciation deductions as ordinary income. Thus 31 percent of an improvement's value can be deducted as depreciation in the first three years (35 percent if it is occupied by low-income households). This increase in tax shelter slightly more than offsets the reduced value of such shelter to high-bracket investors caused by the decline in maximum tax rate from 70 to 50 percent. For investors not previously in brackets above 50 percent, the new tax law greatly enhances the attraction of rental housing. Nevertheless, I expect construction of new rental units will remain low in the first half of the 1980s because the negative factors cited above will continue to outweigh the positive ones.

One rental market likely to be profitable for developers in the 1980s consists of meeting the demand for high-turnover occupancy by small households. In 1980 one of the nation's largest multifamily developers (Lincoln Property Company) successfully built thousands of units in Texas to serve such households.[36] These small units ranged from 500 to 850 square feet. Annual turnover rates of 50–70 percent allowed owners to increase average rents sharply each year without antagonizing tenants because owners could raise rents when units change occupants. But such almost transient accommodations are not appropriate for most renting households, even though renters move much more often than owners. Profitable development of new high-turnover rental units will not offset the negative impacts on total new rental construction of the recent revolution in real estate finance.

36. Data on Lincoln Properties come from personal conversations of the author with Mac Pogue and Preston Butcher of that firm in 1980–81.

4
Future Demand for Rental Housing

THE FUTURE of rental housing cannot be studied apart from the future of ownership housing, since these two are close substitutes for one another. The analysis in the remainder of this book considers markets for both types of housing from 1980 to 2000. The methods I will use to quantify future housing demand and supply include the following steps.[1]

1. *Estimating future demand for additional housing units generated by population growth and requirements for more vacant units.* Separate estimates for homeowning and renting households are presented in this chapter.

2. *Estimating recent and likely future additions to the housing inventory.* These estimates represent the supply side of the market and include an analysis of net replacement. They are set forth in chapter 5.

3. *Comparing these two initial estimates of the number of new housing units demanded with the number likely to be supplied.* If these initial estimates are similar, continuation of current trends will produce a

---

1. In theory, the best way to estimate how much new rental housing will be created is through a comprehensive but reliable econometric model. However, no such model exists. Models of housing markets alone either apply only to individual metropolitan areas or are not reliable enough to predict all the variables involved. Most models of the entire economy have housing sectors, but they do not focus on rental housing. Both the Urban Institute and the National Bureau of Economic Research have developed housing market models. See Frank de Leeuw and Raymond J. Struyk, *The Web of Urban Housing* (Urban Institute, 1975); and John Kain and William C. Apgar, Jr., "Analysis of the Market Effects of Housing Allowances," discussion paper D76-3 (Harvard University, Department of City and Regional Planning, October 1976). The National Association of Home Builders has also developed an econometric model of housing markets in association with Kenneth Rosen of the University of California at Berkeley.

DEMAND FOR RENTAL HOUSING

roughly balanced outcome in future housing markets. If the initial estimate of demand is much larger than that of added supply, shortage conditions are likely. If the initial estimate of demand is much smaller than that of added supply, surplus conditions are likely. Separate comparisons of this type for rental and owner-occupied housing are made in chapter 7.

4. *Identifying the adjustments likely to occur in future housing markets to balance additions to demand and supply.* Market pressures arising out of any projected imbalance will cause adjustments on both sides of the market. For example, if demand appears likely to exceed supply, rents and prices of rental units will rise. That will cause fewer separate households to form, thus reducing demand. It will also motivate developers to build more new units and landlords to use existing units longer, thus increasing supply. These adjustments will equalize the numbers of units demanded and supplied at any given moment. The most likely adjustments and their relative magnitudes are discussed in chapter 7.

Need versus Demand

Many housing studies discuss the number of units "needed" in the future, rather than the number "demanded" or "likely to be supplied." In fact, housing needs are often treated by the press, housing experts, and government officials as something that can be scientifically defined and accurately measured. But this view of needs usually includes housing units desired by households that cannot afford to pay for them without direct public subsidies. Many poor households live in physically substandard units because they cannot afford better ones. They would have to receive some form of subsidy to upgrade or replace their substandard units, but such subsidies would increase the taxes of the general citizenry for the benefit of a minority.

Thus, estimating how many older units need replacement inescapably involves making value judgments about what social priority to place on aiding poor households. It also involves making such judgments about what quality of housing units should be considered "decent" as opposed to "substandard." These judgments cannot be made scientifically because little evidence links any particular quality or size of housing to specific conditions of health, safety, security, or happiness among occupants.

Demand, in contrast to need, includes only those desires that households can back with enough purchasing power to occupy available housing units at their market rents or prices. Estimates of future housing demand are thus forecasts of how many households will be able and willing to pay specific prices for housing, including poor households actually subsidized by various government programs. Consequently, forecasts of demand can be relatively independent of subjective judgments about what ought to be done. This study deals throughout with estimates of housing demand rather than housing need.

Rental Demand to Accommodate Population Growth

Estimation of future rental housing demand generated by population growth must deal with several uncertainties. There are, for example, limitations to the data available. The Census Bureau's household projections (as of early 1982) are based on Current Population Survey data that do not reflect the unexpectedly large number of people revealed by the 1980 census. Furthermore, the census projections called Series B extend only to 1995, whereas this study extends to 2000. Therefore, I have adjusted the Series B household projections upward and outward.

Then, too, population growth alone does not determine the number of people seeking housing. Many people's decisions about whether to establish separate households will be influenced by their income and the added costs of living apart. Therefore, I use two sets of future household projections. One is relatively high to reflect economic conditions favorable to rapid household formation, similar to those in the 1970s. A second is 15 percent lower to reflect less favorable economic conditions. They are shown in table 4-1. The increases in numbers of households in each projection are shown in table 4-2.[2]

Whether many households own or rent their homes will also depend

---

2. The low-growth projection assumes far fewer small households will be formed in the 1980s than in the 1970s. From 1970 through 1979, 85.4 percent of the 13.9 million additional households consisted of one-person and two-person households, according to the U.S. Bureau of the Census, *Statistical Abstract of the United States, 1981* (U.S. Government Printing Office, 1981), p. 46. If 85 percent of the additional 16.9 million households to be formed in the 1980s under the high-growth projection were also one- and two-person households, they would equal 14.4 million. The low-growth projection shown in table 4-2 for the 1980s is 2.5 million lower than the high-growth projection. If *all* this decline consisted of fewer one- and two-person households, then expansion of such households under the low-growth projection would be 17.6 percent lower than under the high-growth projection. I believe that is a plausible outcome, given the much higher housing costs likely to prevail in the 1980s.

Table 4-1. *Projections of the Number of Households, Selected Years, 1980–2000*
Thousands of households

Year	High growth	Low growth
1980	80,400	80,400
1985	89,150	87,838
1990	97,291	94,757
1995	104,541	100,920
2000	110,816	106,254

Source: For 1980, U.S. Bureau of the Census, *1980 Census of Population and Housing: Provisional Estimates of Social, Economic, and Housing Characteristics,* PHC80-S1-1 (U.S. Government Printing Office, 1982), p. 3. Data for other years are estimates by the author as described in appendix A.

Table 4-2. *Projections of the Increase in Households, Selected Periods, 1980–2000*
Thousands of households

Period	High growth		Low growth	
	Increase in households	Annual increase	Increase in households	Annual increase
1980–85	8,750	1,750	7,438	1,488
1985–90	8,141	1,628	6,919	1,384
1990–95	7,250	1,450	6,163	1,233
1995–2000	6,275	1,255	5,334	1,067
1980–90	16,891	1,689	14,357	1,437

Source: Estimates by the author as described in appendix A.

on economic conditions, including housing costs. In the 1970s homeownership rose sharply among husband-and-wife households, but remained relatively constant among households with other male heads or female heads. Because the real costs of homeownership will be much higher in the 1980s than the 1970s, homeownership among husband-and-wife households may not rise as fast as it has. To deal with uncertainty concerning this variable, I have used two alternative projections of the speed of decline in renting among husband-and-wife households.

The details of these procedures are presented in appendix A. The results are four alternative projections of renting and homeowning households for 1980–2000. These involve high and low projections of the total number of households and slow and fast projections of the rate at which renting declines among husband-and-wife households. The four combinations of these traits (low growth with slow decline, low growth

Table 4-3. *High-Growth Projections of the Number of Households, by Type of Tenure, Selected Years, 1980–2000*

Year	Total households	Slow decline[a]		Fast decline[a]	
		Renters	Owners	Renters	Owners
1980					
Number (thousands)	80,400	27,235	53,165	27,235	53,165
Percent	100.0	33.9	66.1	33.9	66.1
1985					
Number (thousands)	89,150	30,059	59,091	29,224	59,926
Percent	100.0	33.7	66.3	32.8	67.2
1990					
Number (thousands)	97,291	32,723	64,568	31,190	66,101
Percent	100.0	33.6	66.4	32.1	67.9
1995					
Number (thousands)	104,541	35,190	69,351	33,092	71,449
Percent	100.0	33.7	66.3	31.7	68.3
2000					
Number (thousands)	110,816	37,147	73,669	34,569	76,247
Percent	100.0	33.5	66.5	31.2	68.8

Source: For 1980, Bureau of the Census, *1980 Census of Population and Housing.* Data for other years are estimates by the author as described in appendix A.

a. Speed of decline in renting among husband-and-wife households.

with fast decline, high growth with slow decline, and high growth with fast decline) are projected in tables 4-3 and 4-4. Changes in the number of renting and homeowning households for each are shown in tables 4-5 and 4-6.

These projections can be used to estimate how future housing demand might be influenced by changes in housing prices and other variables. Conditions favorable to expansion of demand would include relatively low real after-tax interest rates and other housing costs, compared with consumer income. Conditions unfavorable to expansion of demand would include relatively high real after-tax interest rates and other housing costs, compared with consumer income.

Under favorable conditions, more households would be formed from a given population, since the cost of living separately would be relatively low, and a higher fraction of husband-and-wife households would purchase rather than rent homes, since most such households prefer homeownership. Therefore, situations highly favorable to the expansion of demand would resemble the high-growth, fast-decline projection; situations least

Table 4-4. *Low-Growth Projections of the Number of Households, by Type of Tenure, Selected Years, 1980–2000*

Year	Total households	Slow decline[a]		Fast decline[a]	
		Renters	Owners	Renters	Owners
1980					
Number (thousands)	80,400	27,210	53,190	27,210	53,190
Percent	100.0	33.8	66.2	33.8	66.2
1985					
Number (thousands)	87,838	29,393	58,445	28,561	59,277
Percent	100.0	33.5	66.5	32.5	67.5
1990					
Number (thousands)	94,757	31,454	63,303	29,929	64,828
Percent	100.0	33.2	66.8	31.6	68.4
1995					
Number (thousands)	100,920	33,383	67,537	31,303	69,617
Percent	100.0	33.1	66.9	31.0	69.0
2000					
Number (thousands)	106,254	34,942	71,312	32,398	73,856
Percent	100.0	32.9	67.1	30.5	69.5

Source: For 1980, Bureau of the Census, *1980 Census of Population and Housing*. Data for other years are estimates by the author as described in appendix A.

a. Speed of decline in renting among husband-and-wife households.

favorable to the expansion of demand would resemble the low-growth, slow-decline projection.

The following conclusions can be derived from tables 4-3, 4-4, 4-5, and 4-6.

—The fraction of households renting declines steadily from 1980 to 2000 in all four projections. However, lower growth in the number of households produces smaller fractions of renters because it implies higher percentages of husband-and-wife households, who rent less than the other types.

—From 1970 to 1980 the actual net increase in renting households equaled 26.4 percent of the net increase in all households (see chapter 1). From 1980 to 1985 the equivalent projected fraction of renters varies from a high of 32.3 percent to a low of 18.2 percent.

—The absolute number of rental units required to meet population growth varies greatly in these projections, and these differences increase over time. As of 1990, the highest projection of demand for rental units is 32.7 million and the lowest is 29.9 million, or 2.8 million less (8.6

Table 4-5. *High-Growth Projections of the Increase in Households, by Type of Tenure, Selected Periods, 1980–2000*

Period	Total households	Slow decline[a]		Fast decline[a]	
		Renters	Owners	Renters	Owners
1980–85					
Change (thousands)	8,750	2,824	5,926	1,989	6,761
Percent	100.0	32.3	67.7	22.7	77.3
1985–90					
Change (thousands)	8,141	2,665	5,476	1,966	6,175
Percent	100.0	32.7	67.3	24.1	75.9
1990–95					
Change (thousands)	7,250	2,466	4,784	1,902	5,348
Percent	100.0	34.0	66.0	26.2	73.8
1995–2000					
Change (thousands)	6,275	1,957	4,318	1,477	4,798
Percent	100.0	31.2	68.8	23.5	76.5
1980–90					
Change (thousands)	16,891	5,489	11,402	3,955	12,936
Percent	100.0	32.5	67.5	23.4	76.6
1990–2000					
Change (thousands)	13,525	4,423	9,102	3,379	10,146
Percent	100.0	32.7	67.3	25.0	75.0

Source: Estimates by the author as described in appendix A.
a. Speed of decline in renting among husband-and-wife households.

percent). As of 2000, the highest projection is 37.1 million and the lowest is 32.4 million, or 4.7 million less (12.7 percent).

—Average absolute annual increases in the number of renting households are largest in the early 1980s, then decline steadily. Projections for the early 1980s that assume high growth and a fast decline in renting among husband-and-wife households or low growth and a slow decline in renting among husband-and-wife households are similar to recent experience:

	Average annual gain in renting households
High-growth, slow-decline projection	564,800
Low-growth, slow-decline projection	436,600
High-growth, fast-decline projection	397,800
Low-growth, fast-decline projection	270,200
Actual change, 1973–78	440,000

DEMAND FOR RENTAL HOUSING

Table 4-6. *Low-Growth Projections of the Increase in Households, by Type of Tenure, Selected Periods, 1980–2000*

Period	Total households	Slow decline[a] Renters	Slow decline[a] Owners	Fast decline[a] Renters	Fast decline[a] Owners
1980–85					
Change (thousands)	7,438	2,183	5,255	1,351	6,087
Percent	100.0	29.3	70.7	18.2	81.8
1985–90					
Change (thousands)	6,919	2,060	4,859	1,368	5,551
Percent	100.0	29.8	70.2	19.8	80.2
1990–95					
Change (thousands)	6,163	1,930	4,233	1,374	4,789
Percent	100.0	31.3	68.7	22.3	77.7
1995–2000					
Change (thousands)	5,334	1,559	3,775	1,095	4,239
Percent	100.0	29.2	70.8	20.5	79.5
1980–90					
Change (thousands)	14,357	4,243	10,114	2,719	11,638
Percent	100.0	29.6	70.4	18.9	81.1
1990–2000					
Change (thousands)	11,497	3,489	8,008	2,469	9,028
Percent	100.0	30.3	69.7	21.5	78.5

Source: Estimates by the author as described in appendix A.
a. Speed of decline in renting among husband-and-wife households.

—Demand for rental units to accommodate additional population will be much lower in the 1990s than the 1980s. For 1995–2000 the highest projected annual increase in renters is 378,200, while the lowest is 226,200. The former is 22 percent less and the latter 53 percent less than the average annual addition to rental occupancy recorded from 1974 to 1980.

Rental Demand Overall

Efficient operation of any large housing market requires some vacancy to cope with household turnover. Therefore, estimates of future housing demand normally include an allowance for additional vacant units. Estimated vacancy rates in recent years are shown in table 4-7.

This study assumes the market will demand enough additional vacant

Table 4-7. *Vacancy Rates, Selected Years, 1970–80*
Percent

Year	Rental units	Ownership units
1970	6.6	1.2
1973	5.8	1.0
1974	6.2	1.2
1975	6.0	1.2
1976	5.6	1.2
1977	5.2	1.2
1978	5.0	1.0
1979	5.4	1.2
1980	5.4	1.4

Source: Bureau of the Census, *Statistical Abstract of the United States, 1977; 1978;* and *1981.*

units to constitute 5.26 percent of all rental units and 1.21 percent of all owner-occupied units. The specific numbers involved are shown later.

In tables 4-8 and 4-9 on pages 71 and 72 I have projected overall demand for housing to 2000 for each of the four sets of assumptions about household growth and the speed of decline in renting among husband-and-wife households. Each projection includes both occupied and vacant units.

Table 4-8. *High-Growth Projections of the Housing Inventory, Selected Years, 1980–2000*
Thousands of units

Assumption and year	Rental units			Ownership units			Total units		
	Occupied	Vacant	Total	Occupied	Vacant	Total	Occupied	Vacant	Total
Slow decline[a]									
1980	27,235	1,433	28,668	53,165	643	53,808	80,400	2,076	82,476
1985	30,059	1,581	31,640	59,091	715	59,806	89,150	2,296	91,446
1990	32,723	1,721	34,444	64,568	781	65,349	97,291	2,502	99,793
1995	35,190	1,851	37,041	69,351	839	70,190	104,541	2,690	107,231
2000	37,147	1,954	39,101	73,669	891	74,560	110,816	2,845	113,661
Fast decline[a]									
1980	27,235	1,433	28,668	53,165	643	53,808	80,400	2,076	82,476
1985	29,224	1,537	30,761	59,926	725	60,651	89,150	2,262	91,412
1990	31,190	1,641	32,831	66,101	800	66,901	97,291	2,441	99,732
1995	33,092	1,741	34,833	71,449	865	72,314	104,541	2,606	107,147
2000	34,569	1,818	36,387	76,247	923	79,170	110,816	2,741	115,557

Source: For 1980, Bureau of the Census, *1980 Census of Population and Housing*. Data for other years are estimates by the author as described in appendix A.
a. Speed of decline in renting among husband-and-wife households.

Table 4-9. *Low-Growth Projections of the Housing Inventory, Selected Years, 1980–2000*
Thousands of units

Assumption and year	Rental units			Ownership units			Total units		
	Occupied	Vacant	Total	Occupied	Vacant	Total	Occupied	Vacant	Total
Slow decline[a]									
1980	27,210	1,431	28,641	53,190	644	53,834	80,400	2,075	82,475
1985	29,393	1,546	30,939	58,445	707	59,152	87,838	2,253	90,091
1990	31,454	1,654	33,108	63,303	766	64,069	94,757	2,420	97,177
1995	33,383	1,756	35,139	67,537	817	68,354	100,920	2,573	103,490
2000	34,942	1,838	36,780	71,312	863	72,175	106,254	2,701	108,950
Fast decline[a]									
1980	27,210	1,431	28,641	53,190	644	53,834	80,400	2,075	82,475
1985	28,561	1,502	30,063	59,277	717	59,994	87,838	2,219	90,057
1990	29,929	1,574	31,503	64,828	784	65,612	94,757	2,358	97,115
1995	31,303	1,647	32,950	69,617	842	70,459	100,920	2,489	103,409
2000	32,398	1,704	34,102	73,856	894	74,750	106,254	2,598	108,852

Source: For 1980, Bureau of the Census, *1980 Census of Population and Housing.* Data for other years are estimates by the author as described in appendix A.
a. Speed of decline in renting among husband-and-wife households.

5
Recent Changes in Housing Supply

THIS CHAPTER focuses on shifts in the size and composition of the housing inventory, emphasizing 1974–79. That emphasis results partly from better data availability for that period. It also results partly from my belief that, concerning housing activity, the 1980s will more closely resemble the late 1970s than the early 1970s, when the nation had a unique home-building boom.

Changes in the Inventory of Rental Housing

According to the Annual Housing Survey, the rental inventory expanded by 3,534,000 units from April 1970 through October 1979, an average net gain of 372,000 units every twelve months.[1] Inventories for rental and owner-occupied units are shown in table 5-1.

This average annual growth was less than the net inventory gains required to meet three of the four projections of annual demand for occupied housing and vacancies calculated in tables 4-8 and 4-9 for 1980–85:

	Average annual gain in demand for rental units
High-growth, slow-decline projection	594,400
Low-growth, slow-decline projection	459,600
High-growth, fast-decline projection	418,600
Low-growth, fast-decline projection	284,400
Actual change, 1970–79	372,000

1. Occupied rental units increased 3.6 million, but vacant units for rent declined by 66,000. U.S. Department of Housing and Urban Development and U.S. Bureau of the Census, *Annual Housing Survey, 1979, Part A* (U.S. Government Printing Office, 1980), p. 1.

Table 5-1. *Housing Inventory, by Type of Unit, Selected Years, 1970–79*[a]

Thousands of units

Year	Occupied and vacant units[b]		Change from preceding date[b]	
	Rental	Owner-occupied	Rental	Owner-occupied
1970	25,226	40,387	...	...
1973	26,229	45,155	287[c]	1,362[c]
1974	26,676	46,331	447	1,266
1975	27,145	47,444	469	1,113
1976	27,645	48,521	500	1,077
1977	28,047	49,361	402	840
1978	28,429	50,907	382	1,546
1979	28,760	52,088	331	1,181
Average, 1970–79	26,993	46,238	372	1,232
Average, 1974–79	27,718	49,210	417	1,151

Source: U.S. Department of Housing and Urban Development and U.S. Bureau of the Census, *Annual Housing Survey*, Part A, years shown.
a. 1970 data are for April; all other years are for October.
b. Includes only vacant units for rent or for sale, plus all occupied units.
c. Annual average, 1970–73 (3.5 years).

Net inventory change in any period equals total new construction minus total withdrawals from use plus total creation of units through means other than new construction. These three major components are examined in detail below. Changes within the inventory, such as the conversion of existing units from rental to condominium ownership, are also examined.

New Construction

New construction of rental housing occurs mainly from:

—Construction of new multifamily units, less those bought as condominiums or cooperatives and not rented out by their owners.

—Construction of new single-family units bought by persons who rent them out.[2]

2. Some rental units are created through conversion of ownership units to rental use, but in recent years the net result of all tenure conversions has been a decline in rental units and an increase in ownership units. Therefore, conversion is not considered a form of creating additional rental units in this analysis.

Table 5-2. *Multifamily Housing Starts, by Type of Unit, Selected Years, 1970–79*
Thousands of units

Year	Total multi-family starts	Condo-miniums and coop-eratives	Subsidized starts[a]			Nonsubsidized starts for private rental	
			By HUD	By FMHA	Total	Number	Percent[b]
1970	656.0	131.0	253.8	3.0	256.8	268.2	40.9
1971	934.0	233.0	218.3	2.8	221.1	480.0	51.4
1972	1,070.0	290.0	154.6	5.2	159.8	620.2	58.0
1973	925.0	253.0	90.2	8.2	98.4	573.6	62.0
1974	464.0	131.0	42.4	11.4	53.8	279.2	60.2
1975	279.0	45.0	38.8	19.3	58.1	175.9	63.0
1976	386.0	63.0	59.2	23.6	82.8	240.2	62.2
1977	551.0	90.0	101.3	19.1	120.4	328.6	61.0
1978	603.0	131.0	148.0	25.6	173.6	285.4	48.4
1979	566.0	173.0	142.2	29.0	172.2	205.8	37.4
Total	6,434.0	1,540.0	1,248.8	147.2	1,397.0	3,451.1	54.1

Source: For total multifamily starts, Bureau of the Census, *Statistical Abstract of the United States, 1979* (U.S. Government Printing Office, 1979), p. 777; and Council of Economic Advisers, *Economic Indicators*, February 1981, p. 19. For condominiums and cooperatives, Bureau of Census, *Housing Starts*, construction report C-20, May 1980, p. 11; and Department of Housing and Urban Development, special tabulations, March 1981. For subsidized starts, Department of Housing and Urban Development, special tabulations, March 1981.
a. Starts subsidized by the Department of Housing and Urban Development and the Farmers Home Administration.
b. Percentage of all multifamily units started.

—Shipment of new mobile homes used as rental dwellings.

Most new rental construction consists of new multifamily units, fewer of which have been built recently than in the early 1970s (see table 5-2). The average number of multifamily units (all those in structures with more than one unit) started each year was 474,800 from 1974 to 1979, compared with 896,000 from 1970 to 1973.

Some were not for rent, however. A U.S. Department of Commerce series shows that 147,250 new condominiums and cooperative units were started each year from 1972 through 1979.[3] The fraction of all multifamily units that were first sold rather than rented was 27–28 percent from 1972 through 1974, 16 percent from 1975 through 1977, 22 percent in 1978, and 30.6 percent in 1979—averaging 23.0 percent over all eight years.[4]

3. Bureau of the Census, *Housing Starts*, construction report C-20, various issues. The 1980 data include a few cooperative ownership units as condominiums.
4. I have extended the series backward by assuming this fraction was 20 percent in 1970 and 25 percent in 1971.

In 1980 condominium units alone composed 42.3 percent of all multifamily starts.[5]

Some of those units were purchased by investors and placed on the rental market. A U.S. Department of Housing and Urban Development (HUD) study suggests that about 20 percent of rental units converted to condominiums are "permanently" used for rental.[6] Since the Department of Commerce series includes cooperatives, which are rarely rented out, I will assume 15 percent of all new multifamily ownership units remained in the rental market. These assumptions generate an estimate of 125,800 new multifamily units used for owner occupancy for each year from 1970 to 1979. Since 643,400 multifamily starts occurred annually during that period, yearly additions to the rental market averaged 517,600. From 1974 to 1979 they averaged 382,000.

Almost a third of all renters live in single-family units, which are not included in this figure. From 1970 to 1979 there was a net *decline* of 140,000 single-family rental units (1.6 percent) because many shifted to owner occupancy.[7] Nevertheless, thousands of investors have in recent years bought and rented out single-family units while waiting for them to appreciate, thus adding to the rental inventory. I will arbitrarily assume 5 percent of all new single-family units built from 1974 to 1979 entered the rental market, or an average of 58,500 units a year.[8]

Other new rental dwellings consist of new mobile homes not occupied by their owners. During the 1970s an average of about 17 percent of mobile homes were rented.[9] This adds about 61,200 newly shipped units a year to new rental construction for the whole decade, and about 45,800

---

5. The resulting series is shown in table 5-2. The figure for 1980 is 132,200 units.

6. The study showed that 37 percent of all converted units were being rented, but about 18 percent were rented from the converting developers and would presumably be sold eventually to occupants. Hence it is reasonable to assume that 20 percent are "permanently" on the rental market—that is, until their owners resell them in the future after some appreciation has occurred. See Department of Housing and Urban Development, *The Conversion of Rental Housing to Condominiums and Cooperatives* (GPO, 1980), p. VI-14.

7. This net change included a fall of 585,000 in detached single-family rental units and an increase of 445,000 in attached single-family rental units. *Annual Housing Survey, 1979, Part A*, p. 1.

8. From 1970 to 1979 the total number of occupied single-family units (including detached, attached, and mobile homes) rose 11,307,000. The number of renter-occupied single-family units rose only 210,000, or 1.86 percent of the total increase in single-family units. Hence my assumption that 5 percent of all new single-family units built during this period were rented may overestimate the actual number. See *Annual Housing Survey, 1979, Part A*, p. 1.

9. Exact percentages rented were 15.5 in 1970, 14.6 in 1973 and 1974, and 18.6 in 1979. See *Annual Housing Survey, Part A*, p. 1, for the indicated years.

Table 5-3. *New Construction of Rental Housing, 1970–80*
Thousands of units

Year	Multi-family units[a]	Single-family units[b]	Mobile homes[c]	Total
1970	545	41	68	654
1971	736	58	84	878
1972	823	65	98	986
1973	710	57	96	863
1974	353	44	56	453
1975	241	45	36	322
1976	332	58	42	432
1977	474	73	47	594
1978	491	72	47	610
1979	419	60	47	526
1980	291	43	38	372
1970–73	2,814	221	346	3,381
Annual average	704	55	87	845
1974–80	2,601	395	313	3,309
Annual average	434	56	45	473
1970–80	5,415	616	659	6,690
Annual average	492	56	60	608

Source: *Housing Starts*, January 1983, pp. 3, 8.

a. Data are the proportion of all non-single-family housing starts assumed to be for the rental market. For 1974–79, 85 percent of all new condominium and cooperative units started are assumed to be for owner occupancy; for 1980, 80 percent are assumed to be for owner occupancy, as shown in table 5-5.

b. Assumed to be 5 percent of all single-family housing starts. All other single-family housing starts are assumed to be for owner occupancy, as shown in table 5-5.

c. Assumed to be 17 percent of all mobile home shipments. All other mobile home shipments are assumed to be for owner occupancy, as shown in table 5-5.

a year for 1974–79. It also brings the annual average number of rental units from 1974–79 to 489,500.[10] Combining this with 1980 data produces an average of 472,709 new rental units constructed each year from 1974 to 1980 (table 5-3).[11] For convenience, I will round that to 470,000.

Withdrawals

For 1974–79, 489,500 new rental units were built each year, but the annual rental inventory gain was 417,000 units. That seems to imply only

10. In the highest year—1978—the total was 610,000, or 24 percent above the average. Data from *Housing Starts*, June 1981, pp. 3, 8. This estimate of new rental construction has not been adjusted for losses of rental units due to conversion to condominiums, which are discussed later.

11. The text here focuses on the period 1970–79 because 1980 data reflect changes in real estate finance and markets that are unrepresentative of the experience of the preceding decade, as noted in chapter 3.

72,500 existing rental units were being withdrawn from the inventory and replaced by new ones each year. Yet many more rental units were being lost each year through both permanent and retrievable withdrawals, as noted in chapter 1.[12] I estimate that 318,800 rental units were permanently removed and 531,300 retrievably removed each year from 1974 to 1979—an annual total of 850,100. Withdrawal of that many existing rental units from the inventory each year, plus construction of only 489,500 new ones, implies an annual net loss of 360,600 rental units. Nowhere near enough rental units were being constructed to replace those being withdrawn from use.

Creation through Other Means

Nevertheless, the rental inventory rose 417,000 units a year from 1974 through 1979. This implies that 777,600 additional rental units a year were being created through means other than new construction—59 percent more than were being newly built. This is a residual from other estimates, so I have little confidence in its precision. It nonetheless indicates that from 1974 to 1979 the creation of rental units through means other than new construction added much more to the inventory than new construction itself. Moreover, if 777,600 rental units were being added each year through means other than new construction and 531,300 were being *retrievably* removed each year, then 246,300 more units were being added annually than could be created by putting past retrievable removals back into use.[13] These other units were presumably being created by conversion of nonresidential space to residential use or division of larger units into smaller ones.

Thus, if future rental housing demand is to be met, public policies should strongly focus on (1) trying to reduce the number of rental units

12. The Annual Housing Survey for 1979 estimated an average of 1,416,800 units of all types had been removed each year from October 1974 through October 1979. Of these, 37.5 percent were permanently lost and 62.5 percent were retrievable. According to 1979 data, an average of 721,000 units that were present in 1973 had been removed in each of the following six years. About 60 percent had been rental units in 1973 (either occupied or vacant for rent). *Annual Housing Survey, 1979, Part A,* pp. xvii, 28. I will therefore assume that rental units also composed 60 percent of all permanent and retrievable removals from 1974 through 1979. In subsequent calculations concerning annual removals, I used 1,416,800 as a base rather than 721,000 because the latter did not include units not present in 1973 that had been removed by 1979, whereas the former included all removals.

13. When conversions of rental units to condominiums are taken into account, this number rises to 317,800, as noted later in this chapter.

CHANGES IN HOUSING SUPPLY

removed from the inventory each year and (2) encouraging creation of additional rental units through means other than new construction. These goals are as important as encouraging new rental construction.

Conversions to Ownership

The composition of the total housing inventory is also affected by conversion of existing rental units to condominium or cooperative ownership. HUD's study indicated a total gross conversion of 366,000 rental units from 1970 to 1979.[14] If 15 percent of these units were retained for rental, the net decreases in rental inventory caused by such conversions from 1970 to 1980 were about as follows:[15]

	Rental units removed each year
1970–75	11,000
1976	16,000
1977	36,000
1978	64,000
1979	122,000
1980	120,000
1974–79	43,300
1970–80	38,500

These decreases have already been taken into account in the preceding analysis of rental inventory changes (and as increases in the ownership inventory in table 5-1 and later). Conversions also affect housing demand by reducing the number of renting households, many of which buy converted units to live in. That effect has been implicitly accounted for in chapter 4.

How many rental units will be converted in the future? That depends on whether renting continues to produce lower economic returns than owning a home. I believe this will remain true in the near future, but what happens after 1985 is much more uncertain. I also believe conversion will accelerate in the 1980s (as the HUD study forecasts) for reasons

14. Department of Housing and Urban Development, *Conversion of Rental Housing*, p. i. This study also stated that there was a *net loss* of only 18,000 rental units in this period, in relation to rental "needs." It reached this conclusion because the number of renting households declined as renters shifted to ownership in transactions related to the conversion process.

15. Ibid., p. IV-6. Data for 1980 are the author's calculation.

explained in chapter 6. Therefore, I will arbitrarily assume conversion to condominium ownership of 125,000 rental units a year from 1980 to 1990 and 100,000 units a year from 1990 to 2000. I will also assume 20 percent of these converted units are retained as rentals, while the other 80 percent switch to occupancy by their owners. Therefore, projected 1980–90 *rental* inventories will be reduced by 100,000 units a year (80 percent of 125,000) and projected *ownership* inventories raised by the same amount, compared with what they would have been in the absence of conversions.[16]

Summary

The annual flows of new construction, withdrawals, non-new creation, and tenure conversions for 1974–79 derived above are summarized in table 5-4. Clearly, the U.S. economy has recently been constructing far fewer new rental housing units each year than are likely to be demanded annually during the next two decades. Only large-scale creation of added rental units by means other than new construction has prevented the rental inventory from declining significantly.

Changes in the Inventory of Ownership Housing

According to the Annual Housing Survey, the ownership inventory (including vacant ownership units for sale) expanded by 10,520,000 units from April 1970 through October 1979, an average gain of 1,237,650 units every twelve months (see table 5-1).[17] This growth was less than the net inventory gains required to meet only one of the four projected annual demands for the period 1980–85 calculated in tables 4-8 and 4-9.

	Average annual gain in units
High-growth, fast-decline projection	1,368,600
Low-growth, fast-decline projection	1,232,000
High-growth, slow-decline projection	1,199,600
Low-growth, slow-decline projection	1,063,600
Actual change, 1970–79	*1,237,650*

16. The actual adjustments made in chapter 7 for 1980–90 involve subtracting only 50,000 units a year cumulatively from rental inventories and adding corresponding amounts to ownership inventories. See footnote 4 in chapter 7 for a further explanation of these adjustments.

17. *Annual Housing Survey, 1978*, Part A, p. 1.

CHANGES IN HOUSING SUPPLY

Table 5-4. *Average Annual Change in the Rental Housing Inventory, 1974–79*

Type of unit	Additions	Removals
Newly built units	489,500	...
Old units removed		
Permanently	...	318,800
Retrievably	...	531,300
By conversion to condominiums	...	43,300
Units added by non-new construction		
From previous retrievable losses	531,300	...
From other sources	289,300	...
Total	1,310,100	893,100
Net change	417,000	...

Source: Author's calculations.

Actual annual ownership inventory growth was only 10 percent below the highest 1980–85 demand projection. In contrast, the average actual growth of the rental housing inventory from 1970 to 1979 was 37 percent below the highest 1980–85 demand projection. The main components of change in the inventory of ownership housing, discussed below, are the same as those in rental housing.

New Construction

New construction of ownership housing occurs mainly from:

—Construction of new single-family units (less those destined for rental, estimated earlier as 5 percent of annual starts).

—Shipment of new mobile homes (less those destined for rental, estimated earlier as 17 percent of annual shipments).

—Construction of new multifamily units for use as condominiums or cooperatives (estimated earlier as 85 percent of total condominium and cooperative starts).

Table 5-5 indicates that 1,486,000 new ownership units were constructed each year, on the average, from 1970 to 1980. The annual average from 1970 to 1979 was 9.7 percent higher than that from 1974 to 1980. I will use 1,400,000 as the average annual construction of new ownership units in the late 1970s.[18] Comparing table 5-5 with table 5-3

18. The average for the period used earlier in analyzing rental housing (1974–79) was 1,425,000; adding 1980 data reduces it to 1,385,100. Since 1,400,000 is about midway between these two and is a conveniently rounded total, I use that in the subsequent analysis.

Table 5-5. *New Construction of Ownership Housing, 1970–80*
Thousands of units

Year	Multi-family units[a]	Single-family units[b]	Mobile homes[c]	Total
1970	111	772	333	1,216
1971	198	1,093	412	1,703
1972	247	1,244	478	1,969
1973	215	1,075	471	1,761
1974	111	844	273	1,228
1975	38	847	177	1,062
1976	54	1,104	204	1,362
1977	77	1,378	230	1,685
1978	112	1,361	229	1,702
1979	147	1,134	230	1,511
1980	149	809	184	1,142
1970–73	771	4,184	1,694	6,649
Annual average	193	1,046	424	1,662
1974–80	688	7,477	1,527	9,692
Annual average	98	1,068	218	1,385
1970–80	1,459	11,661	3,221	16,341
Annual average	133	1,060	293	1,486

Source: *Housing Starts*, January 1983, pp. 3, 8.
a. Data are the proportion of all non-single-family housing starts assumed to be for owner occupancy. For 1974–79, 15 percent of all new condominium and cooperative units are assumed to be rented out by their owners; for 1980, 20 percent are assumed to be rented out, as shown in table 5-3.
b. Assumed to be 95 percent of all single-family housing starts. All other single-family housing starts are assumed to be rented out by their owners, as shown in table 5-3.
c. Assumed to be 83 percent of all mobile home shipments. All other mobile home shipments are assumed to be rented out by their owners, as shown in table 5-3.

shows that construction of new ownership housing maintained a steadier pace throughout these eleven years than construction of new rental housing, which declined more sharply in the late 1970s.

Withdrawals, Conversions, and Creation through Other Means

From 1974 to 1979 the average annual inventory gain was 1,151,000 units. That seems to imply 249,000 existing units were being withdrawn from the inventory and replaced by the 1,400,000 new ones each year. But actually such annual losses averaged about 212,500 permanent removals and 354,200 retrievable removals, or 566,700 altogether. Also, previous analysis shows that 43,300 existing rental units a year shifted to

CHANGES IN HOUSING SUPPLY

Table 5-6. *Average Annual Change in the Ownership Housing Inventory, 1974–79*[a]

Type of unit	Additions	Removals
Newly built units	1,400,000	...
Old units removed		
Permanently	...	212,500
Retrievably	...	354,200
Net units converted from rental use	43,300	...
Units added by non-new construction		
from previous retrievable losses	274,400	...
Total	1,717,700	566,700
Net change	1,151,000	...

Source: Author's calculations.
a. Rough estimations based on data from this period.

ownership through net conversion to condominiums.[19] These annual flows are summarized in table 5-6.

Thus non-new creation is important to meeting ownership housing demand, but not nearly as important as for rental units. From 1974 to 1979 creation of ownership units through new construction and conversion from rental units exceeded non-new creation by 5.3 to 1. In contrast, new construction of rental units equaled only 60 percent of non-new creation. Moreover, new construction of ownership units from 1974 to 1979 exceeded gross removals of such units by 2.5 to 1, whereas new construction of rental units equaled only 55 percent of gross removals. The U.S. economy will not have to greatly surpass the level of new constuction set in the late 1970s to meet the future demands for ownership housing projected in chapter 4. But that is not true for rental housing, as pointed out earlier.

19. New construction of 1,400,000 new units a year, plus loss of 566,700 existing ones, would result in a net inventory gain of 833,300 units a year. But the inventory actually gained 1,151,000 units a year; about 317,700 units must have been created each year through means other than new construction. If 43,300 existing units a year were converted to ownership from rental (excluding converted units still used as rentals), 274,400 other ownership units must have been added each year through other forms of non-new creation. If annual retrieval of previously removed units equaled the average of 354,200 such removals for the period, then other sources of non-new creation must have equaled a *loss* of 78,800 units a year. This probably means not all previously removed but retrievable units were actually retrieved each year.

Net Replacement Rates

Another way to analyze housing inventory change focuses on *net replacement* of each type of existing housing. That variable equals total new construction of each type minus total inventory change for that type. Policies affecting net replacement can be considered supply-side strategies, because they involve changing the inventory's composition, rather than its total size. However, the withdrawals from use implicit in most replacement also generate demands for additional units. For example, if fire destroys an occupied home, the displaced household seeks another unit either on the same site or elsewhere. Thus the total demand for additional housing in any period is the sum of (1) demand generated by growth in the number of households, (2) demand generated by the need for more vacancy, and (3) net replacement demand. Even so, because net replacement is so closely related to other supply-side components, I analyze it in this chapter and chapter 7.

The equation for net replacement has the same components as the one for inventory change, but rearranges them. The inventory change equation is:

$$\text{Inventory change} = \text{new construction} - \text{withdrawals} + \text{non-new creation}.$$

Shifting new construction to the left side of the equation yields:

$$\text{Inventory change} - \text{new construction} = -\text{withdrawals} + \text{non-new creation}.$$

Reversing the signs on both sides results in:

$$\text{New construction} - \text{inventory change} = \text{withdrawals} - \text{non-new creation}.$$

This is now defined as net replacement:

$$\text{Net replacement} = \text{new construction} - \text{inventory change} = \text{withdrawals} - \text{non-new creation}.$$

Net replacement can then be converted to an annual rate to facilitate comparisons among periods or among different types of housing:

$$\text{Net replacement rate} = (\text{net replacement} / \text{years in period}) \div (\text{average total housing inventory}).$$

CHANGES IN HOUSING SUPPLY

This reformulation has a crucial advantage over the inventory change equation: much more reliable information is available about new construction and net inventory changes than about withdrawals and non-new creation. It is also simpler to make future projections using net replacement rates than all those other components. For these reasons, I have analyzed both recent and future housing supply changes in terms of such rates.

However, future net replacement can be viewed two ways. Descriptively, it is the amount the analyst believes is likely to occur in a given period. Normatively, it is the amount the analyst believes ought to occur. The normative approach is customary in studies that project "desired requirements" for future new construction by quantifying the amount of housing needed to replace units removed by demolition, fire, accident, conversion to nonresidential uses, abandonment, and so forth, along with demands likely to be generated by future household growth. But estimates of such "replacement needs" vary enormously[20] and inherently involve value judgments. How many occupied units in poor physical condition should be withdrawn and replaced with new units each year? To what extent should limited public subsidy funds be used to better the housing of the poor, rather than to raise their income directly, to help them pay for additional health care, or to pursue entirely different goals? To avoid these thorny ethical issues, I will only treat net replacement descriptively by examining past net replacement rates and estimating those likely to prevail in the future.

Past Net Replacement Rates

Net replacement rates have varied tremendously for different types of housing and for different periods. Table 5-7 estimates net replacement rates for all housing from 1950 to 1978. Replacement rates were generally higher in the 1950s and especially in the 1960s than in the 1970s. This reflects the greater removal of old and obsolete housing units in the first two decades of high housing production after World War II.

Table 5-8 shows that net replacement rates for each type of unit vary tremendously over time. For example, rates for conventionally built single-family homes hit a high of 0.80 percent in the 1960s, followed by a low of −0.34 percent in the early 1970s. (A negative rate means total

20. Jeanne E. Goedert and John L. Goodman, Jr., *Indicators of the Quality of U.S. Housing* (Urban Institute, 1977), pp. xi–xii.

Table 5-7. *Net Replacement of Housing Units, Selected Periods, 1950–78*[a]

Period	New housing production[b] (thousands)	Change in inventory (thousands)	Units replaced (thousands)	Annual net replacement (thousands)	Average total inventory[c] (thousands)	Average annual net replacement rate (percent)
1950–60	16,072.1	11,440.7	4,631.4	463.1	49,278.4	0.940
1960–70	17,533.5	12,670.3	4,863.2	486.3	61,333.9	0.793
1970–73	8,906.5	7,624.0	1,282.5	366.4	71,481.0	0.513
1973–78	9,528.4	7,540.0	1,988.4	397.7	78,599.5	0.503
1950–78	51,105.3	39,275.0	11,830.3	415.1	63,195.5	0.657
1970–78	18,434.9	15,164.0	3,270.9	388.8	75,266.2	0.511

Source: *Annual Housing Survey*, indicated years; *Statistical Abstract*, 1956, p. 779, 1961, p. 760, 1963, p. 755, and 1979, p. 782; Bureau of the Census, *1950 Census of Housing*, vol. 1, part 1 (GPO, 1953), p. 1-3, and 1960, vol. 1, Part 1, pp. 1-4, 1-6.

a. Inventory data from Annual Housing Surveys based on October collection dates; data from decennial censuses based on April collection dates; and housing production data based on calendar years. Therefore, housing production totals have been reduced to correspond to October-to-October data by subtracting fractions of annual construction totals in the beginning and ending years of each period shown. Thus, the period shown as 1950–60 actually extends from April 1950 to April 1960 and includes 1950 production times 0.75 and 1960 production times 0.25. The period shown as 1960–70 extends from April 1960 to October 1970 and includes 1960 production times 0.75 and 1970 production times 0.75.

b. Including mobile home shipments.

c. Includes all occupied units and all vacant units ready for occupancy, but not other vacant units. Hence this total is smaller than all year-round units.

inventory grew more than new construction, implying that non-new creation exceeded total withdrawals from use.) In contrast, all multifamily units had a peak net replacement rate of 1.7 percent in the early 1970s, followed by a low of −0.55 percent in the late 1970s.

Table 5-8 also documents the striking impact of high mobile-home replacement rates on overall rates for single-family housing. From 1950 to 1978 the average net rate for mobile homes was 7.9 times as high as that for conventionally built single-family homes. This raised the overall single-family rate to more than double the rate for conventionally built single-family units alone, even though mobile homes averaged only 4.2 percent of the entire single-family inventory. Clearly, overall replacement rates can be misleading if their components are not analyzed separately.

Estimates of net replacement rates for rental and ownership housing can be derived from table 5-8 by creating weighted averages of each by type of unit. Rental housing from 1970 to 1978, for example, consisted on the average of 33.5 percent conventionally built single-family units, 64.6 percent multifamily units, and 1.9 percent mobile homes. Multiplying each of these percentages by the net replacement rate for that

Table 5-8. *Annual Net Replacement Rates, by Type of Unit, Selected Periods, 1950–78*[a]

Percent

	Single-family units			Multifamily units		All units
Period	Total	Conventional	Mobile homes	Total	In buildings of 5+ units	
1950–60	0.257	0.118	9.301	1.398	0.654	0.940
1960–70	1.006	0.804	7.237	−0.074	0.801	0.793
1970–73	0.009	−0.336	6.339	1.743	3.894	0.513
1973–78	0.892	0.568	5.878	−0.553	0.064	0.503
1950–78	0.582	0.367	5.183	0.387	0.831	0.657
1970–78	0.556	0.215	6.613	0.329	1.520	0.511

Source: Author's calculations.

a. Calculated by (1) subtracting actual inventory change from actual new construction to get a total net replacement, (2) dividing that into an annual average for the period, and (3) dividing that average by the average total inventory of that type of unit during that period.

type of unit during the 1970s generates a weighted average for all rental housing.[21] This procedure produces the following estimates of weighted annual average net replacement rates (in percent):

	Rental units	Ownership units
1970–73	1.093	0.149
1973–78	0.047	0.828
1970–78	0.411	0.555

These rates show remarkable variations within the 1970s, similar to those noted earlier for types of units. The net replacement rate for rentals was moderately high during the early 1970s when multifamily housing construction peaked, but it dropped 95.7 percent when multifamily starts fell off sharply. Exactly opposite movements occurred in the net replacement rate for ownership housing. It more than quintupled when single-family construction peaked in 1977 and 1978, even though such construction had been nearly as great in 1972 and 1973. For the entire period net replacement rates were higher for ownership housing than rental

21. The percentages used in calculating this weighted average were derived only from occupied rental housing, not vacant units for rent. A similar exclusion of vacant units occurs in my computation of the weighted average for all ownership housing. The number of vacant units is included in the total inventory figures used in computing these weighted averages, but the composition of vacant units by structure type is not taken into account in deriving the weights. However, this procedure produces only a minor distortion in the results.

housing, in spite of the latter's greater age, because of the statistical influence of mobile homes.[22]

Future Net Replacement Rates

The general quality of the U.S. housing inventory has undoubtedly improved greatly since 1950. Nevertheless, a large but not precisely measurable number of poor units still exists.[23] Although some of these units could be upgraded, it would also be socially desirable to replace much of the existing substandard housing at a relatively rapid rate. Yet the favorable conditions in housing markets that generated so much rental housing construction from 1970 to 1973 will probably not occur again soon, if ever. Basing future projections on an annual net rental replacement rate as high as that attained in the early 1970s would be unrealistic.

Moreover, there has been a policy shift in the U.S. economy toward conservation of existing resources rather than production of new ones. This change will probably be reflected in housing markets by more

---

22. If net replacement rates are calculated from the data in tables 5-1, 5-3, and 5-5, the results are somewhat different from those shown in the text. Average annual net replacement rates calculated from tables 5-1, 5-3, and 5-5 are as follows (in percent):

	Rental units	Ownership units
1970–73	2.219	0.819
1973–78	0.183	0.506
1970–78	0.988	0.629

These replacement rates are generally much larger than those shown in the text. This variance occurs mainly because the inventory data underlying the rates in the text include all year-round housing units, whereas the inventory data in table 5-1 include only occupied units or those vacant units explicitly for sale or rent. There is a large disparity between these two figures because many vacant units are classified as already sold or rented, held for occasional use, or "other." In 1979, for example, the Annual Housing Survey indicated a total of 6,014,000 vacant units, of which 2,277,000 (38 percent) were for sale or rent, but 3,737,000 (62 percent) were otherwise classified. See *Annual Housing Survey, 1979, Part A*, p. 1. I believe it is more accurate to calculate net replacement rates using complete inventory figures rather than smaller figures, although only the latter can be broken down into rental and ownership units. That is why I have derived future replacement rates mainly from past rates calculated on the basis of more complete inventory data. Besides, the general relationships between net replacement rates for different periods are roughly the same, regardless of which method of calculation is used. The main exception is that ownership replacement rates calculated from tables 5-1, 5-3, and 5-4 are lower in the late 1970s than in the early 1970s, like rental rates; ownership rates calculated in the text are higher in the late 1970s.

23. See David Birch and others, *America's Housing Needs: 1970 to 1980* (Joint Center for Urban Studies of the Massachusetts Institute of Technology and Harvard University, December 1973), pp. 4–8.

Table 5-9. *Annual Net Replacement as a Percentage of the Housing Inventory*

Replacement rate	All units	Rental units	Ownership units	Ratio of rental to ownership rates
Low	0.457[a]	0.375	0.500	1.35
High	0.615[a]	0.500	0.675	1.35
Estimated actual rate, 1970–78	0.511	0.411	0.555	1.35

Source: Author's calculations.
a. Weighted average for the occupied inventory based on 1979 percentages of occupied rental and ownership units. This overall net replacement rate is merely illustrative; only the separate rates for rental and ownership housing are used in calculating future replacement demands.

Table 5-10. *Projections of New Housing Construction Needed for Replacement with Low Net Replacement Rates, Selected Periods, 1980–2000*
Thousands of units

Projection[a] and period	Rental units	Ownership units	Total units	Average units a year
High growth, slow decline				
1980–85	565.4	1,420.2	1,985.6	397.1
1985–90	619.5	1,564.4	2,183.9	436.8
1990–95	670.2	1,694.2	2,364.4	472.9
1995–2000	713.8	1,809.4	2,523.2	504.6
High growth, fast decline				
1980–85	557.1	1,430.7	1,987.8	397.6
1985–90	596.2	1,594.4	2,190.6	438.1
1990–95	634.3	1,740.2	2,374.5	474.9
1995–2000	667.7	1,893.6	2,561.3	512.3
Low growth, slow decline				
1980–85	558.6	1,412.3	1,970.9	394.2
1985–90	600.4	1,540.3	2,140.7	428.1
1990–95	639.8	1,655.3	2,295.1	459.0
1995–2000	674.2	1,756.6	2,430.8	486.2
Low growth, fast decline				
1980–85	550.4	1,422.9	1,973.3	394.7
1985–90	577.2	1,570.1	2,147.3	429.5
1990–95	604.2	1,700.9	2,305.1	461.0
1995–2000	628.6	1,815.1	2,443.7	488.7

Source: Author's estimates.
a. Based on rate of household growth and speed of decline in renting among husband-and-wife households.

Table 5-11. *Projections of New Housing Construction Needed for Replacement with High Net Replacement Rates, Selected Periods, 1980–2000*
Thousands of units

Projection[a] and period	Rental units	Ownership units	Total units	Average units a year
High growth, slow decline				
1980–85	753.8	1,917.2	2,671.0	534.2
1985–90	826.1	2,112.0	2,938.1	587.6
1990–95	893.6	2,287.2	3,180.8	636.2
1995–2000	951.8	2,442.7	3,394.5	678.9
High growth, fast decline				
1980–85	742.9	1,931.5	2,674.4	534.9
1985–90	794.9	2,152.4	2,947.3	589.5
1990–95	845.8	2,349.2	3,195.0	639.0
1995–2000	890.3	2,556.3	3,446.6	689.3
Low growth, slow decline				
1980–85	744.8	1,906.6	2,651.4	530.3
1985–90	800.6	2,079.4	2,880.0	576.0
1990–95	853.1	2,234.7	3,087.8	617.6
1995–2000	899.0	2,371.4	3,270.4	654.1
Low growth, fast decline				
1980–85	733.8	1,920.9	2,654.7	530.9
1985–90	769.6	2,119.6	2,889.2	577.8
1990–95	805.7	2,296.2	3,101.9	620.4
1995–2000	838.2	2,450.4	3,288.6	657.7

Source: Author's estimates.
a. Based on rate of household growth and speed of decline in renting among husband-and-wife households.

rehabilitation of older units. Furthermore, the high overall replacement rates of the 1950s and 1960s partly resulted from massive clearance of big-city neighborhoods in both the urban renewal and highway programs. Such large-scale clearance is not likely again.

Because of these considerations and the uncertainties inherent in forecasting, I have used both low and high rates for projecting net replacement housing demand. I selected rates for rental and ownership housing separately, but chose them so as to preserve approximately the same relationship between them as in the past. They are summarized in table 5-9.

These rates can be used to project future demand for new construction to replace net withdrawals from the inventory (all withdrawals less units formed through non-new creation). Calculations for five-year periods

CHANGES IN HOUSING SUPPLY

from 1980 to 2000 are set forth in tables 5-10 and 5-11 for low and high replacement rates, respectively. Each replacement rate is multiplied by the average annual inventory of that type of housing during each five-year period to obtain the number of new units needed for replacement each year. That total is then multiplied by five. Separate calculations have been made for rental and ownership housing, using future inventory projections from chapter 4.

6
Future Profitability of Rental Housing

THIS CHAPTER develops a simple model for analyzing the relationship between financial conditions and market values for rental housing. The model shows that rental property values in real terms have fallen sharply since 1960, even though investors in such properties have made substantial profits. This chapter explores the implications of this finding for future rental housing profitability and production.

Influences on Market Value

Most economists believe the market value of a rental property equals the discounted present value of its future stream of rents.[1] When no general inflation exists, the appropriate discount rate is the prevailing nominal rate of interest,[2] and future rent each year is equal to current rent. Thus market value equals the current operating profit capitalized at the prevailing interest rate, or

Market value = (rents − operating expenses)/nominal interest rate.

When inflation in general prices occurs, both rents and operating

[1]. "The market value of an asset, whether it is a mortgage, an apartment building, a house, or something else, is equal to the discounted value of the annual benefits from holding it." This is a quotation from a review of an earlier draft of this book by John Yinger of Harvard University. It is typical of academic economists' views on how real estate market values are actually determined.

[2]. The interest rate can be seen as either real or nominal, because there is no difference without inflation.

PROFITABILITY OF RENTAL HOUSING

expenses are expected to rise in the future, but not necessarily at identical speeds or at the same speed as prices generally. As noted in chapter 2, from 1960 to 1980 rents did not rise as fast as consumer prices overall. Inflation also increases current interest rates because lenders want to offset its negative effect on the future purchasing power of the dollars with which they will be repaid. Nominal interest rates will thus exceed real rates to an extent roughly reflecting the rate at which prices generally are expected to rise. But only if rents and operating expenses are both expected to rise at exactly the same rate as prices generally will inflation have no effect on the market values of rental properties, as computed in the preceding equation.

Expectations, not actual experiences, are what influence current market prices. However, yesterday's experiences certainly can influence today's expectations about tomorrow's rate of inflation. In the 1950s and 1960s lenders did not anticipate increases in inflation; they made long-term fixed-rate loans at low nominal rates, which turned out to be negative in real terms. Burned by this experience, lenders became extremely cautious in the early 1980s. They then demanded very high nominal interest rates reflecting not only their expectations that rapid inflation would continue, but also a premium for the uncertainty and volatility associated with it. In early 1983 nominal mortgage interest rates were as much as eight percentage points above the current rate of inflation in the consumer price index (CPI). That high before-the-fact real rate was more than double the after-the-fact real rate realized by lenders in the 1950s before inflation became acute.[3]

Most real estate practitioners equate a property's current market value with the sum of the present value of its future rents and the present value of its future sales price.[4] This implies that the future sales price is not necessarily equal to the discounted value of future rents beyond the moment of sale. Past experience indicates that some purchasers are willing to pay more for a property than appears warranted from discounting its most likely future rent stream.[5]

Another influence on market value is the tendency of current interest

---

3. See Anthony Downs and S. Michael Giliberto, "How Inflation Erodes the Income of Fixed-Rate Lenders," *Real Estate Review* (Spring 1981).

4. This is my personal impression from talking to many such practitioners throughout the United States during the past fifteen years.

5. Perhaps this merely reflects widely differing opinions about how fast its rents will escalate after the sale. In any event, this phenomenon is encountered often enough to justify treating future rents separately from the future sales price.

rates to change much faster than current residential rents. Interest rates are set in national money markets encompassing many activities besides those associated with real estate. The past few years prove that interest rates can swiftly move up and down by large amounts. But residential rents are set locally and are influenced by ongoing contractual and other relationships between landlords, tenants, and local governments. Rent levels are relatively "sticky" because of both the fixed term of most leases and the unwillingness of many landlords to antagonize their good tenants. Moreover, information about prevailing rents, supply, and demand is quite imperfect in many markets. Thus, even during inflation, the interest rates facing landlords can rise (or fall) much faster than landlords can raise (or lower) their rents. From June 1979 to May 1980, for example, the contract interest rate on conventional home mortgages shot up 30 percent, whereas residential rents increased only 8.7 percent.[6] So the negative impact of every inflationary increase in interest rates on property values is not necessarily offset by an equal positive impact of inflation on expected future rents.

Another reality not reflected in economic theory is that expectations concerning inflation held by capital suppliers can diverge from those held by developers and property owners. In the early 1970s many developers and investors anticipated more rapid inflation than most lenders; hence the former borrowed heavily to build or buy rental properties. In fact, it is typical of real estate developers to be more optimistic and to take more risks than capital suppliers, who are supposed to be prudent fiduciaries. By the early 1980s the expectations of most capital suppliers had changed to more closely match those of developers and investors, as noted in chapter 3. That change raised the real interest rates charged by capital suppliers without raising the future rents expected by developers and property owners, who were already anticipating inflation. This asymmetrical change helped create the refinancing problem described later in this chapter.

Nevertheless, inflation is certainly likely to raise rents in the future, not just operating costs and interest rates. The current market value of a property can therefore rise because expected future rent increases tend to offset the present increases in interest rates caused by expected

6. Interest rate data are from the *Federal Home Loan Bank Board Journal*, vol. 13 (August 1980), p. 64. Rent data are from Lowry's index cited in chapter 2, with the 9.6 percent increase from 1979 to 1980 reduced by one-twelfth. Ira S. Lowry, "Inflation Indexes for Rental Housing," working draft WD-1081-HUD (Rand Corporation, May 1981).

PROFITABILITY OF RENTAL HOUSING

inflation. In such cases the property's current market value is much greater than appears warranted by its current profitability. Other factors can also cause current market value to exceed what appears justified from current profitability. They include the availability of very low real interest rates, the impact of leverage during inflation, the advantages of tax shelter, and the expected rapid appreciation in the property's market value. These factors explain why investment in rental housing has been profitable even though rents have often failed to cover operating expenses by enough of a margin to produce operating profits competitive with yields on other investments.

Much of this chapter uses an analytic approach involving "required rent increases." These are the current rent increases necessary to sustain certain market values for a typical rental unit under different conditions. This approach consists of three steps. The first is changing key variables on the cost side of operating rental property to reflect recent trends. The second step is determining what rent increases on the revenue side would be necessary to sustain or achieve a certain market value, given those cost changes. The last step is judging the plausibility that such rent increases can actually occur. This method does *not* imply that inflation affects only costs but not rents. But it questions whether the rent increases required by certain circumstances are truly feasible.

Influences on Profitability

One factor inhibiting large capital suppliers from investing in rental apartments is the relatively high cost of managing them. For any given asset value, management costs for rental housing greatly exceed those for other forms of property, such as office or industrial real estate and stock or bond portfolios. This results from the small amount of space occupied by the average renter and the high turnover among renters.

A second inhibiting factor is fear of political interference by local governments. Examples are rent controls, limitations on conversion of rental units to condominium ownership, and tenant-management statutes strongly favoring tenants' rights.

Another negative factor is fear that the present tax laws might be made more adverse to rental housing ownership. Changes in tax laws since 1969 have already slashed rental housing's ability to shelter unrelated income.[7] Although the Economic Recovery Tax Act of 1981 aided rental profitability by instituting shorter-life depreciation schedules, it also reduced the value of tax shelter to high-bracket investors by cutting the highest marginal rate from 70 to 50 percent.[8]

Proposals to build new rental housing tend to provoke opposition from a variety of groups, including environmentalists, upholders of social exclusion, and antigrowth advocates. Resulting delays and legal expenses required to obtain permission for new rental projects further reduce their economic feasibility.[9]

Some investors are also inhibited by the population's age distribution. In the 1970s household formation soared, partly because young people born in the postwar baby boom began living apart from their parents. This greatly expanded the market for rental units, since most new households had relatively low incomes and no children. In the 1980s many of these households will seek homeownership, but few new households will be entering the rental market because there were low birth rates in the late 1960s and throughout the 1970s. Hence new rental units built now might experience falling occupancy in the late 1980s and early 1990s, with no long-range cure in sight. However, my projections in chapters 4 and 7 show a rising number of renting households through 2000, though at a declining rate of increase.

These inhibiting factors, plus lagging rents, have made most long-term capital suppliers much warier about investing in rental housing than they were in the early 1970s. As a result, developers have not been able to "mortgage out" new construction with little or no equity investment,

---

7. These included recapture as normal income of any depreciation in excess of straight-line, inability to deduct interest on initial investments as current expenses, and imposition of minimum tax rates on otherwise tax-free income.

8. It is too soon to judge the impact of these changes. Some practitioners of rental apartment syndication think these two effects will offset each other. The model used later in the chapter shows their combined effect produces some gain in yield on down payment (including tax benefits). However, it is not large enough to offset the adverse impact of the high interest rates prevalent in most of 1982, because the cost and availability of long-term financing are still the most important factors influencing profitability. I am indebted to Preston Butcher of Lincoln Properties and Sedg Mead of the Charles Shaw Company for their views on this subject.

9. Bernard Frieden's recent analysis of applications to build multifamily units in northern California showed that an overwhelming percentage were denied, often for reasons unrelated to either the need for such housing or its environmental impacts. See Bernard Frieden, "The Exclusionary Effect of Growth Controls," in M. Bruce Johnson, ed., *Resolving the Housing Crisis* (San Francisco: Pacific Institute for Public Policy Research, 1982), pp. 19–34.

as they did in the past. By early 1982 the construction of new rental units had almost stopped in most U.S. markets.

The Refinancing Problem

The recent shift from relatively low to much higher real interest rates described in chapter 3 raised the debt-service costs of proposed new rental units. It thereby increased the rents necessary to make new units with any given construction cost economically feasible.[10] Higher interest rates also make it harder to sell existing units or to pay for their modernization or maintenance. With higher rates, a given level of rents will support a smaller mortgage. When the owner tries to sell a property, the buyer must therefore put up a larger down payment even if the price remains the same. Or the price must be cut if the buyer refuses to increase the down payment beyond the traditional percentage of the price. Or secondary financing must be introduced to fill the "investment gap" between the price the seller wants and the funds the buyer and the first mortgagor are willing to supply.[11]

A numerical example illustrates this refinancing problem. Assume an existing twelve-unit apartment building had a 1980 market value of $30,000 a unit, or 8.3 times its gross annual rent (100 times its monthly rent).[12] Total rent for each unit was $300 a month, or $3,600 a year. Someone who bought this unit in 1980 would typically have paid 25 percent down with the remaining $22,500 financed by the seller at an interest rate of 10.5 percent. That was below the current market rate of about 13 percent for apartment mortgages in 1980. But sellers usually

---

10. This rise in interest rates was caused by a change in expectations of capital suppliers concerning future inflation, as explained in chapter 3. However, those new expectations did not allow owners of rental property to raise rents immediately in response to higher interest rates, as noted in the preceding section. Purchasers of rental units who also expected more inflation could anticipate rising rents in the future, and they might be willing to pay more for those properties than previously. But they still faced the difficulties described in this section when trying to finance their purchases.

11. The term "investment gap" was first used in this manner, as far as I know, in Cain and Scott, Inc., *The Cain and Scott Apartment Market Study* (Seattle: Cain and Scott, Inc., 1981), pp. 14–16. I have also taken much of the analysis and data in this section from that study, to which I am greatly indebted.

12. In computing the gross income multiplier in this example, no allowance is made for possible vacancy during the year. Hence it differs slightly from the model set forth later in this chapter. These values are from the 1980 Seattle apartment market, but the basic relationships apply anywhere.

finance transactions at below-market rates during "credit-crunch" periods.[13]

If the mortgage was amortized over twenty-five years, annual debt service equaled $2,549. Operating expenses were 33 percent of rents, or $1,200 a year; debt service and operating expenses combined were $3,749—or $149 more than gross rents. This property had a slightly negative cash flow before tax effects. Therefore the *debt-service ratio*—the ratio of net rental income after subtracting operating costs to total debt service—was only 0.94. (The four main reasons buyers are willing to accept negative cash flows are discussed later.)

Now assume the new owner seeks to sell or refinance the same property in 1981 at an interest rate of 13 percent. The higher rate may be necessary either because rates generally rose (as they did in 1981) or because the owner must resort to institutional financing, as in refinancing the property. If any financing from a bank or savings and loan is involved, the owner cannot expect a below-market rate such as that provided by the seller in the original transaction. If the interest rate rises to 13 percent, debt service increases to $3,045 a year. If operating profit still equals only 94 percent of debt service, rents would have to rise to $338.50 a month (up 12.8 percent) even if other expenses remained the same. But financial institutions also demand debt-service ratios above 1.0 to reduce the risk of default. That means the property must produce a positive cash flow after debt service—even though the debt service has gone up because of higher interest rates. Assume the institution requires the typical debt-service ratio of 1.25. Net operating profit would then have to be $3,806, up 58.6 percent over the original situation. Therefore, even if operating costs remained $1,200 each year, rents would have to rise to $5,006 a year—a jump of 39 percent![14]

Housing markets are almost never tight enough to permit a rent increase of 39 percent in one year (although they might permit the 12.8 percent increase required by the higher interest rate alone).[15] That means rents cannot be increased enough to support the same-sized mortgage at the new higher debt-service ratio and interest rate. If rents were raised

13. A similar low rate would have prevailed if the unit had been bought earlier, say, in 1977. But this example uses 1980 because I have more complete data for the Seattle market in that year.

14. About two-thirds of this required increase results from the higher debt-service ratio and one-third from higher interest rates.

15. If such a severe local shortage existed, landlords would have been raising rents faster in the past, achieving positive cash flows with much higher debt-service ratios.

15 percent and operating costs remained the same, the net operating income would be $2,940.[16] With a debt-service ratio of 1.25, $2,352 would be available for debt service, which supports a 13 percent mortgage of $17,378. Thus the biggest traditional mortgage a new buyer can get is much smaller than the one already on the property. If that new buyer does not want to pay more than 25 percent of the sales price down, then the current owner must reduce the sales price to $23,170—a loss of 22.8 percent from the price one year earlier.[17] Thus, at these high interest rates, properties cannot produce debt-service ratios greater than 1.0 without down-payment ratios larger than 25 percent. But most developers and many investors are not willing to put up large fractions of the total required investment in cash.

To avoid such a loss, the seller can fill the investment gap with a second mortgage the seller supplies. But in the early 1980s the buyer would probably not make such a mortgage unless it had a below-market interest rate. Then the seller could not sell this mortgage on the market except at a discount from its face value because of the low rate. In the example above, with a first mortgage of $17,378 and a down payment of $7,500 on the $30,000 sales price, the seller would have to take back a second mortgage for $5,122 to fill the investment gap. In such situations sellers often use short-term "balloon" second mortgages. Assume one is used here with interest payments only at 10 percent for five years and then full repayment. If the seller wanted to cash out this mortgage by selling it to another investor, the mortgage would be discounted to a value of $3,940 so that it yielded 13 percent to that other investor. Thus the true sales price of the unit is really $1,182 less than the reported price of $30,000—a discount of 3.9 percent.

These calculations assume the unit is being sold for the same price

---

16. The residential rent component of the consumer price index rose 8.5 percent from December 1980 to December 1981; *Economic Report of the President, January 1982*, p. 291. This probably understates the actual increase somewhat, as noted in chapter 2. Nevertheless, it indicates that a 15 percent rent increase would have been sizable under 1981 market conditions.

17. The year-earlier *stated* price is really exaggerated because the buyer received a loan from the seller at a below-market interest rate. This is equivalent to discounting the market price. Since the $22,500 mortgage was financed at an interest rate 19.2 percent below the prevailing market rate, the true value of the mortgage was $4,327 less than its nominal value. This is equivalent to a 14.4 percent discount on the stated sales price of $30,000, reducing it to $25,673. Thus the decline in true value caused by a rise in interest rates is less in this example than it appears from looking only at the original stated or nominal value.

the owner paid one year earlier. But it is more usual for the seller to demand a higher price. This requires taking back a bigger second mortgage and therefore accepting a bigger discount from the stated price.

The situation becomes even less favorable to the seller if interest rates rise still higher, as occurred in mid-1981. If the first mortgage is at 16 percent, rents must rise 60.7 percent to sustain a market value of $30,000 without a second mortgage.[18] If rents can be raised only 15 percent, they will support a 16 percent first mortgage of $14,424 with a 1.25 debt-service ratio. To sustain a price of $30,000, either the buyer must make a 52 percent down payment or the seller must take back a second mortgage of $8,076 if the buyer will pay only 25 percent down. If that second mortgage is at 12 percent, it has a value of only $6,057 when discounted to yield 16 percent. So the seller is getting a true price 6.7 percent less than the stated price.

Thus rapid increases in debt-service ratios and interest rates reduce the ability of rental properties to support given market prices much faster than rents can be raised to offset that effect. Sellers of existing properties can partly mitigate these difficulties by using self-financing at below-market interest rates, but doing so is equivalent to accepting discounted prices. And owners cannot do this when refinancing to obtain funds for maintenance or renovation, nor can developers of new rental properties. Both must borrow from financial institutions that demand full market rates and positive cash flows after debt service.

A Model for Profitability and Market Value

Previous analysis shows that ownership of rental housing will not become profitable enough to call forth much new supply unless rents increase greatly. But how much do they have to rise? And if enough added supply to meet future demand can be created only through enormous rent increases, what is the economic or political feasibility of the policies required to produce such rent increases? To answer these questions, it is important to estimate reliably how much rents need to rise to make rental housing profitable.

This can be done with a simple model of the investment profitability

18. Of this rise, 29.1 percentage points result from increasing the interest rate from 10.5 to 16 percent, whereas 31.6 percentage points result from increasing the debt-service ratio from 0.94 to 1.25.

PROFITABILITY OF RENTAL HOUSING

of individual units. The model estimates how large a market value for a rental unit is generated by various amounts of rent under different conditions. It is based on the following definitions and assumptions.

—The operating-cost ratio is the ratio of all operating expenses to total rents from each unit.

—Gross rental revenues minus operating expenses forms net operating income. This is used to pay debt service and to provide any cash flow to the investors.

—The property is financed with a fixed-rate mortgage amortized over twenty-five years. Long-term fixed-rate mortgages are no longer widely available, but the model focuses on financial conditions in the first year. Hence roll-over mortgages amortized for long periods but with rates renegotiated in one to five years can also be used in the model.

—The nominal mortgage interest rate is, in most cases, assumed to be the average nominal rate attained on commercial and industrial mortgages by fifteen large insurance companies from 1951 through 1980.[19] Some calculations are based on other interest rates, which are explained when used.

—The amount available for debt service equals net operating income divided by the debt-service ratio. For example, if total rents are $200 a month and the operating-cost ratio is 0.40, then net operating income is $120 a month ($200 less operating costs of $80). That amount divided by a debt-service ratio of 1.25 equals $96 a month.

—Owners always pay the maximum allowable amount for debt service to reduce the size of their initial equities (that is, their down payments). Hence the entire $96 above will be used to make monthly mortgage payments.

—When institutional lenders require debt-service ratios larger than 1.0, properties must have positive cash flows after debt service. In the example above, cash flow equals $24 ($120 operating income minus $96 debt service). However, many recent sales partly financed by sellers have involved negative cash flows.

—The monthly mortgage payment and the nominal interest rate determine the total amount of the mortgage. Once that amount and the

19. Data are from the American Council of Life Insurance. Although this rate is for nonresidential properties, it is likely to be closer to the rental-apartment borrowing rate than the rate for single-family mortgages—the only other one for which data are available. That is true because nonresidential and rental apartment properties are both financed purely as investments, whereas single-family homes are partly financed as the owners' shelter.

down-payment ratio are known, the property's market value is established. Thus the market value of the property in this model is what rental revenues can carry, given the other key variables. It is generated internally, *not* by current market conditions. They enter the analysis in a different way. In this model, the size of tax shelter affects the yield on equity, but not market value.

—First-year depreciation is 1.5 times the straight-line depreciation at the assumed lifetime of the property, which is also a variable. In most calculations, a life of twenty-five years has been used, since it would fit the entire inventory reasonably well. Besides, in this model variations in depreciation also affect yield on equity, but not market value.[20]

—The owner is assumed to be in a 50 percent marginal tax bracket; hence the tax benefit equals half the reportable tax loss. Tax loss is calculated as net operating income minus depreciation minus the entire mortgage payment.[21]

—Cash flow equals rent minus operating costs minus the entire mortgage payment, without subtracting depreciation. Thus depreciation is not treated as a real expense, but purely as a tax shelter. That is a common real estate practice.

—The down payment is considered the investor's equity, and yield is computed with that as the base. Down-payment ratios can be varied in the model, but most calculations assume a 25 percent down payment.

—The benefits used in calculating yield on equity include all tax savings resulting from a reportable loss, plus any positive cash flows paid the investor. This means yield includes tax benefits—a departure from normal real estate practice.

Given past rents, operating-cost ratios, and interest rates, this model determines what market values of rental units prevailed at certain past dates. Then it analyzes what present rent levels would be necessary to sustain equivalent real market values for such units. Data on past conditions come mainly from Ira S. Lowry's analysis of rent levels and operating costs, plus a few other sources.[22] The model calculates market value by capitalizing first-year profits (via the mortgage) rather than projecting future costs and revenues and deriving an internal rate of

20. A twenty-five-year life was used instead of the fifteen-year life permitted in the Economic Recovery Tax Act of 1981 because the model applies to a period before that act took effect.

21. This method erroneously includes amortization as an expense, but since calculations are for only the first year the resulting distortion is minor.

22. See Lowry, "Inflation Indexes for Rental Housing."

PROFITABILITY OF RENTAL HOUSING

return. The former procedure more closely corresponds to actual real estate valuation practices in the 1960s and 1970s.

Allowing for Changes in the Interest Rate

Because interest rates have been gradually rising for two decades, most properties have mortgages with lower rates than those prevailing at any given moment. Hence estimating the average market value of all existing units with the current year's interest rate may understate their value. If an older unit were sold or refinanced during the current year, the current interest rate would be applicable, unless the buyer assumed the old mortgage and the seller took back a second mortgage (as has been occurring in 1980 and 1981). Such assumptions would produce lower average interest rates than the prevailing ones during periods of generally rising rates, as from 1960 through 1980. Those interest rates would depend on the age of the mortgages assumed.

I have been unable to find reliable information on the age of mortgages outstanding on rental housing, but most owners sell or refinance their rental housing every ten years or sooner. Holding mortgages longer than that reduces the tax advantages of interest deductibility and depreciation. To allow for the possibility of assumptions, I have made two calculations of the market value of the average rental unit in each year from 1960 through 1980. One is based on that year's interest rate applied to the entire inventory (table 6-1). The second is based on a moving-average rate covering that year and the preceding nine years, giving every year equal weight (table 6-2). The results of both are quite similar. Consequently, I have used only the current-rate calculation in the following discussion.

Deriving Market Values and Required Rent Increases

According to the Annual Housing Survey, median gross rent among all unsubsidized renter-occupied units was $208 a month in 1978.[23] That number is used as a base for the remainder of the analysis. Its precise accuracy is not important because the analysis focuses on *relative* changes. Using Lowry's quality-adjusted rental revenue index, I derived rents

23. U.S. Department of Housing and Urban Development and U.S. Bureau of the Census, *Annual Housing Survey, 1978, Part A* (U.S. Government Printing Office, 1978), p. 12.

Table 6-1. *Estimated Market Values for Rental Units, Based on Current-Year Interest Rates, 1960–80*

Year	Monthly rent (dollars)	Operating-cost ratio[a] (percent)	Mortgage interest rate (percent)	Current market value (dollars)	Real market value (1967 dollars)	Index of real market value
1960	99.2	41.0	6.25	9,463.8	10,669.4	108.5
1961	100.4	41.5	6.04	9,686.8	10,811.2	110.0
1962	102.4	41.8	5.99	9,875.8	10,900.4	110.9
1963	103.4	42.4	5.90	9,992.8	10,897.3	110.8
1964	105.4	42.5	5.90	10,129.2	10,903.3	110.9
1965	107.5	43.0	5.95	10,282.0	10,880.4	110.7
1966	110.9	43.2	6.42	10,025.2	10,313.8	104.9
1967	115.2	43.6	6.97	9,832.2	9,832.2	100.0
1968	119.8	44.0	7.66	9,548.6	9,163.7	93.2
1969	125.1	44.7	8.69	9,020.3	8,215.2	83.6
1970	131.3	45.4	9.93	8,461.1	7,275.2	74.0
1971	138.2	46.2	9.07	9,396.8	7,746.7	78.8
1972	143.8	47.0	8.57	10,037.0	8,010.4	81.5
1973	150.8	47.4	8.76	10,282.7	7,725.2	78.6
1974	158.8	48.5	9.47	10,008.4	6,776.2	68.9
1975	168.6	49.4	10.22	9,845.6	6,107.7	62.1
1976	179.8	49.9	9.83	10,714.9	6,284.4	63.9
1977	193.0	50.6	9.34	11,789.7	6,495.7	66.1
1978	208.0	51.7	9.46	12,304.4	6,297.0	64.0
1979	223.7	51.7	9.98	12,702.7	5,843.0	59.4
1980	245.3	52.6	12.53	11,351.3	4,599.3	46.8

Source: Ira S. Lowry, "Inflation Indexes for Rental Housing," working draft WD-1081-HUD (Rand Corporation, May 1981), p. 62; Anthony Downs and S. Michael Giliberto, "How Inflation Erodes the Income of Fixed-Rate Lenders," *Real Estate Review* (Spring 1981), p. 46; and *Federal Home Loan Bank Board Journal* (June 1981), p. 58.

a. For all dates after 1960, values increase over the 1960 value by one-half the amount shown in Lowry, "Inflation Indexes for Rental Housing," p. 62.

from the 1978 base for three decennial years, as shown in table 6-3, along with operating-cost ratios calculated by Lowry and the interest rate prevailing in each year. From these data the model can generate market values of rental units sustainable in the years shown. Initially, I used an operating-cost ratio of 41 percent for all years to be conservative.

In 1960 a unit with a $99.20 gross rent and an operating-cost ratio of 41 percent could sustain a market value of $9,464 with a 6.25 percent mortgage interest rate. If its market value had increased at the same rate as consumer prices measured by the CPI, it would be worth $26,333 in 1980. By 1980, however, the mortgage interest rate had doubled to 12.53

PROFITABILITY OF RENTAL HOUSING

Table 6-2. *Estimated Market Values for Rental Units, Based on Weighted-Average Interest Rates, 1960–80*

Year	Monthly rent (dollars)	Operating-cost ratio[a] (percent)	Annual interest rate (percent)	Weighted interest rate[b] (percent)	Current market value (dollars)	Real market value (1967 dollars)	Index of real market value
1960	99.2	41.0	6.25	5.14	10,531.7	11,873.4	111.3
1961	100.4	41.5	6.04	5.30	10,403.4	11,611.0	108.8
1962	102.4	41.8	5.99	5.45	10,402.4	11,481.7	107.7
1963	103.4	42.4	5.90	5.56	10,324.9	11,259.4	105.6
1964	105.4	42.5	5.90	5.69	10,335.2	11,125.1	104.3
1965	107.5	43.0	5.95	5.81	10,329.6	10,930.8	102.5
1966	110.9	43.2	6.42	5.96	10,468.0	10,769.5	101.0
1967	115.2	43.6	6.97	6.09	10,665.2	10,665.2	100.0
1968	119.8	44.0	7.66	6.30	10,797.2	10,362.0	97.2
1969	125.1	44.7	8.69	6.58	10,848.3	9,934.4	93.1
1970	131.3	45.4	9.93	6.94	10,878.1	9,353.5	87.7
1971	138.2	46.2	9.07	7.25	10,972.2	9,045.5	84.8
1972	143.8	47.0	8.57	7.51	10,991.1	8,771.8	82.2
1973	150.8	47.4	8.76	7.79	11,162.7	8,386.7	78.6
1974	158.8	48.5	9.47	8.15	11,158.4	7,554.7	70.8
1975	168.6	49.4	10.22	8.58	11,225.8	6,963.9	65.3
1976	179.8	49.9	9.83	8.92	11,524.7	6,759.4	63.4
1977	193.0	50.6	9.34	9.15	11,971.6	6,595.9	61.8
1978	208.0	51.7	9.46	9.33	12,433.0	6,362.9	59.7
1979	223.7	51.7	9.98	9.46	13,233.2	6,087.0	57.0
1980	245.3	52.6	12.53	9.72	13,950.3	5,652.5	53.0

Source: Lowry, "Inflation Indexes for Rental Housing," p.62; Downs and Giliberto, "How Inflation Erodes the Income of Fixed-Rate Lenders," p. 46; and *Federal Home Loan Bank Board Journal* (June 1981), p. 58.

a. For all dates after 1960, values increase over the 1960 value by one-half the amount shown in Lowry, "Inflation Indexes for Rental Housing," p. 62.

b. Ten-year moving average, with equal weights on rates from each year.

percent. At that rate, with an operating-cost ratio of 41 percent, the unit would have to obtain a monthly rent of $457.15 to sustain a 1980 market value of $26,333. But Lowry's rent revenue index indicates that actual rents in 1980 were $245.30 a month for the average unit. Thus rents would have had to be 86 percent higher in 1980 than they actually were to sustain the same real market value that the average rental unit had in 1960. To put it another way, the current market value sustained by the actual 1980 rent at the 1980 interest rate (but using the 1960 operating-cost ratio) was only $14,129—or 54 percent of the 1960 value adjusted to 1980 prices. A similar calculation using 1970 as a base shows that 1980

Table 6-3. *Estimated Monthly Rent, Selected Years, 1960–80*

Year	Monthly rent (dollars)	Operating-cost ratio (percent)	Mortgage interest rate (percent)
1960	99.2	41.0	6.25
1970	131.3	49.7	9.93
1978	208.0	62.4	9.46
1980	245.3	64.1	12.53

Source: Lowry, "Inflation Indexes for Rental Housing," p. 62; Downs and Giliberto, "How Inflation Erodes the Income of Fixed-Rate Lenders," p. 46.

rents should have been 37 percent higher than they actually were to sustain the real value that the average rental unit supported in 1970 (using the 1970 operating-cost ratio).

Even larger increases in 1980 rents would have been necessary to sustain these earlier real values if interest rates similar to those prevailing in mid-1981 were used in the calculations. With a 16.0 percent mortgage interest rate but operating costs at 41 percent, the model shows a need for 1980 rents 58 percent higher than they actually were to sustain the 1970 unit value and 132 percent higher to sustain the 1960 unit value.

If Lowry is correct that operating costs have risen much faster than rents, this situation is even less favorable. In the extreme case of an operating-cost ratio of 64 percent in 1980, taken from Lowry's estimates, 1980 rents would need to be 107 percent higher than they actually were to sustain the 1970 rental unit value at a 12.53 percent mortgage interest rate.

Thus the real value of residential rental properties sustainable from their rents has declined sharply in the past fifteen years. Table 6-1 presents estimates of the market values of rental units derived from the model, using the prevailing nominal interest rates for each year's calculation. It also uses rent and operating-cost inputs from Lowry's computations. For all years after 1960, however, operating-cost ratios have been scaled down from Lowry's estimates to be conservative. I arbitrarily reduced by one-half the amount his estimate of each year's operating-cost ratio had risen above the 41 percent he estimated for 1960. For 1980, for example, I used 52.6 percent instead of the 64.1 percent in his series. However, I used his rental revenue index to estimate annual rents.

PROFITABILITY OF RENTAL HOUSING

Table 6-1 shows startling declines in the real market value of rental housing units from 1960 to 1980, especially after 1965. By 1980 rental housing units had lost 57 percent of the real value they possessed two decades earlier. Moreover, these estimated losses would be even greater if Lowry's estimates of operating-cost ratios had been used.

If these data are even roughly correct, rapid increases in operating costs and interest rates, plus lagging rents, have wiped out much of the real value of the nation's rental housing inventory over the past two decades. This conclusion seems contrary to the widespread belief that all real estate has been an excellent hedge against inflation. This apparent inconsistency is discussed in detail later.

Testing the Model with 1980 Data

How reliable is the simple model from which these dramatic conclusions have been derived? Its predictions of 1980 market values are close to the actual values of a 1980 sample of 226 apartment project sales from three counties in the Seattle area. This is a limited sample from which to derive conclusions about the entire nation, but it is difficult to find current sales data both detailed enough to check the model's operations and broad enough to cover an entire metropolitan market. These data meet both criteria.[24]

The model's estimates of 1980 values are somewhat below actual values in the Seattle area. For example, for the 167 apartment projects that were sold in 1980 in King County (which includes Seattle), the median values of key variables for these sales were a down-payment ratio of 24 percent, an operating-cost ratio of 34.3 percent, a monthly rent of $253, a mortgage interest rate of 10.5 percent, and a debt-service ratio of 0.92.[25] The model indicates these inputs could sustain a 1980 market value of $25,293 a unit. The actual median market value was $28,125; hence the model's result was 10.1 percent too low. Using actual 1980 inputs from other areas, the model produced market value estimates 1.3

---

24. Cain and Scott, *Apartment Market Study*. I am indebted to this organization for keeping such excellent records and publishing them over several years.

25. Median values were used instead of separate calculations for each transaction because I did not have data on individual transactions.

percent high for thirty-eight sales in Pierce County and 9.6 percent low for twenty-one sales in Snohomish County.[26]

The model's tendency to underestimate actual 1980 market prices probably arises from its failure to take account of possible future rent and value appreciation. Buyers are willing to pay a higher price for a property than can be sustained by its current characteristics alone when they expect its rents and market value to rise with inflation. They also take account of the possibility of converting rental units to condominiums at a substantial profit. The study by Cain and Scott, Incorporated, showed that 20 percent of the Seattle-area buyers in 1979 and 21 percent in 1980 said they either would certainly or might convert their properties.[27] As of 1980, recent past experience also supported expectations of higher prices because most rental properties had previously risen in nominal value, if not real value. The Cain and Scott index of Seattle-area prices shows that "in constant 1969 dollars, apartment properties [as of 1980] are almost 13 percent less today than in 1969, and rents are 9.9 percent below their 1969 level."[28] The rents shown in table 6-1 fell 13 percent in real terms in that period, quite similar to the Seattle experience. However, the 13 percent decline in real value in Seattle is much smaller than the 44 percent decline nationwide shown by table 6-1 for the same

---

26. The number of *sales* is not the same as the number of *rental units sold*, since all projects in the sample contained five or more units. In King County, for example, the distribution of sales was as follows: projects with five to eleven units, 26.3 percent of sales; projects with twelve to twenty-four units, 32.9 percent of sales; projects with twenty-five to seventy-four units, 28.1 percent of sales; and projects with seventy-five or more units, 12.7 percent of sales.

The size of these errors was not clearly related to the age of the buildings concerned, as shown by the following data for 1980 sales in King County, taken from Cain and Scott, *Apartment Market Study*, pp. 26–36:

Period when units were built	Median unit sale price (dollars)	Error of model estimate (percent)
1920–30	20,880	+2.5
1955–64	28,125	−15.5
1965–70	28,889	−13.2
1975–80	32,884	−7.6
New construction	36,833	−4.6

27. Ibid.
28. Cain and Scott, Inc., *The Cain and Scott Apartment Report*, vol. 5 (Winter 1981), p. 3.

period. After a local recession in the early 1970s, the Seattle housing market has been much stronger than markets in many older northeastern and midwestern metropolitan areas. Moreover, the rents and prices in table 6-1 are presumably for units of constant quality, based on Lowry's analysis. The Seattle data, in contrast, do not hold quality constant, and it may have risen significantly over this period. These empirical tests of the model confirm that current residential rents would have to rise greatly in order to sustain the real market values of past investments in such properties.

Why Rental Housing Has Been Profitable despite Lagging Rents

If real market values sustainable from rents have declined, why has so much investment in rental housing occurred during the past two decades? And why do so many such investors claim to have made handsome profits? The answer is that the *rate of return on equity* was excellent until 1980 because it was influenced by four major factors other than net operating incomes. These were tax shelter, leveraging, low real interest rates, and anticipated appreciation. As long as excellent yields on investment could be obtained because of these factors, investors were willing to buy and operate rental housing without raising net incomes enough to keep pace with inflation and rising interest rates. Therefore, market prices derived mainly from net operating income (as in the model) did not rise nearly as fast as the general price level.

This can be shown by using actual values from 1970 to 1979 in the model. The rent, interest rate, and operating-cost ratio for 1970 produce an estimated market value in current dollars of $8,461, as shown in table 6-1. From 1970 to 1979 compound annual rates of increase were 6.1 percent for rents and 7.6 percent for operating costs. The interest rate increased to 10.0 percent. These inputs generate a 1979 market value in current dollars of $12,703, up 50 percent from 1970. But, because consumer prices rose 86.9 percent during that period, real market value actually fell about 20 percent. Even so, if the property were sold in 1979 for $12,703, there was a nominal profit before capital gains taxes of $4,242. That is what remains after paying off the full mortgage balance and subtracting the down payment (assuming for simplicity no amortization of the outstanding mortgage balance). After a capital gains tax of

25 percent (the rate then prevailing), the profit rate on the initial down payment was 4.6 percent compounded.

This sales profit does not include cash flow. In the first year, cash flow plus tax savings equaled 13.9 percent of the down payment. Since the property showed a net loss, the cash flow was tax free. This rate declined in subsequent years, but would average about 10 percent. Hence the overall after-tax yield in current dollars was about 15 percent a year. The annual inflation rate as measured by the CPI was 7.2 percent in this period, making the real after-tax yield on equity 7.3 percent a year—a healthy real profit rate. Thus an investor who purchased the typical rental housing unit in 1970 for the market value computed by the model and sold it in 1979 for its market value, as then computed, made a good return on the investment, *even though the market value fell 20 percent in real terms*.

This surprising result springs from tax shelter, leveraging, and low real interest rates. Rental housing investors benefit from accounting losses that reduce their taxes on other income. This return on equity does not depend on profits from operations; in fact, it gets bigger the more money their properties lose.

In the example just discussed, the investor also leveraged initial equity by borrowing 75 percent of the property's cost. Such leverage causes every 10 percent rise in the property's overall market value to produce a 40 percent rise in initial equity. Any other benefits proportional to the entire property, such as depreciation deductions, also have multiplied impact on equity profits.

A third factor is low real interest rates. The real, after-the-fact interest rate received by the lender in this example on a ten-year mortgage loan made in 1970 was only 1.02 percent. Because interest payments are a tax deduction, the real after-tax interest rate paid by a borrower in the 50 percent tax bracket was *negative* 2.5 percent.[29]

Although increased yields from these factors do not depend on a property's ability to generate net operating profits, rents had to produce enough net income to cover debt service, assuming the lender demanded a debt-service ratio of at least 1.0. However, thousands of rental properties sold at prices so high in relation to rents that negative cash flows resulted.

That outcome reflects the fourth factor mentioned earlier: anticipated appreciation. Most investors bought rental properties partly as a hedge

---

29. Downs and Giliberto, "How Inflation Erodes the Income of Fixed-Rate Lenders," p. 46.

PROFITABILITY OF RENTAL HOUSING

against inflation. They believed prices would rise faster for such properties than for alternative investments, such as stocks and bonds. One support for that belief was the possibility of converting rental units to condominium ownership. Moreover, many real estate investors were trying to switch their assets out of the stock market, the bond market, and cash. The advantages that the three other factors gave to their real estate equity investments further strengthened their belief in future appreciation. Hence they bid the prices of many rental properties well above levels justified by current earning power, especially new units in rapidly growing areas. That is why most of the apartments sold in the Seattle area in 1980 involved negative cash flows. My conversations with realtors, developers, and lenders across the nation indicate this was true in most markets. When current cash flows are negative, *all* the benefits of ownership are either tax shelter or anticipated future appreciation.

Anticipated appreciation can become a self-fulfilling prophecy for at least a while. If more investors start believing rental apartments will go up in price, more people bid for the available supply, driving prices up—and thereby confirming their original belief. That attracts even more investors, continuing to increase prices without any close relationship to the properties' current or even future earning power. During the 1970s investors from all over the world sought equity ownership of U.S. real estate as a hedge against inflation. Prices were driven up and current yields down, since investors were counting future appreciation as part of their total yields. Market prices therefore became higher than those the model would indicate were sustainable from current operating profits. Even so, actual prices did not increase enough to maintain the real values of such properties.

Nevertheless, the market prices of rental units rose much faster than those of either bonds or common stocks, on the average, during most of the 1970s. Table 6-1 indicates that the nominal price of a rental housing unit sustainable from its rents increased 45.4 percent from 1970 to 1978. It then declined 7.7 percent from 1978 to 1980, ending the decade 34.2 percent above its 1970 level. In contrast, the nominal price of corporate bonds purchased in 1970 fell 9.7 percent by 1978 and then plunged another 25.5 percent from 1978 to 1980. By 1980, 1970 bonds had lost 32.8 percent of their nominal value.[30] Standard and Poor's index of 500

---

30. The yield shown by Moody's index of corporate bonds rose from 8.51 percent in 1970 to 9.07 percent in 1978 and 11.94 percent in 1980. Bureau of the Census, *Statistical Abstract of the United States, 1981* (GPO, 1981), p. 524; and Council of Economic Advisers, *Economic Indicators*, February 1982, p. 30.

stocks rose 15.4 percent from 1970 to 1978.[31] From 1978 to 1980 that index rose 23.8 percent; hence in 1980 it was 42.8 percent above its 1970 level. Common stock prices thus did much better in the late 1970s than rental unit prices, as measured by table 6-1, and somewhat outperformed them over the entire decade. But actual market prices of rental units probably rose about as much as common stock prices during the 1970s and vastly more than bond prices.

Another reason many investors in rental apartments made large profits in the 1970s springs from the "cream-skimming" nature of certain syndicated investments. For example, executives of the Lincoln Property Company, one of the nation's largest rental housing developers, claim many of their projects doubled in market value within seven years after construction.[32] Those projects were designed to serve high-turnover rental markets mainly in fast-growing areas. Hence Lincoln's average rental unit contained only 700 square feet, had an annual turnover rate of 70 percent, and was rented from month to month with no lease. Management could therefore raise rents continually during periods of inflation or housing shortages. By serving this limited market and exercising close control over costs, Lincoln was able to raise rents about 10 percent each year, while operating costs were rising only 8 percent.

I have used these numbers in the model, along with a depreciable life of twenty-two years (Lincoln's average), an initial monthly rent of $250 (though rent does not affect the results), an operating-cost ratio of 47 percent (from table 6-1 for 1972), and an interest rate of 8.57 percent (the actual rate in 1972). I also assumed the property was sold at the end of the seventh year with 75 percent financing at a rate of 9.98 percent (the actual rate for 1979). With these inputs, the model shows a seven-year increase in sustainable market value of 92.6 percent—almost doubling. It also shows a first-year yield (cash flow plus tax benefits) of 12.8 percent and a sales profit rate on equity of 24.8 percent a year compounded. The initial market value exactly doubles if the property is sold after 7.35 years. Thus the model's predictions are consistent with Lincoln's actual results.

But these characteristics are surely not typical of the entire rental inventory, which includes millions of older units in markets that are growing slowly or declining. Hence the average rental housing units

31. Ibid.
32. These comments about Lincoln Property Company's projects are based on personal conversations I held with Preston Butcher and Mac Poague of that organization in 1981.

almost certainly did not perform nearly as well, or rise nearly as fast in price, as these selective newer investments.

Why Profitability Is Changing

Changes have occurred recently in three of these four key factors, mainly because of dramatic increases in real interest rates since 1980. Those increases abolished low real interest rates and slowed the appreciation of all types of residential real estate.

For example, the median price of existing single-family homes sold in December 1981 was only 5.7 percent higher than one year earlier, whereas the CPI rose 8.9 percent. Thus the real price of such homes fell 3.2 percent from December 1980 to December 1981.[33] Moreover, this calculation overstates the December 1981 price. In both 1980 and 1981 sellers supplied large fractions of total sales revenue by taking back mortgages at about a 25 percent discount from the market interest rate then prevailing.

I estimate that about 15 percent of total home sales revenue was so supplied in 1980 and 25 percent in 1981.[34] If so, the proper price index for 1980 in year-to-year comparisons is not 100, but 96.25 (reflecting a 25 percent discount of 15 percent of the price). Similarly, the proper price index for 1981 is not 106.2, but 99.56 (reflecting a nominal rise of 6.2 percent, but a 25 percent discount of 25 percent of that price). Since the CPI rose 8.9 percent from 1980 to 1981, restating that 99.56 in 1980 dollars yields a 1981 real adjusted price index of 91.42. Thus the real adjusted median price of existing single-family homes sold fell from 96.25 in December 1980 to 91.42 in December 1981, or 5.0 percent. This negative appreciation occurred because of high financing costs. They have greatly reduced the number of households eligible to purchase homes at existing prices and have discouraged many eligible households from entering the market.

A similar slowdown in appreciation has affected rental housing, though no nationwide data are available to confirm it. Many people had purchased

---

33. National Association of Realtors, *Monthly Report: Existing Single-Family Home Sales*, January 1982, p. 3; and Council of Economic Advisers, *Economic Indicators*, January 1982, p. 23.

34. These estimates are based partly on a study of the financing of over 300 sales of existing homes in California in early 1981. See California Association of Realtors, *Financial Survey: Preliminary Findings* (Los Angeles: CAR, August 1981).

single-family homes or condominium units as investments, renting them out temporarily while waiting for prices to rise in the homeownership market. Slower appreciation reduces the attractiveness of such investments. Converting rental units to condominium ownership is now more difficult, too, because it is harder to finance sales of the converted units to individual buyers.

Even more important, most insurance companies and other suppliers of capital are no longer willing to make long-term fixed-rate mortgage loans on rental housing. Some have withdrawn from the rental housing market altogether. Others will enter it only in joint ventures with large-scale developers. Still others will make mortgage loans, but only at high variable or renegotiable rates. Thus the possibility of highly leveraging initial equity with borrowed money has been drastically reduced, especially for small-scale investors. As of early 1982, these changes had almost shut down the syndications that formerly provided much of the newly built rental housing across the nation. When interest rates fell considerably below their 1981 and early 1982 levels in early 1983, those operations began again.[35] Even so, syndicators' traditional leveraging was hard to accomplish. Lenders would not make long-term, fixed-rate loans but demanded some protection against possible future inflation by sharing in equity or in cash flows above debt service.

Future Profitability and Market Value

Three of the four factors that helped support market prices of rental housing above levels justifiable by current profits are thus likely to become much weaker in the future. This will occur even if interest rates decline well below their 1981 levels. Only tax shelter will remain undiminished in force. More of the future market value of each rental unit will therefore depend on its current net operating income.

But rents have lagged far below the levels necessary to support real market values anywhere near their past levels. Because there are few reliable data concerning market prices of rental housing, it is not clear whether they have fallen as low as indicated by table 6-1. In my opinion, current average prices for the entire inventory are well above that low level because of the past effects of the four factors discussed above. Yet

---

35. However, syndicators have begun aggregating capital through partnership arrangements that supply all the necessary funds without use of debt.

PROFITABILITY OF RENTAL HOUSING

current prices are still far below the levels necessary to preserve their 1960 or even 1970 real values. This is less true for relatively new units than for the inventory as a whole and for older units.

Even if current financial conditions improve considerably, there will still be a gap between present rents and those required to sustain existing market values. That means pressure will build in rental housing markets to raise rents.

If there were no change in the balance of supply and demand in the rental market, this would be impossible. But the demand for rental units will rise significantly in the 1980s. More households will want to rent, and many households that want to buy will be forced to rent because of the increased costs of homeownership. Yet new construction of rental units will virtually cease for a while, except for directly subsidized units (see chapter 7). Hence demand will be rising much faster than supply in most rental markets, except where many non-new units are created. This will permit owners of rental units to increase rents faster than in the past, thereby underpinning the market values their units have already attained.

Nonetheless owners will be unable to raise rents fast enough to eliminate the rent gap overnight. During most of the remaining 1980s, therefore, rental housing markets will paradoxically experience both rapid increases in rents and some weakness in the market values of existing rental units. Residential rents are likely to increase faster than the general price level, reversing the trend dominant during the past twenty years. This dramatic change was disguised at first by the 1981–82 recession. During recessions, rental vacancy typically rises as renters pressed by unemployment or the fear of it double up. In fact, rental vacancy rose in 1982. Even so, for every month in 1982 except January, the consumer price index for rent showed larger percentage gains over the same index one year earlier than did the overall consumer price index.[36] After the recovery beginning in early 1983 is well under way, rental demand should expand rapidly, stimulating unusually fast increases in rents.

After an initial period of rent increases, building of new rental housing may become economically feasible again, especially if interest rates decline. When that happens also depends on how fast construction costs go up relative to rents. Development of new rental housing will first become economically feasible in rapidly growing areas with relatively

36. *Economic Report of the President, January 1983*, p. 221.

small existing rental inventories. Small, high-turnover units will be developed sooner than larger, lower-turnover units, which are costlier to build and suffer more competition from homeownership. But new development will not become feasible for any rental units unless long-term financing becomes available again.

This forecast assumes no widespread adoption of local rent controls. As rent increases accelerate, pressure for such controls will increase, too, especially in big cities containing many elderly renters. If rent controls become widespread, rents will not rise enough relative to construction and other costs to make new building of rental units feasible.

7
Future Housing Construction and Potential Shortfalls

IF POTENTIAL SHORTFALLS of new rental housing construction arise because expected future production is below projected increases in demand, developers, investors, and households will adjust their behavior in ways that alter the forecast in demand or supply. These adjustments will "clear the market"—that is, equate supply and demand at the prevailing price. Hence no *actual* shortfalls will occur, but the failure of projected supply changes to meet projected demand changes will greatly affect housing market behavior.

This chapter estimates likely future housing production. It then explores whether potential shortfalls will arise, how large they would be under various circumstances, and what behavioral adjustments they would generate.

Projected New Housing Construction

Without public policy intervention, incentives to produce new rental housing will remain weak in the near future. Although the Economic Recovery Tax Act of 1981 reduced the allowable period for depreciating rental housing, it also cut the highest tax brackets from 70 to 50 percent. Moreover, federal subsidies for more new rental units have already been slashed from 400,000 units a year in fiscal 1977 to 150,000 in fiscal 1982 and a proposed 10,000 from 1983 onward.[1] If rents climb enough to

1. U.S. Department of Housing and Urban Development, *Fiscal Year 1983 Budget: Summary* (U.S. Government Printing Office, February 1982), pp. H-1–H-3.

justify building new rental units, political pressures on local governments to adopt rent controls will escalate sharply.

These conditions, combined with the likelihood of continued high interest rates and the attractiveness of homeownership, may reduce average annual creation of new rental units in the 1980s to below its level in the late 1970s, as already happened in 1980 and 1981. Nevertheless, I will consider 475,000 units a year as a moderate projection of future new rental production in the 1980s. This is about 0.4 percent above the average new rental construction from 1974 to 1980. I will use a high projection of 590,000 units a year (24 percent above the moderate projection) and a low projection of 350,000 units (26 percent below the moderate projection). From 1974 to 1980, annual new rental construction (as shown in table 5-3) exceeded the high projection only in 1977 and 1978, and fell below the low projection only in 1975. Hence these projections roughly correspond to experience in the late 1970s.

Nevertheless, they may seem low, since the moderate projection is 44 percent below the actual average of 1970–73, shown in table 5-3. But the latter was abnormally high because new multifamily construction then averaged 896,000 units a year, compared with only 187,000 during the 1950s, 518,000 during the 1960s, and 470,000 from 1974 through 1980.[2] The huge multifamily construction surge in the early 1970s was caused by a unique combination of factors. They included record federal subsidies, massive funding by real estate investment trusts, initial entry into real estate development by many big industrial corporations, and low real interest rates. None is likely to recur soon. Therefore that surge should be regarded as a deviation from normal construction levels for multifamily housing.

Financial conditions in the 1980s will also be less favorable to new construction of ownership housing. It would be unrealistic to project big increases in such construction over its level in the 1970s, in spite of rising demand. Even continuation of the 1970s levels may be overly optimistic.

I therefore assume moderate future construction of ownership housing will equal 1,500,000 units a year. This is just 1 percent above the 1970–80 average. I also assume a high level 20 percent greater (1,800,000 units

2. U.S. Bureau of the Census, *Statistical Abstract of the United States, 1956* (GOP, 1956), p. 773; *1961*, p. 760; *1963*, p. 755; and *1979*, p. 779. The average for the 1950s is based on an older data series; it might be as high as 200,000 units a year if that series is expanded to conform to later data series.

HOUSING CONSTRUCTION AND POTENTIAL SHORTFALLS

Table 7-1. *Projections of Annual New Housing Construction, 1980–90*
Thousands of units a year

Ownership housing construction rates	Rental housing construction rates		
	Low (350)	Moderate (475)	High (590)
Low (1,200)	1,550	1,675	1,790
Moderate (1,500)	1,850	1,975	2,090
High (1,800)	2,150	2,275	2,390

Source: Author's estimates.

a year) and a low level 25 percent smaller (1,200,000 units a year). From 1970 to 1980 actual new construction of ownership units (as shown in table 5-5) exceeded the high projection only in 1972 and was lower than the low projection only in 1975 and 1980.[3]

Expected levels of total housing construction during the 1980s are shown in table 7-1. The columns indicate three alternatives for annual rental construction; the rows indicate three alternatives for annual ownership construction. The resulting nine projections of average annual construction (including mobile home shipments) range from 1.55 million units a year to 2.39 million.

Projected Demand for New Housing Construction

Total demand includes estimated demand for housing arising from household growth and requirements for added vacancies (see chapter 4) and from estimated net replacement (see chapter 5). In calculating potential future shortfalls, each unit required for net replacement can be viewed either as a subtraction from the existing supply (as in chapter 5)

---

3. These ownership projections are higher than the rental projections in relation to overall experience with both types of production throughout the 1970s. One reason is the unique surge of rental production in the early 1970s, which produced an abnormally high average for the entire decade. In addition, production of new subsidized rental units is likely to be much lower in the 1980s than in the 1970s. No comparable production decline will occur in the ownership market because few new ownership units have been directly subsidized. In contrast, higher real capital costs are likely to affect both types of production adversely. Therefore, the moderate projection for rental production is much lower than the overall average for 1970–80, whereas the moderate projection for ownership production is not.

Table 7-2. *Projections of Demand for New Housing Construction with Low Net Replacement Rates, Selected Periods, 1980–2000*[a]
Thousands of units

	High growth[b]		Low growth[b]	
Type and period	Slow decline[c]	Fast decline[c]	Slow decline[c]	Fast decline[c]
Rental housing				
1980–85	3,787	2,900	3,107	2,222
Annual average	757	580	621	444
1985–90	3,675	2,916	3,018	2,267
Annual average	735	583	604	453
1990–95	3,416	2,786	2,822	2,201
Annual average	683	557	564	440
1995–2000	2,924	2,372	2,465	1,931
Annual average	585	474	493	386
Ownership housing				
1980–85	7,168	8,024	6,480	7,333
Annual average	1,434	1,605	1,296	1,467
1985–90	6,856	7,594	6,208	6,938
Annual average	1,371	1,519	1,242	1,388
1990–95	6,386	7,003	5,789	6,398
Annual average	1,277	1,401	1,158	1,280
1995–2000	6,029	6,600	5,428	5,956
Annual average	1,206	1,320	1,086	1,191
All housing				
1980–85	10,955	10,924	9,587	9,555
Annual average	2,191	2,185	1,917	1,911
1985–90	10,531	10,510	9,226	9,205
Annual average	2,106	2,102	1,845	1,841
1990–95	9,802	9,789	8,611	8,599
Annual average	1,960	6,958	1,722	1,720
1995–2000	8,953	8,972	7,893	7,887
Annual average	1,791	1,794	1,579	1,577

Source: Author's estimates.
a. Includes adjustments for accelerated condominium conversions. Figures are rounded.
b. Rate of household growth.
c. Speed of decline in renting among husband-and-wife households.

or an addition to the demand for new construction. For convenience, I will treat net replacement here as added demand for new construction.

Chapters 4 and 5 used a variety of alternatives to cope with uncertainty about the future values of variables such as rates of household growth and net replacement. This approach expands the number of possible outcomes tremendously, making it hard to grasp all of them at once. Instead of presenting all possible combinations of total future housing demands under various assumptions, I show in table 7-2 only a summary

HOUSING CONSTRUCTION AND POTENTIAL SHORTFALLS

of four cases, assuming low net replacement rates to be conservative. Because the demands in table 7-2 have been adjusted to account for future condominium conversions, they do not exactly equal the sums of the two types of demand from chapters 4 and 5.[4]

Total annual demand for all types of new housing for 1980–85 ranges from 2.1 million to 2.4 million. Within each projection, annual demand for new units declines steadily in every subsequent five-year period, mainly because of slowing household growth. By the late 1990s annual demand for new housing will be about 23 percent lower than in the early 1980s. Actual new housing construction (including mobile homes) from 1970 through 1980 averaged about 2.1 million units (the sum of the two averages derived from tables 5-3 and 5-5). That is 1 percent below the lowest estimate of total demand for the first half of the 1980s and 14 percent below the highest estimate. But it is also 13 percent higher than the highest projected demand for 1995–2000.

These data imply that any failure of new housing construction to meet projected demand in the 1980s could probably be made up by achieving new construction levels above current demands in the 1990s. However, that would still leave some potential demand in the 1980s "unsatisfied" until long after its initial appearance.

Comparing Future Construction and Demand

To estimate the potential shortfall in new construction of rental housing, I compared projections of total demand from table 7-2 with projections

---

4. In chapter 5 I estimated that conversion of existing rental units to condominium ownership would accelerate in the 1980s to about 100,000 units a year, then remain in the 1990s at about 80,000 a year (after adjusting for converted units replaced on the rental market). The net rates used to calculate the total replacement demands shown in chapter 5 inherently contained an allowance for about 50,000 net conversions a year. That was the approximate average for the late 1970s. (Future rental replacement rates exceed the actual rate in the late 1970s because the latter was low.) But the conversion levels forecast for the 1980s and 1990s exceed that historical average by 50,000 and 30,000 units, respectively. Further adjustments must be made to account for this future acceleration of net conversions. Those adjustments have been made in table 7-2 and in all subsequent tables in this chapter. Appropriate amounts have been added to net replacement and total demand for rental housing and have been subtracted from net replacement and total demand for ownership housing, leaving demand for all housing unaffected. For the 1980s, 250,000 units were added to five-year rental demand and 50,000 units were added to annual rental demand. For the 1980s, 150,000 were added to five-year rental demand and 30,000 were added to annual rental demand. Identical amounts were subtracted from analogous ownership demand for the same years.

Table 7-3. *Projections of Potential Shortfalls in Rental Housing, 1980–90*[a]

Thousands of units

Replacement rate, demand, and shortfall	High growth[b]		Low growth[b]	
	Slow decline[c]	Fast decline[c]	Slow decline[c]	Fast decline[c]
Low net replacement rates				
Average annual demand				
For additional households	548.9	395.5	424.3	271.9
For replacement	168.5	165.3	165.9	162.8
For vacancies	28.8	20.8	22.3	14.3
Total	746.2	581.6	612.5	449.0
Average annual shortfall				
With low levels of new construction[d]	396.2	231.6	262.5	99.0
With moderate levels of new construction[e]	271.2	106.6	137.5	−26.0
With high levels of new construction[f]	156.2	−8.4	22.5	−141.0
High net replacement rates				
Average annual demand				
For additional households	548.9	395.5	424.3	271.9
For replacement	208.0	203.8	204.5	200.3
For vacancies	28.8	20.8	22.3	14.3
Total	785.7	620.1	651.1	486.5
Average annual shortfall				
With low levels of new construction[d]	435.7	270.1	301.1	136.5
With moderate levels of new construction[e]	310.7	145.1	176.1	11.5
With high levels of new construction[f]	195.7	30.1	61.1	−103.5

Source: Author's estimates.
a. Includes adjustments for accelerated condominium conversion. Negative shortfalls are surpluses.
b. Rate of household growth.
c. Speed of decline in renting among husband-and-wife households.
d. Assumed to be 350,000 units a year.
e. Assumed to be 475,000 units a year.
f. Assumed to be 590,000 units a year.

of new rental housing construction from table 7-1. Table 7-3 shows these comparisons for 1980–90, under a variety of assumptions about replacement rates, household growth, and rates of decline in renting among husband-and-wife households. Four conclusions can be derived from table 7-3.

First, if new rental housing is constructed at a low rate, significant

HOUSING CONSTRUCTION AND POTENTIAL SHORTFALLS 123

potential shortfalls would arise from 1980 to 1990 under three of the four projections based on low net replacement rates. Shortfalls would range from 99,000 to 396,200 units a year. As of 1980 there were about 2.2 million vacant units for rent nationwide, according to the 1980 census.[5] Even if all those units became occupied, a potential shortfall of over 1.76 million rental units would arise by 1990 if the high-growth, slow-decline projection was realized. That projection calls for 32.7 million occupied rental units as of 1990. So a shortage of 1.76 million units would amount to 5.4 percent of projected total demand. But such an assumption of zero vacancy is unrealistic and undesirable. Hence the potential shortfall would be a higher fraction of projected total demand.

With moderate production, significant but smaller potential shortfalls would arise by 1990 under three of the four projections assuming low net replacement. Shortfalls would range from 137,500 to 271,200 units a year. A slight surplus would occur under the low-growth, fast-decline projection. Even if all units vacant in 1980 became occupied by 1990, there would be a shortfall of 512,000 units under the high-growth, slow-decline projection, or 1.6 percent of projected total demand. But since the elimination of vacancy is unlikely, the shortfall would be a greater fraction of projected total demand. Even so, the shortfall would probably be small enough so that overcoming it would not require much adjustment in market conditions. If new rental construction occurs at high levels, potential shortfalls will be negative or quite low in all but the high-growth, slow-decline projection.

A second conclusion is that the potential rental construction shortfall

---

5. The number of vacant units for rent revealed by actual count in the 1980 census is much larger than those projected by the Annual Housing Surveys from samples. The rental vacancy rate in the fourth quarter of 1980 was 5.0 percent, according to the Council of Economic Advisers, *Economic Indicators,* June 1981, p. 19. In October 1979 there were 28,760,000 units either occupied by renters or vacant and for rent, according to the U.S. Department of Housing and Urban Development and Bureau of the Census, *Annual Housing Survey, 1979, Part A* (GPO, 1980), p. 1. If this inventory rose 300,000 by October 1980, it equaled about 29,060,000 units. Five percent of that total equals 1,450,000 vacant units for rent. However, the 1980 census counted 28,595,000 renter-occupied units, of which 2,179,000 were vacant and for rent; Bureau of the Census, *1980 Census of Population and Housing: Provisional Estimates of Social, Economic, and Housing Characteristics,* PHC80-S1-1 (GPO, 1982), p. 70. This implies a rental vacancy rate of 7.6 percent. This implies 2,185,000 units were vacant and for rent. No explanation for this discrepancy had been supplied by the Census Bureau at the time this book was written. To be conservative about the extent of possible future rental housing shortages, I have used the larger estimate of 1980 vacancy in the analysis.

Table 7-4. *Projections of Potential Shortfalls in Ownership Housing, 1980–90*[a]
Thousands of units

Replacement rate, demand, and shortfall	High growth[b]		Low growth[b]	
	Slow decline[c]	Fast decline[c]	Slow decline[c]	Fast decline[c]
Low net replacement rates				
Average annual demand				
For additional households	1,140.2	1,293.6	1,011.4	1,163.8
For replacement	248.5	252.5	245.3	249.3
For vacancies	13.8	15.7	12.2	14.0
Total	1,402.5	1,561.8	1,268.9	1,427.1
Average annual shortfall				
With low levels of new construction[d]	202.5	361.8	68.9	227.1
With moderate levels of new construction[e]	−97.5	61.8	−231.1	−72.9
With high levels of new construction[f]	−397.5	−238.2	−531.1	−372.9
High net replacement rates				
Average annual demand				
For additional households	1,140.2	1,293.6	1,011.4	1,163.8
For replacement	352.9	358.4	348.6	354.0
For vacancies	13.8	15.7	12.2	14.0
Total	1,506.9	1,667.7	1,372.2	1,531.8
Average annual shortfall				
With low levels of new construction[d]	306.9	467.7	172.2	331.8
With moderate levels of new construction[e]	6.9	167.7	−127.8	31.8
With high levels of new construction[f]	−293.1	−132.3	−427.8	−268.2

Source: Author's estimates.
a. Includes adjustments for accelerated condominium conversion. Negative shortfalls are surpluses.
b. Rate of household growth.
c. Speed of decline in renting among husband-and-wife households.
d. Assumed to be 1,200,000 units a year.
e. Assumed to be 1,500,000 units a year.
f. Assumed to be 1,800,000 units a year.

depends greatly on household growth and rental preferences. High household growth and slow decline in renting among husband-and-wife households produce by far the largest shortfall at every level of new rental construction. Low household growth and fast decline in renting produce either a small shortfall or a surplus. Both the rate of household formation and the ability of husband-and-wife households to buy homes are influenced by economic conditions. If low levels of new housing

HOUSING CONSTRUCTION AND POTENTIAL SHORTFALLS 125

construction cause major housing shortfalls, the overall cost of housing will go up. This could slow the rate of household formation and reduce the ability of husband-and-wife households to buy homes. Hence the relationship between these key assumptions and future rental shortfalls involves two-way causality. This relationship is crucial to analyzing possible adjustments to potential shortfalls, as discussed later.

Third, new construction may provide enough units to accommodate additional renting households; the greatest shortfalls will involve replacement. If new rental construction remains low, there will be enough new units to accommodate all additional households only under the low-growth, fast-decline projection. But only the high-growth, slow-decline projection involves so many additional households that moderate new construction would fail to serve them. Yet replacement demands are fully met only under the low-growth, fast-decline projection with high new construction. This implies continued strong pressure in the 1980s to make more intensive use of the existing rental housing inventory.

Fourth, high replacement rates would make potential rental housing shortfalls more severe. For example, using high rather than low net replacement rates increases total demand in the high-growth, slow-decline projection and potential shortfalls by 395,000 units over the decade. High net replacement rates imply that withdrawals from use greatly exceed non-new creation. Yet if there is strong pressure to use existing housing intensively, withdrawals will probably decline, and non-new creation will increase. That means net replacement will fall to low levels. Strong pressure to use existing housing arises under conditions like those generated by large potential shortfalls. Thus large potential shortfalls are in reality inconsistent with high net replacement rates. High replacement rates are probably possible only at high levels of new housing construction when potential shortfalls are small or nonexistent.

Table 7-4 shows that large potential housing shortfalls in the 1980s are less likely for ownership housing than for rental housing.[6] If low net

---

6. The main reason lies in the relationship between future demand projections and levels of different types of housing production in the late 1970s. The projections of both future housing demand and future construction used in this analysis are largely based on experience in the late 1970s. During that period both household formation and new construction of ownership housing occurred at relatively high levels compared with historical experience. But new construction of rental housing took place at relatively low levels, even excluding any comparison with the unique surge in the early 1970s (see chapters 2 and 3). This disparity between additions to demand and additions to supply for rental and ownership housing is likely to persist in the 1980s.

replacement rates prevail for ownership housing, high levels of new construction would produce large potential market surpluses in all four projections. Even moderate levels of new construction would produce a sizable potential shortfall only under the high-growth, fast-decline projection. However, low levels of new construction throughout the 1980s would create large shortfalls in ownership housing under all projections except low growth and slow decline. Yet even low new building would produce enough new ownership units to accommodate almost all added households.

High net replacement rates would produce much larger potential shortfalls in ownership housing, though high levels of construction would still avoid them almost completely. With high net replacement rates, low new construction would generate potential shortfalls ranging from 149,500 to 467,700 units a year. Even moderate new building would also create big potential shortfalls under two projections and some shortfalls under two others.

Avoiding Shortfalls through Other Means

As chapter 5 indicated, from 1974 to 1979 about 820,000 additional rental units were created annually through means other than new construction. These non-new units greatly outnumbered units created by new construction in that period and largely offset the 850,100 units either permanently or retrievably removed from rental use each year. That is why the 1973–78 net replacement rate for rental housing was low.

Although these data are not very reliable, they prove that any analysis of potential future shortfalls must take non-new units into account. Some withdrawals and non-new creation have already been accounted for in calculating future net replacement demand. Those calculations assume the continuation of "typical" past relationships between withdrawals and non-new creation. Additional allowances have to be made for either withdrawals or non-new creation only if they will markedly depart from these past relationships.

The four demand projections for rental housing in the 1980s (table 7-2) assume annual net replacement of 162,800 to 168,500 rental units under low rates and 200,300 to 208,000 units under high rates. Each such figure is the net result of subtracting total units arising from non-new creation from total withdrawals. The size of these figures implies that withdrawals will substantially exceed non-new creation. That has generally been the case, except in the late 1970s. The net replacement rate for rental housing was then low, apparently because of a combination of little new rental construction and considerable non-new rental creation.[7] Both total removals and non-new creation were much greater in the late 1970s than at any other time since 1950, according to studies done by the Department of Housing and Urban Development.[8]

Undoubtedly, changing past relationships between withdrawals, non-new creation, and new construction is one way housing markets can adjust to potential housing shortfalls. Low levels of new housing construction create greater pressure to use the existing inventory, thereby reducing withdrawals and increasing non-new creation. During the 1980s decreasing removals from the inventory and creating additional non-new rental units will play crucial roles in reducing potential rental shortfalls. Variations in these activities will affect shortfalls just as directly as variations in new construction. Thus public policies should encourage longer use of existing units and creation of more non-new ones, especially since both are typically far less costly per unit than new construction.

Market Adjustments to Potential Shortfalls

Predicted shortfalls in rental housing construction cannot actually persist. If the number of households demanding rental units exceeds the number of units available at some moment, competition among the demanders will drive up prices until equilibrium is reached. That will occur when some demanders drop out because they cannot afford the increased prices and more suppliers offer units for rent at those prices. Eventually the number of demanders remaining will just equal the number of units supplied, and relative prices will stabilize. Such adjustments do not occur instantaneously, however. The rental market can be in disequilibrium for some time while they are taking place.

---

7. See Duane McGough, "Housing Inventory Losses as a Requirement for New Construction," paper prepared for the Economic Commission for Europe Seminar on Housing Forecasting and Programming, January 1981, p. 17. Also see *Annual Housing Survey, Part A, 1974* through *1978*, especially the introductions where these variables are discussed.

8. Ibid.

These adjustments also indicate how the behavior projected earlier is likely to change if shortfalls appear imminent. For example, initial demanders who adjust by dropping out of the rental market as prices rise will not purchase units of the same quality, since that is even more costly than renting. Instead, they may continue living in accommodations with others from whom they would like to separate. Temporary or even long-range postponement of household separation is especially likely among people with a high propensity to rent, such as young unmarried persons leaving their parents' homes for the first time.

Some households now living apart will merge so they can afford to rent or buy a unit that would otherwise be too costly. This adjustment is especially likely among unrelated single persons, whether young or old. Thus potential rental housing shortfalls are likely to increase crowding and decrease the rate of separate household formation compared with what they would be if rental housing were plentiful. Many households will accept a lower quality of housing than they would if rental units were plentiful, and they will be more likely to spend a greater proportion of their income on housing.

Suppliers of rental housing will be able to get higher rents for marginal-quality units if shortfalls occur; hence they will tend to keep using such units longer. Consequently, the rate at which older units are withdrawn from the existing inventory will decline, and the average age of the rental inventory will increase. Whether this will cause its average quality to decline is not clear. Older units tend to be more deteriorated, but higher rents will enable many owners to maintain older properties better than they otherwise would.

As relative rents increase, more rental units will be added through means other than new construction. This will include conversion of nonresidential structures into housing, retrieval of units that had been removed from the market, and division of large older units into two or more smaller units. Non-new creation will be especially important in large cities and older suburbs containing big single-family homes. Nonresidential structures likely to be converted into housing include obsolete strip stores, surplus school buildings, and old loft or industrial buildings. However, converted units will often bring higher prices on the ownership market than the rental market; most will be sold to owner-occupants rather than rented. Nevertheless, some purchasers of such units will rent them out while waiting for them to appreciate. In other cases converted units will not be sufficiently large or well located to sell well, though they can be rented.

As a result of reduced withdrawals and increased creation of non-new units, future net rental replacement rates will be relatively low compared with average past experience. Even if new housing construction is sustained at moderate rather than low levels, most new units will be absorbed by household growth rather than used for replacement.

Because housing shortfalls are likely to be much greater among rental units than ownership units in the 1980s, rents will go up faster than both home prices and the general price level. This is likely in spite of the many forces described earlier that have restrained rent increases over the past two decades. This conclusion is highlighted by the dramatic slowing of price appreciation for owner-occupied housing from 1980 to 1982, due mainly to higher real mortgage interest rates.[9]

The implications of potential housing shortfalls for future conversion of rental units into condominium ownership are unclear. On the one hand, the higher real costs of buying detached single-family homes will increase demand for converted condominium units among households seeking homeownership at relatively low cost. On the other hand, slower price appreciation of other owner-occupied housing will reduce the profits entrepreneurs can earn by converting rental units into condominiums. The possibility of obtaining higher rents will also motivate more apartment owners to continue renting, and it may cause more owners of converted units to rent their units as investments.

As a result, pressures to convert existing rental units to condominiums will probably be strongest in the moderately priced market. In the high-priced market, converted units will face much stronger competition from detached single-family homes, newly built multifamily units for sale, and already-converted condominiums. In the low-priced market, conversion will not be profitable at all.[10]

All of these adjustments to potential housing shortfalls can affect the housing market just as profoundly as potential demographic developments. Any initially rapid household growth, for example, will generate

9. The Bureau of Labor Statistics has recently proposed changing the measure of housing costs in the consumer price index from home purchase prices and interest rates to residential rents. This shift is aimed at reducing the exaggeration in living costs caused by faster increases in home prices and mortgage interest rates than in either rents or the "true" costs of shelter. The shift is designed to take effect at about the time when I believe home prices will stop rising faster than inflation generally and rents will start doing so. Ironically, this shift is therefore likely to have exactly the opposite effect from what is intended and the opposite effect from continuing the present arrangements in spite of their clear past distortions.

10. Adjustments for an acceleration of condominium conversions in the 1980s and 1990s over their levels in the 1970s have already been made, as described earlier.

large potential housing shortfalls. Adjustments to the resulting shortage conditions will lead to formation of fewer households than in the high-growth projections.

Fast declines in renting among husband-and-wife households also seem unlikely. They would imply rapid increases in homeownership among such households, but the real costs of homeownership will be much higher in the 1980s than in the 1970s. Hence shifts out of renting will probably slow down.

Similarly, replacement rates will probably remain low. Low levels of new rental construction seem most likely in the near future, but moderate new construction is more probable over the whole decade. The rising prices implied by large potential rental shortfalls will eventually call forth higher levels of new rental construction than the low projections (unless real interest rates remain extremely high throughout the decade).

In fact, the adjustments described above imply that rental housing markets in the 1980s are likely to reach equilibrium at a point resembling the low-growth, slow-decline, low-net-replacement demand projection. That projection involves demands for averages of 612,500 new rental housing units a year in the 1980s and 528,500 a year in the 1990s (including adjustments for accelerated condominium conversions). With moderate new rental housing construction, that projection indicates a potential shortfall of 1.38 million rental units over the entire decade, according to table 7-3. Of course, actual shortfalls cannot persist because market forces will move toward equilibrium by increasing prices, reducing demand, and expanding supplies. But this analysis indicates further adjustments would have to be made to reach equilibrium even after household growth fell, husband-and-wife shifts out of renting slowed, and net replacement rates remained low. Such further adjustments could be larger new construction, more non-new creation of rental units, fewer withdrawals of existing units, even lower household growth, and perhaps faster shifting of husband-and-wife households out of renting. However, the last would occur only if rents had risen so far compared with home prices by the end of the 1980s that home purchase was relatively easier again.

This forecast assumes that such market responses will not be thwarted by widespread adoption of rent controls. This possibility and its implications are discussed in the next chapter.

8
Future Rental Housing Policies

THE U.S. Congress has established as a basic goal for all federal housing policies "the realization as soon as feasible of . . . a decent home and a suitable living environment for every American family."[1] This goal was first stated in 1949 and has been reaffirmed for over thirty years, but has never been fully attained because Congress has not appropriated enough funds. Given the Reagan administration's drive to reduce federal nondefense spending, the realization of this goal is not likely to be feasible soon. Hence this goal must be regarded primarily as an aspiration, not as a guarantee that individual families can use to demand publicly financed fulfillment of their "rights" to decent housing and a suitable environment. Even so, this goal expresses both a moral and legal basis for possible public policies related to rental housing. In fact, many subsequent laws affecting housing refer to it as their justification.[2] Because of the unequal

---

1. *Basic Laws and Authorities on Housing and Community Development, Revised through January 3, 1979,* Committee Print, House Committee on Banking, Finance, and Urban Affairs, 94 Cong. 1 sess. (U.S. Government Printing Office, 1979), p. 1.

2. Congress has established several other primary objectives for housing policy as means of pursuing the basic goal stated above. These are the following.

—Providing housing assistance to low-income households. This includes enabling those now living in substandard or overcrowded housing to occupy decent units and financially aiding those who now pay very high fractions of their income to live in decent units. "Low-income households" are usually defined as those with annual income less than 80 percent of the median household income in the area concerned. This definition is used to establish eligibility for the Section 8 housing subsidy program. Because 80 percent of the median household income is now about double the poverty-level income, this definition includes many households with incomes well above the official poverty level. Hence the term "very low income" is sometimes applied to households with income below 50 percent of the

131

distribution of incomes and wealth in the United States and the high cost of "decent" housing, attaining this goal implies redistributing at least some resources to the poor.

Rental housing is also greatly affected by many local, state, and federal policies and programs not primarily aimed at housing. Accounting for the many goals of all these policies relevant to rental housing would be overwhelmingly complicated. I have therefore condensed all such goals into four major objectives, two affecting supply and two affecting demand. The supply objectives are stimulating the production of new rental housing and making more intensive use of existing structures as rental housing. The second includes encouraging (1) proper maintenance of existing rental housing units, (2) conversion of nonresidential structures into rental units, (3) return of retrievable units to current rental use, (4) division of large single-family units into two or more units, some used for rental, and (5) continued use, rather than removal, of rental units now in the active inventory.

The first demand objective is helping poor renters by enabling those now living in substandard housing to occupy better units or by providing financial aid to those who pay excessive fractions of their income for rent, including many who already occupy decent units. (The latter really suffer from inadequate income rather than inadequate housing.) The second objective is encouraging homeownership among all income groups. This

---

median household income in the area. The term "moderate income" was initially used in the Housing Act of 1968, applying to households with income between the "very low income" and "low-income" levels as defined above. Therefore, the goal of serving moderate-income households can be considered as encompassed within the goal of serving low-income households, as they are now defined.
—Encouraging homeownership among households at all income levels.
—Stimulating the economy by increasing activity in the housing industry.
—Increasing the total available supply of decent housing units.
—Improving the quality of deteriorated neighborhoods.
—Providing housing assistance to numerous specific groups, such as the elderly, Indians, and persons displaced by government actions. The assistance is the same as described above concerning low-income households.
Congress has also adopted several other housing goals I consider secondary because of the lesser emphasis they have received. These include providing housing assistance to colleges, stabilizing annual housing output at a high level, encouraging housing innovations, creating employment and training opportunities for residents of low-income areas, encouraging maximum feasible participation of private enterprise and capital in meeting housing needs, and achieving reduced concentration of low-income households in deteriorated urban neighborhoods. This list of goals is taken from Anthony Downs, *Federal Housing Subsidies: How Are They Working?* (Lexington Books, 1973), pp. 1–2.

is relevent to rental housing markets because implementing it tends to shift households from renting to owning their homes.

The Tension between Supply and Demand Objectives

Achieving both supply objectives requires improving the profitability of rental housing, which in turn requires raising rents substantially. Developers are not building many new unsubsidized rental units, and financial institutions are not funding many, because rents are not high enough in relation to construction and operating costs to make doing so profitable. Similarly, many owners of existing rental units are converting them to condominiums because it is much more profitable to sell them than to continue renting them. Other owners are allowing their rental properties to deteriorate because spending the money to maintain them is not justified by the added profits gained. Furthermore, non-new rental units will not be added to the inventory unless they promise profitability, and substantial numbers of non-new units must be created in the 1980s if major rental shortfalls are to be avoided.

To make rental housing profitable enough to call forth an adequate future supply, rents will have to increase for at least several years much faster than operating costs, building costs, the general price level, or consumer incomes—reversing the trend prevailing from 1960 to 1981.[3] Only in that way can enough revenues be generated to justify the investments required to create additional new and non-new units and to maintain and operate existing units. The only alternative is a massive infusion of government subsidies, which seems unlikely in the present political and budgetary climate.

Undoubtedly, such rent escalation would be bitterly opposed by most tenants and would be especially onerous for poor tenants. Rapidly rising rents would make achievement of the first demand objective much more difficult because the cost of helping poor renters occupy decent housing would increase accordingly. That would reduce the number of households that could be effectively aided with any given amount of subsidy, or it would decrease the effectiveness of any given subsidy distributed to all needy households.

3. From July 1981 to December 1982, the consumer price index component for residential rent rose faster than the overall index; *Economic Report of the President, January 1983*, p. 221. Hence this change has already begun.

Table 8-1. *Ownership of Rental Housing Units, 1979*

Type	Number of units (thousands)	Estimated average units per separate owner	Number of separate owners (thousands)
Single-family units	8,390	1.0	8,390
Multifamily structures			
2–4 units	7,475	2.5	2,990
5–19 units	6,100	7.5	813
20–49 units	2,082	30.0	69
50 or more units	2,442	55.0	44
Mobile homes	671	2.0	336
Total	27,160	2.1	12,933

Source: U.S. Department of Housing and Urban Development and Bureau of the Census, *Annual Housing Survey, 1979, Part C* (U.S. Government Printing Office, 1980), p. 4, and author's estimates.

Thus there is a fundamental tension between the two supply objectives and the first demand objective. This tension makes it difficult to formulate any set of public policies concerning rental housing that will be both balanced and effective. The supply must be increased greatly to meet future needs, and that requires raising the price (rents). Yet raising the price worsens the situation of low-income renters and increases the public subsidy costs of assisting them.

This underlying tension makes it hard to formulate policies on rental housing that have a real chance of being adopted. The number of people whose short-run welfare would be reduced by higher rents is vastly greater than the number who would gain from them. In 1979, 63.3 million persons were renting 27.2 million units from their owners. I estimate that a maximum of 12.6 million other persons owned those units (see table 8-1), and the correct number may be much smaller.[4] At least twice as many households contain tenants as contain landlords, and the number of tenants is five times the number of landlords. Elected officials are thus likely to be more sensitive to the demands of tenants than of rental owners, especially in areas where tenants are heavily concentrated.

Renters compose over 70 percent of the residents of New York City and over 80 percent of the residents of Santa Monica, California. It is

4. My estimate of the average number of units held by each owner is a conservative one; if the average is in fact higher, the number of separate owners would be smaller than my estimate.

not surprising that both cities have stringent rent controls. Nonetheless, many cities do not have such laws. Perhaps the relatively widespread ownership of rental housing compared with other forms of wealth in our society (such as stocks and bonds or small businesses) makes local governments more sensitive to the drawbacks of rent controls than sheer numbers would indicate was likely.

The Importance of Federal Policies

Because the federal government is uniquely able to influence the flow of capital and the distribution of income nationwide, a broad range of federal policies on interest rates, taxes, access to credit markets, and subsidies to the poor profoundly affect housing markets. Until recently, these policies created a sheltered position for housing within the economy, and many argue that this sheltered position should be restored. This section examines a variety of federal policies that influence rental housing; subsequent sections consider the limitations of federal policies and recommend specific policy changes.

Interest Rates

Federal monetary policies profoundly influence the economic feasibility of building new rental units and selling, modernizing, or refinancing existing ones. Throughout 1981 and well into 1982 very high real and nominal interest rates severely constrained all types of mortgage lending. That constraint depressed both the building of new rental units and transactions concerning existing ones. These high interest rates were caused by a combination of continuing inflation, strictures on the growth of the money supply by the Federal Reserve, and fears of large future federal deficits.

There is great disagreement among economists about how to lower nominal and real interest rates in the long run. I cannot resolve this issue here, but, assuming there is *some way* to reduce interest rates, I would like to look at the implications for rental housing.

Lower interest rates would greatly improve the profitability of building, buying and operating, or refinancing rental housing. For example, a 21.9 percent fall in mortgage interest rates from 16.0 percent to 12.5 percent with constant rents would raise the market value sustainable from a given property by 24.6 percent.[5]

For real estate activity to return to the level normal before 1980, nominal mortgage interest rates would have to fall from early-1982 levels of about 16–17 percent to about 12–13 percent. But even that level of activity would not add much new rental housing, as pointed out in chapter 7. That result would probably require further declines in nominal mortgage rates to around 8 or 9 percent—though no one knows for certain. Thus reducing interest rates in both real and nominal terms is a necessary but not sufficient step to constructing any large number of new rental units.

Credit Markets and Taxes

From 1945 to about 1980 federal credit and tax policies made investing in housing—especially owner-occupied housing—more advantageous than investing in most other widely available assets, such as stocks, bonds, and businesses. Housing's advantages sprang from federal regulations that sheltered mortgage lending in the nation's credit markets and from federal tax benefits that accrued to homeowners. In addition to aiding builders, realtors, and households buying homes, these advantages undoubtedly made the overall flow of financial capital into housing much larger than it would otherwise have been.

Federal regulations protected thrift institutions (savings and loan associations and mutual savings banks) from having to pay full market prices to obtain deposits from small-scale savers. Thrifts were created to borrow money for short terms, mainly as savings deposits, and lend it as long-term home mortgages so as to encourage construction and purchase of owner-occupied housing. For the thrifts to be economically viable, short-term interest rates had to remain lower than long-term rates most of the time. To strengthen that viability, Congress put ceilings on the rates thrift institutions and banks could pay for savings deposits and allowed thrifts to pay slightly higher rates than banks. In return, thrifts had to use most of their loanable funds for home mortgages.

---

5. These results were derived from the model described in chapter 7. They assume a down-payment ratio of 0.25, an operating-cost ratio of 0.41, a debt-service ratio of 1.25, a depreciable life of twenty-five years, a marginal tax rate of 0.5, and monthly rent of $245. However, the precise value of these variables is not critical, as long as they remain the same when interest rates are changed.

This arrangement often reduced mortgage rates below what they would otherwise have been, especially during tight money periods. Lower mortgage rates made it easier for people to buy homes and to buy or develop rental properties. This strategy worked so well that thrifts were the largest source of home mortgage finance from 1950 to 1978.[6]

In addition, households that bought their own homes enjoyed tax benefits not easily obtainable from other investments. Chapter 3 described how these benefits, combined with unanticipated inflation, encouraged people to invest in their own homes rather than in corporate equities, bonds, or unincorporated businesses.

Housing's sheltered financial position was ended in the late 1970s and early 1980s by a combination of inflation and changes in federal regulations. Inflation drove general interest rates above the ceilings for savings rates for much longer periods than previously. Also, regulatory changes allowed small-scale savers to invest in new forms of savings without rate ceilings, such as money market funds. Many savers withdrew their funds from thrift institutions because they could get higher returns elsewhere. To defend thrifts, federal regulators gradually raised the ceilings for savings rates, which helped thrifts slow outflows but also raised their costs. Because most thrifts still held large portfolios of older long-term mortgages paying low yields, their average cost of retaining deposits rose above their average yield on assets. As a result, most thrifts lost money in 1981 and 1982. Their basic strategy—borrowing short and lending long—had been made unviable because short-term rates had risen well above both current and earlier long-term rates.[7] Unless this new relationship among rates for investments of different durations changes, thrifts can no longer finance housing in the traditional way.

Moreover, the relative tax advantages of investing in homeownership were greatly reduced by the Economic Recovery Tax Act of 1981, which increased the tax benefits available from other types of investments, as discussed in chapter 3. Thus both major forms of favorable investment treatment enjoyed by housing investments in the 1970s were notably diminished in 1980–81.

Some people argue that housing should be returned to a sheltered position in the nation's financial structure. Then thrifts could again make

6. *Federal Reserve Bulletin*, 1950–81.
7. The original strategy cannot work as long as the blended average rate from both current and past mortgages in the thrift industry's total portfolio is below the average current rate it must pay for savings and other deposits.

mortgage loans at lower rates than would prevail otherwise. However, any such arrangement requires either that people who save in thrifts receive lower returns than they could find elsewhere or that the government make up the difference with a subsidy. But savers will not accept lower returns voluntarily. In fact, one reason monetary authorities ended housing's sheltered position was to help small savers receive market rates. Therefore, the only politically acceptable way to restore housing's sheltered position is through a federal subsidy to savers in thrift institutions.

Congress passed one such subsidy in 1981 by allowing thrift and bank depositors to receive a limited amount of interest free from federal income taxes. This privilege lasted only one year to help thrifts escape from the squeeze on their earnings described above. However, this subsidy did not remedy the cause of that squeeze: low earnings on thrifts' large portfolio of older mortgages, combined with prolonged periods when short-term rates exceed long-term rates. Also, if this tax-free feature lasted only one year, it would not permanently restore housing's sheltered financial position.

A permanent restoration would encourage larger flows of credit into housing. But more credit would not necessarily increase production of new or even non-new housing units.[8] Wherever local restrictions make building more housing difficult, easier credit availability combined with strong local demand tends to drive up prices of the existing inventory. In California, for example, the median sales price of existing single-family homes rose over 21 percent a year from 1976 to 1980.[9] Moreover, investment in housing was already encouraged by its many tax advantages before tax-free savings were available. These tax advantages distorted the allocation of capital that would have occurred if tax benefits for other investments had been equal to those for housing. The recent extension of greater tax benefits to other investments may therefore actually reduce overall distortions in capital allocation, rather than increasing them.

Restoring the favored financial treatment of housing would have the

---

8. For a discussion of this point, see chapter 3 and Anthony Downs, "Are We Using Too Much Capital for Financing Housing?" in Federal National Mortgage Association, *Housing Finance in the Eighties: Issues and Options* (Washington, D.C.: FNMA, May 1981), pp. 66–79.

9. California Association of Realtors, *California Real Estate Trends Newsletter*, vol. 2 (April 10, 1981), p. 1. The median price rose from $44,800 in February 1976 to $97,481 in February 1980, or at a compound annual rate of 21.5 percent. In the following year, it rose only 6.0 percent, however.

disadvantages of continuing to distort investment decisions and using scarce federal dollars to aid nonpoor mortgage borrowers and high-bracket homeowners while aid to the poor is being cut. Hence this policy is basically undesirable. If short-term interest rates remain high very long, some federal assistance for thrift institutions will be necessary to prevent their collapse. But it need not involve restoring housing's sheltered position in credit markets or its great tax advantages compared with other investments.

Subsidies to Poor Renters

The federal government is a better source of funds for policies that redistribute income than either state or local governments. In fact, it already provides subsidies to a significant fraction of all poor renters in the United States.[10] At the same time it provides much larger implicit subsidies to homeowners who deduct their mortgage interest payments and local property taxes from their federally taxable income. Subsidizing the poor, by definition, requires government to tax affluent households more than poor ones, to aim its spending more at the poor than at affluent households, or to do both. But many relatively affluent citizens taxed heavily by a local government can move to nearby communities that do not tax them as much. Moreover, they can do so without having to change jobs or sacrifice their access to the entire area. Hence, if a local government tries to carry out major income redistribution, it may drive many of its more affluent citizens beyond its taxing jurisdiction.

State governments confront the same problem. Because many major U.S. metropolitan areas contain parts of several states, residents of one state can move to another nearby without having to leave their economic area. The recent burgeoning of luxury homes and corporate headquarters in southern Connecticut was generated in precisely this way by high taxes in New York. But it is difficult to move out of the United States altogether to escape redistributive federal fiscal policies. So public policies aimed at helping poor renters (the first demand objective) should be funded by the federal government, although they can sometimes be effectively administered by state or local governments.

---

10. Jill Khadduri and Raymond J. Struyk estimated that about one-third of all renter households with incomes below 50 percent of their area median income were receiving federal housing subsidies of some type as of 1981. See Jill Khadduri and Raymond J. Struyk, *Housing Vouchers: From Here to Entitlement?* (Urban Institute, 1980), pp. 3–5.

Housing Markets

Another crucial federal role is to reduce obstacles that local governments deliberately erect to the efficient and equitable operation of housing markets. Many suburban communities of middle- and upper-income households do not want poor households as neighbors. One reason is fear that property values might decline as a result. Residents use their political dominance of local governments to pass exclusionary laws, such as zoning regulations, building codes, and subdivision ordinances that require dwellings too expensive for most low- and moderate-income households. Many communities also drastically limit the amount of multifamily rental housing within their borders. This limitation and high land costs raise the rents there beyond what low- and moderate-income households can pay. Such interference with housing markets is not accidental; rather, it is one of the central purposes of many suburban governments.

Some regulation of housing and neighborhood quality is undoubtedly desirable to eliminate inefficient conflicts over land use and to prevent unhealthful substandard conditions. But the regulations adopted by many suburban communities go beyond what is necessary to achieve these reasonable goals. By helping to cause disproportionate concentrations of high-income and low-income residents within different parts of metropolitan areas, exclusionary regulations often produce both inequitable and inefficient patterns of land use.[11]

Another market intervention undesirable in the long run is local rent controls. They are usually adopted only in communities where middle-income renters form a large part of the electorate. However, the short-run beneficiaries of rent controls include low- and moderate-income renters, too. The persons treated inequitably by rent controls are the owners of controlled properties, who are deprived of competitive returns on their investments. Rent controls also have a variety of disadvantages in the long run.

—They reduce the quality of housing services provided to tenants of controlled units because owners cut back on maintenance.

—They cut off additions to the rental housing supply and thereby generate shortages.

11. For a discussion of this point, see Anthony Downs, *Neighborhoods and Urban Development* (Brookings Institution, 1981), chap. 4. See also *The Report of the President's Commission on Housing* (GPO, 1982), pp. 199–222.

—They increase property tax burdens on owner-occupants because the assessed values of rental units decline as a result of deterioration.

—They increase the costs of owner-occupied housing by shifting rental demand to ownership units.

—They somewhat restrict the mobility of renters if moving requires them to give up units with very low controlled rents.[12]

Both exclusionary zoning and rent controls are thus inefficient and inequitable interferences with overall urban housing markets. Both have undesirable impacts not confined to the communities adopting them, but harmful to their overall metropolitan areas. Yet certain local communities adopt them because of the parochial composition of their electorates, compared with the composition of society at large. Politically dominant groups within those communities benefit from such policies, but do not have to pay the social costs. Those costs are borne mainly by people living elsewhere (as with exclusionary zoning) or by groups within the community who are opposed to such interferences (as with rent controls). Local governments in these communities are not likely to sacrifice the benefits most of their residents are receiving in order to aid their metropolitan area as a whole. Only a government with jurisdiction over an entire metropolitan area is likely to have an appropriate perspective on the housing needs of all area residents. Except for the very few metropolitan governments within the United States, only the state and federal governments normally have such broad jurisdictions.

The breadth of federal jurisdiction is a particular advantage in regard to rent controls. Although state governments could also prohibit rent controls, a federal prohibition would be more effective than state actions within metropolitan areas that encompass parts of several states. Furthermore, only federal prohibition of rent controls is likely to convince potential investors in rental housing that the profitability of their investments would not be jeopardized by future actions of individual state or local governments.

The Limitations of Federal Policies

There are major disadvantages to having decisions on local land use made by governments with broad jurisdictions, especially the federal

12. This is most likely if the ordinance concerned allows landlords to raise rents without limit whenever units are voluntarily vacated.

government. The immense diversity of local urban conditions, even within individual metropolitan areas, can rarely be accommodated by distant state and federal governments. Their remote influence is usually effective only in developing rules that can be clearly applied in many different local circumstances. Given the complexity and variety of exclusionary land use practices, it is difficult for the federal government to reduce or inhibit such practices. In contrast, it could very simply influence local rent controls by prohibiting them altogether. That is why I do not believe federal prohibition of rent controls would constitute unwarranted interference in the complexities of local conditions.

Regardless of whether federal interference in local housing markets is desirable, the constitutional separation of state and federal powers makes it legally difficult. The federal government cannot mandate changes over which it has no constitutional authority, and local governments are under the constitutional authority of the states. Federal influence on local regulations is likely to be most effective when accompanied by some large federally funded incentive for local governments to follow federal suggestions.

One such incentive is a believable threat to reduce existing federal financial aid to local governments if those suggestions are not heeded. Many suburbs engaging in exclusionary zoning do not receive much federal financial aid; their behavior would not be swayed by such threats. But urban communities most likely to adopt rent controls often depend heavily on federal funds for fiscal support; they would be quite susceptible to federal financial pressure to prohibit or abolish rent controls. Even if those incentives were not effective, the federal government could devise other ways to make most rental units free from local controls, if Congress were willing to pass them. Congress could, for example, exempt from local rent controls all housing units financed by agencies insured or regulated by the federal government.

Desirable Federal Policies

In addition to helping establish an appropriate overall economic climate, the federal government should perform two principal roles concerning rental housing: (1) helping to reduce the poverty of low-income renters and (2) preventing local governments from adopting rent controls. These roles and the policies they imply are outlined here and analyzed in more detail in appendix B.

Subsidies to Poor Renters

Millions of people throughout the United States have such low income they cannot afford dwelling units with the minimum size and quality regarded as necessary by prevailing middle-class standards. Many would be able to solve their housing problems without subsidies if the overall economy grew more rapidly than it has in the early 1980s, because they could get jobs or increase their earnings. But even sustained prosperity would not eliminate poverty altogether, as experience in the 1960s and early 1970s proves.[13] Enabling all or even most poor households to live in decent dwellings therefore requires providing many with subsidies.

Like most economists, I believe the best way to do that would be for the federal government to provide the poor with jobs or greater direct income assistance. However, this approach faces political obstacles. Congress has been unwilling to fund enough direct aid to eradicate poverty, assuming that would be possible.[14] It prefers aiding the poor through various types of in-kind assistance, such as food stamps and medicare, tied to the consumption of specific goods or services. Such "earmarked" assistance has the practical advantage of attracting political

13. The fraction of U.S. citizens with money income below the official poverty line fell from 22.4 percent in 1959 to 11.1 percent in 1973, but has remained above the latter level ever since. Taking in-kind transfer payments into account, the fraction of citizens with real income below the official poverty level has probably fallen as low as 6–7 percent. Much of this decline, however, must be attributed to government transfer programs, rather than improved earnings from the private sector. See Laurence E. Lynn, Jr., "A Decade of Policy Developments in the Income Maintenance System," in Robert H. Haveman, ed., *A Decade of Federal Antipoverty Programs: Achievements, Failures, and Lessons* (Academic Press, 1977), pp. 88–102; Felicity Skidmore, "Progress Against Poverty: Summary and Outlook for the Future," in Robert D. Plotnick and Felicity Skidmore, *Progress Against Poverty: A Review of the 1964–1974 Decade* (Academic Press, 1977), pp. 169–79; Morton Paglin, "Poverty in the United States: A Reevaluation," *Policy Review*, no. 8 (Spring 1979), pp. 7–24; and James R. Storey, "Income Security," in John L. Palmer and Isabel V. Sawhill, ed., *The Reagan Experiment* (Urban Institute Press, 1982), p. 371. See also Bureau of the Census, *Statistical Abstract of the United States, 1980* (GPO, 1980), p. 465.

14. Poverty probably could be fully eliminated through public policies if it is defined as "income poverty," that is, poverty that results from a combined money and in-kind income below some officially established level. But poverty almost certainly could not be fully eliminated through public action if it is defined as also encompassing certain personal attitudes and behavior patterns.

support from providers of the goods or services concerned. A similar approach could be taken in the case of housing through a nationwide housing voucher program like the one tested in the experimental housing allowance program.[15] Therefore, if Congress remains unwilling to provide more direct aid, I recommend making housing vouchers available to all renting households with income below 50 percent of the areawide median.[16] Based on experience in the experimental housing allowance program, only about half of all eligible households would actually participate in such a program.[17]

This program could be paid for without any net increase in federal spending by modestly reducing the present tax benefits received by homeowners. The Congressional Budget Office (CBO) estimated that homeowners saved $36 billion in federal taxes in fiscal 1982 by deducting mortgage interest and property taxes from their taxable income.[18] CBO calculated that this saving would rise to $53.1 billion by fiscal 1984. In contrast, the total outlays for a full-scale housing voucher entitlement program would probably rise to about $7.3 billion in fiscal 1984.[19] Reducing estimated homeowner tax benefits by only about 14 percent would completely offset the cost of such a program in 1984.

15. For an analysis of the experimental housing allowance program and its effectiveness, see Katharine L. Bradbury and Anthony Downs, eds., *Do Housing Allowances Work?* (Brookings Institution, 1981).

16. For a discussion of the possible form and costs of such a program, see Khadduri and Struyk, *Housing Vouchers*.

17. See Bradbury and Downs, *Housing Allowances*, pp. 21–27, 113–45.

18. Congressional Budget Office, *The Tax Treatment of Homeownership: Issues and Options* (CBO, 1981), p. 7. Homeowners' ability to deduct mortgage interest and property taxes from their taxable income does not constitute a true subsidy, relative to other investments. All investors (except those buying tax-exempt bonds) can deduct interest and other expenses from their taxable incomes. But other investors must also pay income taxes on the net income from their investments, whereas homeowners are free from that obligation. Homeowners do not earn cash income on their homes because they rent those homes themselves. But the imputed rents they receive constitute "real" income to them as investors, on which they do not have to pay income taxes. This freedom from tax liability is a true subsidy not available to investors in stocks, bonds, or other investments. The exact size of the resulting benefit for homeowners is hard to measure because of uncertainty about what the level of imputed rents should be, in the absence of a freely operating market, though there is a market for rental of single-family homes. But past measurement efforts indicate this benefit is at least as large as the tax savings received from deducting both mortgage interest and property taxes from taxable income. Therefore, I have used calculations concerning those tax savings as a surrogate for the true subsidy to homeowners in this part of the analysis. For estimates comparing this surrogate to the true subsidy, see Henry Aaron, *Shelter and Subsidies* (Brookings Institution, 1972), p. 56.

19. Khadduri and Struyk, *Housing Vouchers*, p. 21.

I believe this could best be done by converting homeowners' present tax deductibility benefits to a tax credit and then reducing the rate used to compute that credit enough to pay for the voucher program. CBO estimated that a tax credit of about 25 percent of homeowners' mortgage interest and property tax payments would have produced the same total revenues as current deductions in 1982. But it would yield $7.9 billion more revenues by fiscal 1986. Hence it might be possible to finance a nationwide housing voucher program for poor renters with no net increase in federal costs and without much reduction in the tax credit rate below 25 percent.

Moreover, a tax credit is much fairer than a tax deduction. A credit provides every taxpayer the same amount of tax savings for each dollar of mortgage interest payment or property tax, regardless of the taxpayer's marginal tax rate. In contrast, a deduction provides much greater tax savings to wealthier taxpayers who are in higher marginal tax brackets. This fact alone justifies changing homeowner benefits to a tax credit, whether or not a housing voucher program is adopted.

The Reagan administration has already advocated shifting most federal low-income housing assistance to a housing voucher program.[20] But it also suggested scaling down current funding for such assistance, while leaving homeowners' vastly larger tax benefits intact. The approach I recommend would create a more equitable distribution of federal housing benefits by shifting some from high-income to low-income households. Yet it would still provide immense tax advantages to owner-occupants, thereby continuing to encourage homeownership.

Prohibition of Rent Controls

A nationwide prohibition of rent controls, or the creation of extremely strong federal incentives for local governments to abstain from such controls, would remove a major obstacle to investment in rental housing by private developers and capital suppliers. However, such a prohibition should not be adopted unless it is accompanied by some form of increased financial assistance to low-income renters, such as the housing voucher program described earlier. Added assistance will be necessary to protect

---

20. Department of Housing and Urban Development, *Fiscal Year 1983 Budget: Summary* (GPO, February 1982), pp. H-2–H-5.

them from big rent increases. Housing is by far the largest single expense for most poor households. In 1979 the median fraction of income paid for gross rent was 26 percent for all renters, but over 60 percent for renters with income below $3,000, 44 percent for those with income from $3,000 to $6,999, and 31 percent for those with income from $7,000 to $9,999.[21] It would clearly be inequitable to impose relatively heavy financial burdens on many of the poorest households in order to encourage private developers to add to the overall supply of rental housing. Such encouragement could be achieved without this inequity if a federal prohibition of rent controls were coupled with increased financial assistance to poor renters.

Other Policies

Certain other federal policies concerning rental housing are desirable but should have much lower priority. These include (1) providing some rehabilitation assistance to owners of deteriorated rental units, (2) allowing state housing finance agencies to continue using tax-exempt bonds to finance new construction of rental housing under certain limited circumstances, (3) building a small number of new public housing units each year to meet specialized needs not served by the private market, and (4) turning over surplus units foreclosed by the Federal Housing Administration to local governments or local public housing authorities at nominal cost.

The federal government should definitely *not* adopt certain other policies. These include (1) directly subsidizing construction of new rental units for middle-income households, (2) creating new tax deductions for renters, (3) selling off existing public housing projects to private owners, (4) providing tax benefits to developers or owners of rental housing beyond those already adopted in the Economic Recovery Tax Act of 1981, and (5) creating special housing voucher programs only for occupants of public housing or of units undergoing condominium conversion. These policies are discussed in more detail in appendix B.

21. U.S. Department of Housing and Urban Development and Bureau of the Census, *Annual Housing Survey, 1979, Part C* (GPO, 1981), p. 7. The fractions of total expenditures devoted to housing by very poor households are somewhat lower than these percentages, since such households typically spend more than their current income. I am indebted to Henry Aaron for pointing this out.

Desirable Local Policies

Although local governments cannot directly cope with the poverty underlying most rental housing problems, they can be effective in helping local market forces work more efficiently and in offsetting the inequitable effects of certain nonmarket arrangements, or externalities. Examples of the latter are the lending practices of banks, the steering behavior of real estate brokers, and the laws governing property rights, zoning, building codes, and landlord-tenant relations. The specific policies local governments should follow are discussed briefly here and in more detail in appendix C.

Reconsideration of Local Ordinances

Ironically, the greatest obstacles to efficient operation of rental housing markets in almost every community are local government ordinances. In most cases these ordinances were created to deal with circumstances that cannot be satisfactorily handled by markets alone. Building and housing codes were designed to ensure a minimum quality of housing construction and operation. This was desirable to protect consumers who cannot judge construction quality and to prevent a few substandard dwellings from reducing property values in the surrounding neighborhood. But many codes require unnecessarily expensive materials or processes that add to housing costs. Zoning ordinances were designed to reduce conflicts among adjacent land uses (such as industrial zones that generate heavy truck traffic near residential areas) and to protect the environment of residential areas. But such ordinances often require housing quality far in excess of what is necessary to protect local health and safety, thus excluding low- and moderate-income households. Other laws require builders to have their proposed plans reviewed by local officials and neighborhood groups before they can build. These laws were designed to prevent erection of projects damaging to surrounding areas. But the time necessary to conduct all the reviews and obtain all the permissions required often adds significantly to overall housing costs.

As a result, the most effective way for each local government to make its rental housing market operate more efficiently would be to review all of its own ordinances affecting that market and simplify them as much as possible. Unfortunately, local officials have little incentive to do this. In many areas they *want* local laws to raise housing costs so as to exclude the poor. And in nearly all areas local officials are politically rewarded much more for avoiding mistakes than for expediting positive development. Proceeding with great caution costs them nothing, reduces their chances of overlooking something, and allows them to resolve local controversies about proposed actions. Furthermore, complex and ambiguous laws allow them considerable discretion and power over the process of development. But regardless of the advantages of complicated and time-consuming laws and procedures for local officials, there are serious disadvantages for local housing markets. Reducing the obstacles to efficient operation of housing markets posed by such procedures remains a vital role for local governments.

Decreasing such obstacles is crucial in areas experiencing a large immigration of poor households. Southern California is a prime example. Thousands of poor Hispanic and other immigrants are overcrowding older homes in East Los Angeles and elsewhere because they cannot afford "standard quality" units. The cost of directly subsidizing new housing for these households would be prohibitive. A better approach over the long run would be encouraging the construction of new unsubsidized units, either by making vacant peripheral land more available or by increasing densities in built-up neighborhoods. Middle-income households could then occupy these new units, freeing older units for low-income households. But stringent local regulations in much of California impede the building of new units and raise their costs, even under favorable financing conditions. Ironically, the insistence by local governments on very high quality and low density for new housing is generating burgeoning slums to accommodate the poor. This outcome can only be avoided by radically reducing regulatory barriers to new unsubsidized units.

Such reductions will also help each community make more intensive use of its existing housing inventory. I believe local governments should give very high priority to (1) permitting owners of large, older homes to subdivide them so as to create small units for rent, while maintaining reasonable standards of unit quality, (2) using differential code enforcement by neighborhoods, rather than enforcing all codes identically everywhere, (3) permitting postponement of tax reassessment for units that have been rehabilitated, and (4) encouraging owners of rental apartment buildings to live on the premises.

RENTAL HOUSING POLICIES

Two other policies aimed at this goal should have somewhat lower priority. One is using federal community development block grants to help owners of rental units rehabilitate them. The second is requiring each rental unit to pass a code inspection every time a tenant moves out before a new one can move in.

Other Policies

Local governments should also permit more intensive use of land within the community for multifamily rental units. Specific policies serving that goal include (1) raising allowable densities on land already zoned for multifamily use, (2) increasing the amount of land so zoned, and (3) simplifying the process of getting the permissions required to build new rental units.

Local governments should definitely *not* adopt certain other policies related to rental housing. The most important policy to avoid is residential rent controls. Second is any ordinance that unduly restricts conversion of rental units to condominiums, since such conversions are basically desirable in most communities because they expand opportunities for homeownership. Last is granting tax abatements for new rental housing to be occupied by middle- and upper-income households. These policies are discussed in more detail in appendix C.

The Future of Rental Housing

Privately furnished rental units now vastly outnumber publicly furnished ones in the United States. But coming rapid rent increases in private units could change this balance drastically over the next decade or two, as has happened in Great Britain since 1945. The remainder of this chapter discusses this possibility and relates it to the policies I have recommended.

Rapid rent increases in the near future will make poor households worse off in real terms, if no further government actions are taken to assist them. As rents rise, many injured households will pressure governments to help them. Possible government reactions include local adoption of rent controls and federal provision of various subsidies. But federal officials are now disinclined to expand aid to the poor; in fact, they are substantially reducing such aid in real terms. Hence local controls will be the only immediate public policy response to higher rents that seems both politically and economically feasible.

Rent controls will undoubtedly benefit poor households and many nonpoor ones in the short run. Therefore, powerful political pressures favoring such controls will appear in many cities. These pressures will cause more widespread adoption of rent controls unless the federal government prevents it.

Even if a minority of large cities adopts rent controls, enough might do so to alter the nation's rental housing supply in the long run because the longer rent controls remain in force, the more difficult it is to get rid of them. The gap beween existing rents and those needed to make construction of new rental units economically feasible rises continuously while controls are in force, and shortages of rental housing develop or intensify. Sudden removal of controls generates a rapid increase in rents, causing substantial hardships for many poor households. Yet the private sector does not respond by immediately building many new rental units; that occurs only after rents have risen enough to make it feasible. Thus, right after controls are ended, renters suffer added hardships with no result except the enrichment of landlords. To avoid that unpopular outcome, elected officials are tempted to keep rent controls in force. This is the case in New York City today.

Yet the continuation of rent controls only increases the shortage of rental housing and the deterioration of the existing rental inventory. If these ills became widespread, they would eventually generate strong pressures for the federal government to do something about them. By then, rent controls would have been in operation for several years in many markets and would influence the form of federal policy responses. It may then be politically difficult to abolish controls completely so that rents can rise rapidly to the level at which private developers will build more rental units. It may be equally difficult to use housing vouchers to support the low-income rental market, because vouchers do not work well under rent controls.[22] The federal government may be pressured into aiding the poor by expanding the supply of new subsidized housing. This is especially likely if current attitudes against federal aid to the poor have changed, as such intangible moods typically do in time.

22. Controls prevent owners from meeting the full costs of operation, even if vouchers permit poor tenants to pay allowable rents without undue hardship. Hence units deteriorate and shortages arise in the long run, in spite of vouchers.

Yet building subsidized housing is the costliest way to improve the poor's housing. It would also reduce the relative importance of the private rental sector in housing markets. This is precisely what has happened in several European nations: private rental housing has shrunk dramatically, and public housing has greatly expanded. Ironically, this eventual result of the nation's present conservative mood would generate conditions highly inconsistent with that mood.

Of course, initially failing to prohibit rent controls or adopt additional financial aid to poor renters would not inexorably lead to massive expansion of publicly subsidized housing. Yet this scenario is quite plausible, even though most households at every income level prefer living in privately owned quarters to living in public housing. At the very least, such a scenario shows that decisions on the amount and nature of federal housing subsidies and other aids to the poor are closely related to decisions on local rent controls. Both types of decisions have vital implications for "the realization as soon as feasible of . . . a decent home and a suitable living arrangement for every American family."

APPENDIX A

Projecting Number, Type, and Tenure of Households

PROJECTING the number and type of households used in calculating future rental housing demand is a complex process requiring several arbitrary judgments. This appendix describes the six major components of that process.

Correcting to Reflect Census Results

As of early 1982, the Census Bureau's published household projections for 1980 through 1995 were based on data gathered before the 1980 census. That count revealed 226.5 million persons in the United States—4.3 million more than the Census Bureau had previously estimated.[1] Hence the Census Bureau's household projections need to be adjusted to take account of this larger number.

According to the 1980 census, there were 80.4 million households in 1980.[2] With an average household size of 2.7 persons, the total population in households was 220.8 million, or 97.5 percent of the total estimated residential population.[3] Since there were 63.4 million households in

---

1. This previous estimate is found in U.S. Bureau of the Census, *Statistical Abstract of the United States, 1978* (U.S. Government Printing Office, 1978), p. 8, as the Series II projection for 1980 (the actual value was 222,159,000). This estimate is also consistent with the current estimates and projections found in *Statistical Abstract, 1979*, p. 8.
2. Bureau of the Census, *1980 Census of Population and Housing: Provisional Estimates of Social, Economic, and Housing Characteristics*, PHC80-S1-1 (GPO, 1982), p. 3.
3. Total resident population was 226,545,805 in 1980, according to the 1980 decennial census.

Table A-1. *Original and Adjusted Series B Projections of Households, Selected Years, 1980–95*
Thousands of households

Year	Original Series B	Adjusted	Difference
1980	79,870	80,400	530
1985	88,565	89,150	585
1990	96,653	97,291	638
1995	103,856	104,541	685

Source: Series B data are from U.S. Bureau of the Census, *Projections of the Number of Households and Families, 1979 to 1995*, current population reports P-20, May 1979, p. 11.

1970, the total number increased by 17.0 million from 1970 to 1980, or 1.7 million a year.

Adjusting Household Projections

The Census Bureau's Series B household projections (most recently issued in May 1979) provide a reasonable estimate of future household formation, but need to be adjusted to reflect 1980 census results. The Series B projections assume that trends in marital status and household proportions observed from 1964 to 1978 will continue through 1995 (the latest date presented in this series). Series B shows a rate of household growth lying between very fast growth (Series A) and very slow growth (Series D). The Series B estimate for 1980 was about 79.9 million, so the actual 80.4 million is 0.66 percent higher. Therefore, I have raised each projected Series B value by 0.66 percent, producing the results shown in table A-1.

Extending the Adjusted Series to 2000

Series B household projections do not go beyond 1995, but the analysis in the book extends to 2000. Hence those projections—adjusted as indicated above—have been expanded through the following calculations.

CALCULATING AVERAGE HOUSEHOLD SIZE. Average household size in April 1970 was 3.14 persons; by 1980, it had fallen to 2.75 persons, or 87.6 percent of its 1970 size. Therefore the number of households in each year in the 1970s was 0.9868 times as large as in the preceding year (0.9868 is the tenth root of 0.8758). The decline from 3.31 persons in 1960 to 3.14 in 1970 implied a similar annual rate of decline of 0.9947. Judging from foreseeable demographic trends in the 1980s, household size will keep declining, probably at a rate somewhere between those for the 1960s and 1970s—say, 0.9900. Applying that rate from 1980 to 2000 yields the following average number of persons in each household:

1980	2.75
1985	2.62
1990	2.49
1995	2.37
2000	2.25

ESTIMATING TOTAL RESIDENT POPULATION AT FUTURE DATES. These household size estimates can be used to convert Series B household projections into projections of total population and to estimate total population beyond 1995. For example, the adjusted household projection for 1995 (104.5 million) times the average household size (2.37 persons) equals 247.7 million persons living in households. If the population in households is 97.5 percent of the total resident population, the latter would be 254.1 million in 1995. Similar calculations yield estimates of 239.6 million for 1985 and 248.5 million for 1990.

These estimates can be compared with the Census Bureau's Series II population projections to develop a ratio for projecting total resident population for 2000. Series II projections assume a lifetime fertility rate of 2,100 births for every 1,000 women, plus net legal immigration from abroad of 400,000 persons a year. I believe this lifetime fertility assumption is too high; 1,800 births for every 1,000 women would be more accurate. But this error compensates for the failure of Series II to take account of net illegal immigration from abroad. The excess growth resulting from a fertility assumption of 2,100 instead of 1,800 is statistically equivalent to the growth that would result from additional net illegal immigration from abroad of 400,000 a year. This is as reasonable an estimate of illegal immigration as can be made, so I believe the Series II projections are the most useful—once adjusted for consistency with the actual count in 1980.

The 1985 projection of total resident population calculated above is 2.9 percent higher than the Series II projection for that date, and the 1990 projection is 2.0 percent higher than the Series II projection for that date.[4] Therefore, the total population for 2000 can be estimated by increasing the Series II projection for 2000 (260.4 million) by 2.5 percent to 266.9 million. (This procedure already contains an adjustment for the actual 1980 census count.) If 97.5 percent live in households, then 260.2 million persons will live in households in 2000.

4. *Statistical Abstract*, 1979, p. 8.

DERIVING A HOUSEHOLD ESTIMATE FOR 2000. Dividing that total by the average household size for 2000 set forth earlier produces an estimate of 115.6 million households in 2000. But that would imply an increase of 18.3 million households in the 1990s—surpassing the rise of 16.9 million anticipated for the 1980s. Nearly all demographic analysts believe that household growth will slow markedly in the 1990s because of changes in age distribution. People born in the postwar baby boom will be passing into their late thirties and early forties by the end of the 1990s, so there will be a sharp decline in the number of persons in their twenties and early thirties. Hence this household estimate is clearly too high. It would be more reasonable to assume that household growth each year from 1995 to 2000 will be smaller than the annual increments of 1.6 million from 1985 to 1990 and 1.5 million from 1990 to 1995. Assuming this growth rate will again decline, I have arbitrarily set it at 1.3 million a year from 1995 to 2000. The total number of households in 2000 would then be 111.0 million, based upon the Series II projection, the Series B household projection, and my own adjustments. This implies an average household size in 2000 of 2.34 persons, only slightly below the 1995 size of 2.37 estimated earlier. So this procedure assumes average household size will decline more slowly in the late 1990s than earlier.

Allowing for Variations in Household Formation

The numbers of households projected for 1990 by various analysts[5] are as follows:

This study	97,291,000
Census Bureau	
Series A	98,950,000
Series B	96,653,000
Jaffee and Rosen	
High growth	98,802,000
Moderate growth	96,854,000
Low growth	95,479,000
Pitkin and Masnick	92,700,000 to 97,613,000

---

5. Dwight Jaffee and Kenneth Rosen, "The Demand for Housing and Mortgage Credit: The Mortgage Credit Gap Problem," paper prepared for the Federal National Mortgage Association Symposium on Housing Finance in the 1980s, Washington, D.C., February 1981, p. 11. See also, John Pitkin and George Masnick, *Projections of Housing Consumption in the United States, 1980 to 2000, by a Cohort Method* (Joint Center for Urban Studies of M.I.T. and Harvard University, June 1980), p. 2.

The projections in this study are slightly higher than many of the others partly because they have been corrected for 1980 census results. However, the number of households at each future date will be determined by economic factors as well as demographic ones. Harsh economic conditions or high housing costs may cause fewer people to form separate households than would do so under more favorable circumstances. But the preceding household projections assume continuation of conditions existing in the 1970s, which were extremely favorable for establishing separate households. Conditions in the 1980s will be much less favorable, implying lower projections. But how much lower?

A recent econometric model created by Jaffee and Rosen relates rates at which each age group heads households to various economic and demographic conditions, including changes in real disposable income, divorce rates, marriage rates, and housing costs.[6] They projected household growth from 1980 to 1990 under assumptions of rapid economic growth (3.0 percent annual rise in real disposable income), moderate growth (1.5 percent rise), and low growth (0.1 percent rise).[7] The increase in households under their low-growth projection was 3.4 million (18.3 percent) below that under their high-growth projection. In contrast, the Census Bureau's highest projected household increase for 1980 to 1990 (Series A) is 18.8 million, or 30.9 percent above the lowest increase (Series D).

Joseph C. Hu reviewed earlier approaches to relating household formation to economic conditions before developing his own econometric model of rates at which different age groups head households.[8] It involved two alternative rates of economic growth lower than those he believed were built into the Census Bureau's Series B projections. Hu's projections for the increase in households from 1980 to 1985 were 9.8 million under conditions of moderate growth and 10.1 million under rapid growth, compared with 8.7 million for the Census Bureau's Series B projections and 8.8 million for my projection. Hu's highest projection shows 4.4 percent more household growth than the estimate I set forth earlier.[9]

6. Jaffee and Rosen, "Demand for Housing and Credit," p. 13.
7. Their three projections also involved variations in other variables besides real disposable income, which are not cited here.
8. Joseph C. Hu, "An Econometric Model of Household Headship," paper prepared for the annual meeting of the Southern Regional Demographic Group, Tallahassee, Florida, October 1980.
9. His highest projection for 1985 is actually 0.3 percent lower than the projection in this study, but he started with an uncorrected estimate for total 1980 households considerably below the 80.6 million used in this study. Hence his projected increases are larger than the one in this study.

Table A-2. *High-Growth and Low-Growth Projections of Households, Selected Years, 1980–2000*
Thousands of households

Year	High growth	Low growth
1980	80,400	80,400
1985	89,150	87,838
1990	97,291	94,757
1995	104,541	100,920
2000	110,816	106,254

Source: Estimates by the author as described in this appendix.

Table A-3. *High-Growth and Low-Growth Projections of the Increase in Households, Selected Periods, 1980–2000*
Thousands of households

	High growth		Low growth	
Period	Change in households	Annual change	Change in households	Annual change
1980–85	8,750	1,750	7,438	1,488
1985–90	8,141	1,628	6,919	1,384
1990–95	7,250	1,450	6,163	1,233
1995–2000	6,275	1,255	5,334	1,067
1980–90	16,891	1,689	14,357	1,437
1990–2000	13,525	1,353	11,497	1,150

Source: Estimates by the author as described in this appendix.

After reviewing these studies, I assume that the household projections I presented earlier in this appendix are at the high end of the range of probable outcomes and that growth rates 15 percent lower represent the low end. My resulting estimates are set forth in table A-2. Table A-3 shows changes in the number of households by five-year periods from 1980 to 2000 for both high and low projections.

Projecting Types of Households

As George Sternlieb and James Hughes have pointed out, the percentage of renters among certain types of households has been remarkably stable.[10] From 1970 to 1979 that percentage declined among

10. George Sternlieb and James W. Hughes, "Housing: Past and Future," paper prepared for the Federal National Mortgage Association Symposium on Housing Finance in the 1980s, Washington, D.C., February 1981, p. 48.

Table A-4. *Series B Projections and Actual Percentage of Households, by Type, Selected Years, 1970–95*

Year	Household type (percent)			Total households (thousands)
	Husband- and-wife	Other male- headed	Female- headed	
1970[a]	70.6	8.3	21.1	63,401
1975[a]	66.0	10.4	23.6	71,120
1980[a]	60.9	13.0	26.1	80,400
1985[b]	58.9	14.2	26.9	88,565
1990[b]	56.6	15.4	28.0	96,653
1995[b]	54.5	16.5	29.0	103,856

Source: Bureau of the Census, *Statistical Abstract of the United States, 1981* (GPO, 1981), p. 42; and Bureau of the Census, *Projections of the Number of Households and Families*, p. 3.
a. Actual.
b. Projected using Census Series B data without the adjustment described in this appendix.

households with both husband and wife present, but was almost constant among households headed by females or other males. Therefore, using these three groups in making projections permits more reliable estimates of housing demand by tenure type.

The Census Bureau's household projections through 1995 divide households into these three types. Hence the percentages of each type in its Series B projections can be directly applied to my high-growth projections adapted from Series B. However, my low-growth projections assume slower rates of household formation, with less creation of smaller households. Low household growth would involve higher percentages of husband-and-wife households and lower percentages of the other two types than high household growth. The actual percentages of these types of households in 1970 and 1975, and estimates through 1995 based on the Series B projections, are set forth in two accompanying tables. Table A-4 shows the percentage of each type of household at each date, and table A-5 shows the percentage changes in each type of household during each period.[11] These percentages have been used to estimate the number of households by type for my high-growth household projections.

The percentages used to divide my low-growth household projections into household types were arbitrarily set as shown in table A-6. I raised the percentage of change for husband-and-wife households shown in table A-5 by about 10 percent, and then distributed the required reduction in

11. Estimates for 1995–2000 were made by arbitrarily assuming the total growth of households would have about the same breakdown by type in that period as in the preceding period.

Table A-5. *Series B Projections and Actual Change in Households, by Type, Selected Periods, 1970–2000*

Period	Change in households (percent)			Change in households (thousands)
	Husband-and-wife	Other male-headed	Female-headed	
1970–75[a]	28.7	27.3	44.0	7,719
1975–80[a]	16.5	36.1	47.4	9,280
1980–85[b]	36.6	26.3	37.1	8,695
1985–90[b]	31.9	28.6	39.5	8,088
1990–95[b]	26.7	31.2	42.1	7,203
1995–2000[c]	30.0	30.0	40.0	...

Source: Bureau of the Census, *Projections of the Number of Households and Families*, pp. 11–12.
a. Actual.
b. Projected using Census Series B data without the adjustment described in this appendix.
c. Estimated by the author.

Table A-6. *Low-Growth Projections of Percentage Change in Households, by Type, Selected Periods, 1980–2000*

Period	Change in households (percent)			Change in households (thousands)
	Husband-and-wife	Other male-headed	Female-headed	
1980–85	40.0	24.9	35.1	7,438
1985–90	35.0	27.1	37.9	6,919
1990–95	29.0	29.9	41.1	6,163
1995–2000[a]	30.0	30.0	40.0	5,334

Source: Adjusted from Series B results by the author.
a. No change made in percentages for 1995–2000 from table A-5.

percentages for the other two types about 60 percent to female-headed households and 40 percent to other male-headed households. For example, Series B projections showed that 36.6 percent of household change in 1980–85 consisted of more husband-and-wife households.[12] A 10 percent rise increased that figure to 40.2 percent, rounded to 40.0 percent. This requires reducing the shares of the other two types by 3.4 percentage points (40.0 minus 36.6). The share of female-headed households was cut by 2.0 percentage points (about 60 percent of 3.4) and the share of other male-headed households by 1.4 percentage points (3.4 minus 2.0).

These projections permit estimating the total increase in different

12. Bureau of the Census, *Projections of the Number of Households and Families, 1979 to 1995*, current population reports P-20, May 1979, p. 11.

PROJECTING DATA ON HOUSEHOLDS

Table A-7. *High-Growth Projections of the Increase in Households, by Type, Selected Periods, 1980–2000*
Thousands of households

Period	Change in household type			Change in households
	Husband-and-wife	Other male-headed	Female-headed	
1980–85	3,203	2,301	3,246	8,750
1985–90	2,597	2,328	3,216	8,141
1990–95	1,936	2,262	3,052	7,250
1995–2000	1,882	1,883	2,510	6,275

Source: Estimates by the author as described in this appendix.

Table A-8. *Low-Growth Projections of the Increase in Households, by Type, Selected Periods, 1980–2000*
Thousands of households

Period	Change in household type			Change in households
	Husband-and-wife	Other male-headed	Female-headed	
1980–85	2,975	1,852	2,611	7,438
1985–90	2,422	1,875	2,622	6,919
1990–95	1,787	1,843	2,533	6,163
1995–2000	1,600	1,600	2,134	5,334

Source: Estimates by the author as described in this appendix.

types of households in each time period. The results are presented for high-growth projections in table A-7 and for low-growth projections in table A-8. These increases generate total numbers of each type of household at future dates. They are shown for high-growth and low-growth projections in tables A-9 and A-10, respectively.

Projecting Tenure of Households

Both the proportion and number of all husband-and-wife households consisting of renters have fallen over time, as shown in table A-11. The number of such households renting fell 2.9 million (23.1 percent) from 1970 to 1980, even though total renting households rose 4.0 million, or 17.0 percent.

What will happen to the future number and share of renters among husband-and-wife households? The attractions of homeownership will probably cause such households to continue shifting out of renting. But

Table A-9. *High-Growth Projections of Households, by Type, Selected Years, 1980–2000*

Thousands of households

	Household type			
Year	Husband-and-wife	Other male-headed	Female-headed	Total households
1980	48,964	10,452	20,984	80,400[a]
1985	52,167	12,753	24,230	89,150
1990	54,764	15,081	27,446	97,291
1995	56,700	17,343	30,498	104,541
2000	58,582	19,226	33,008	110,816

Source: Estimates by the author as described in this appendix.
a. Decennial census data.

Table A-10. *Low-Growth Projections of Households, by Type, Selected Years, 1980–2000*

Thousands of households

	Household type			
Year	Husband-and-wife	Other male-headed	Female-headed	Total households
1980	49,044	10,452	20,904	80,400[a]
1985	52,019	12,304	23,515	87,838
1990	54,441	14,179	26,137	94,757
1995	56,228	16,022	28,670	100,920
2000	57,828	17,622	30,804	106,254

Source: Estimates by the author as described in this appendix.
a. Decennial census data.

the real costs of borrowing to buy a home will be much greater than in the 1970s, increases in real income will be slower, and housing prices and monthly mortgage payments will be higher. These factors will restrict the ability of husband-and-wife households to buy their own homes, even though higher proportions will contain more than one person working outside the home. Therefore, I have assumed the fraction of renters among such households will fall at a slower rate than in the 1970s.

That fraction fell from 29.3 percent in 1970 to 20.7 percent in 1980, so its compound annual rate of decline was 0.9659. If it continued to fall at that rate it would be 17.4 percent in 1985, 14.6 percent in 1990, 12.3 percent in 1995, and 10.3 percent in 2000. In 2000 there will be 58.6 million husband-and-wife households, according to the high-growth

Table A-11. *Renting among Husband-and-Wife Households, Selected Years, 1970–80*

Year	Renters as a percentage of all husband-wife households	Number of renters (thousands of households)
1970	29.3	12,759
1973	26.0	11,831
1974	25.0	11,653
1975	24.5	11,517
1976	23.8	11,291
1977	22.9	10,748
1978	21.8	10,182
1979	21.4	10,063
1980	20.7	9,818

Source: U.S. Department of Housing and Urban Development and Bureau of the Census, *Annual Housing Survey, Part A, 1973* through *1980*.

projection. Hence only 6.0 million such households would be renting then—or 4.1 million less than in 1979. That rate of decline seems too precipitous for the 1980s. I will assume a compound annual rate of decline of 0.9829, reflecting just half as rapid a rate of fall. The percentage of renters among husband-and-wife households (using 1980 as a base) would then be 19.0 in 1985, 17.4 in 1990, 16.0 in 1995, and 14.7 in 2000. There would be 8.6 million renters among such households in 2000, or 1.5 million less than in 1979, if the high-growth projection of households prevailed. To test the sensitivity of the overall results to this assumption, I will use both this and the faster annual rate of decline described above in making projections.

The percentages of renters among the other two types of households remained relatively constant from 1970 to 1980, and their absolute numbers increased significantly. Among households headed by other males, renters rose from 3.7 million in 1970 to 6.5 million in 1980, for percentages renting of 58.8 and 58.0, respectively.[13] Among households headed by females, renters went up from 7.1 million to 11.2 million, for percentages renting of 52.2 in each year. Both groups were apparently constrained from increasing their proportions of homeownership by the

---

13. Department of Housing and Urban Development and Bureau of the Census, *Annual Housing Survey, 1980, Part A* (GPO, 1982), pp. 5–6.

relatively high cost of owning homes. Since these costs are likely to rise even higher in the future, such behavior will probably not change. Therefore, I estimate future renting at 58.8 percent of other male-headed households and 52.2 percent of female-headed ones, for both high-growth and low-growth projections.

The last step in estimating the number of renting and homeowning households for 1980–2000 consists of applying the percentages of each household type renting to the numbers of different types of households at each date. This has been done for both high-growth and low-growth household projections and for both fast and slow rates of decline in renting among husband-and-wife households. These four different projections are shown in tables 4-3 and 4-4. Changes in the number of renting and homeowning households for each five-year period are shown in tables 4-5 and 4-6.

APPENDIX B

Possible Federal Policies on Rental Housing

THIS APPENDIX analyzes the effectiveness of thirteen possible federal policies in achieving the objectives discussed in chapter 8. Policies already discussed in detail in chapter 8 (such as a federal prohibition of rent controls) are not included here, nor are policies likely to be highly ineffective. Table B-1 summarizes the evaluations. Appendix C considers possible local policies on rental housing.

1. Expand rental tax shelters.

NATURE AND PURPOSE. Some real estate tax shelters eliminated in 1969 and 1976 could be restored. Examples are, first, writing off all interest and property taxes during the construction period as expenses rather than capitalizing them and, second, not recapturing as income any depreciation in excess of straight-line. Restoration of these advantages would increase the attraction of new rental housing for high-bracket investors.[1]

DISCUSSION. This policy would use scarce subsidy dollars to benefit wealthy investors rather than truly needy households. Also, rent reductions resulting from the increased supply generated by such subsidies would be much smaller than the losses in federal revenue. Hence this is not an efficient policy.

---

1. Accelerated depreciation on rental housing resulted in an estimated tax benefit of $1.0 billion in calendar 1980, according to the Treasury Office of Tax Analysis. Homeowner tax benefits in the same year were $26.9 billion. See David Einhorn, *Federal Tax Incentives and Rental Housing* (U.S. Government Printing Office, 1983).

Table B-1. Evaluation of Possible Federal Policies on Rental Housing

Policy number	Policy	Relationship of policy to objective				Evaluation
		Stimulating new rental construction	Encouraging good maintenance and conversion of non-new structures	Helping low-income renters	Encouraging home-ownership	
	Tax policies					
1	Expand rental tax shelters.	+ +	...	...	...	Undesirable in view of other tax benefits created in 1981.
2	Reduce federal tax advantages of homeownership.	+ +	...	...	—	Desirable, but politically infeasible, except for use of tax credit rather than deductions.
3	Increase federal tax benefits for tenants.	...	...	+	—	Undesirable—too costly and administratively difficult.
	Direct subsidy policies					
4	Create a comprehensive housing voucher program.	...	+ +	+ +	...	Highly desirable but costly.
5	Expand Section 8 new construction subsidies.	+ +	...	+	...	Undesirable, since less costly means are available for attaining same goals.
6	Create a mortgage subsidy for middle-income rental housing.	+ +	...	+	...	Undesirable, since subsidy does not focus on poor.

7	Build more public housing.	+	...	+	...	Undesirable because both costly and unpopular, but some new units are desirable for large families and the elderly.
8	Provide grants or low-interest loans for rehabilitation.	...	++	+	...	Desirable, should have high priority.
9	Develop a voucher program to help renters purchase units converted to condominiums.	...	+	+	+	Undesirable, since subsidy does not focus on the most needy.
10	Expand use of tax-exempt bonds to provide low-interest mortgages for rental housing.	++	...	+	...	Desirable only under very restrictive conditions.
11	Convert public housing subsidies to vouchers for tenants.	...	+	+	...	Undesirable as general policy; should be tested on small scale.

Other policies

12	Sell public housing units to occupants or investors.	...	+	+	+	Undesirable as general policy; should be tested on small scale.
13	Sell surplus FHA and other federal units to local housing authorities.	...	+	+	...	Desirable in a few cities with many FHA-owned units, but not as large-scale federal policy.

Source: Author.
Key: ++ Policy is very effective.
 + Policy is somewhat effective.
 − Policy has negative effect.
 ... not applicable.

NET EVALUATION. Reinstating these tax advantages would be undesirable, particularly in view of the advantages created in the Economic Recovery Tax Act of 1981.[2]

2. Reduce federal tax advantages of homeownership.

NATURE AND PURPOSE. Rental housing demand is reduced by two major attractions of ownership housing. One is the possibility of benefiting from future appreciation in home values. This attraction has already been weakened by the stagnation of home prices in 1981 and 1982. The other consists of the tax advantages of homeownership, which still make buying more appealing than renting, especially for high-income households. Decreasing these tax advantages would increase the relative lure of renting. This would permit owners to raise rents and perhaps make construction of new rental units feasible again.

Possible ways to reduce homeownership tax advantages have been analyzed by the Congressional Budget Office.[3] Among these ways are the following.

—Eliminating the deductibility of mortgage interest and property taxes from taxable income.

—Retaining such deductibility but putting a ceiling on the amount that any taxpayer can deduct.

—Converting such deductibility into a tax credit calculated at a uniform tax rate for all taxpayers.

—Adopting a capital gains tax for profits on the sale of one home before they are invested in another.

DISCUSSION. In 1981 Congress increased from $100,000 to $125,000 the capital gain that taxpayers over age fifty-five could remove from

---

2. The Economic Recovery Tax Act of 1981 contains a complete revision of depreciation procedures that shortens the allowable life of all real property to fifteen years. This greatly affects the profitability of rental housing. When the mortgage interest rate is 12.5 percent, first-year yields on the down payment on a rental housing unit vary with its depreciable life as follows: a forty-year life gives a 10 percent yield; a thirty-year life gives a 12 percent yield; a twenty-year life gives a 16 percent yield; a fifteen-year life gives a 20 percent yield; and a ten-year life gives a 28 percent yield.

These first-year calculations are based on the investment model explained earlier. They somewhat overstate the benefit of shorter remaining lives on yields over longer periods. This is because they reflect yields when the advantages of depreciation are at their maximum and also count tax shelter benefits as part of yields.

3. Congressional Budget Office, *The Tax Treatment of Homeownership: Issues and Options* (GPO, 1981).

housing without paying taxes. It also increased from eighteen to twenty-four months the time permitted for reinvestment of proceeds from the sale of a home without incurring tax liability. Hence Congress hardly seems inclined to adopt this policy at present, perhaps because over 65 percent of all households own their own homes.[4]

Nevertheless, this policy has two key advantages over most others favoring rental housing. First, it would increase federal revenues, rather than reduce them. In fact, revenue gains from adopting it could be huge. The Treasury estimated that the mortgage interest deduction resulted in 1981 tax savings of $21.5 billion for those who used it, and the property tax deduction saved $9.5 billion.[5] These tax savings will be even larger in future years. Second, the wealthiest homeowners receive the largest tax advantages from deductions, so reducing those advantages increases equity.

NET EVALUATION. Eliminating these tax advantages altogether is undesirable because homeownership should be encouraged to some extent. However, reducing or limiting them would increase both equity and efficiency. But Congress probably will not pass tax changes that reduce homeowner benefits.[6] Hence the relative desirability of renting over homeownership probably cannot be increased through this policy. Reducing tax biases favoring homeownership over other investments could probably be best done by increasing the latter's tax benefits. However, more equitable distribution of homeownership tax advantages among income groups would not require any big cut in their total size. That could be done by changing the benefit from a deduction to a tax credit at a uniform rate close to the average for all taxpayers.

3. Increase federal tax benefits for tenants.

NATURE AND PURPOSE. If landlords passed their local property tax bills through to tenants, then tenants could pay those bills and deduct

---

4. As of 1978, however, less than 40 percent of all homeowners and 62 percent of all those with mortgages claimed the mortgage interest deduction on their federal tax returns. Congressional Budget Office, *Tax Treatment of Homeownership*, p. 11.

5. Ibid., pp. 4, 9.

6. In early 1982 the U.S. Senate voted 83–0 against limiting the tax deduction allowed for home mortgage interest payments, shortly after publication of Congressional Budget Office, *Tax Treatment of Homeownership*. This shows the lack of political support for such limitations, at least during a congressional election year. See *Land Use Digest*, vol. 15 (January 15, 1982), p. 3.

them from their taxable incomes. This would increase the relative attraction of renting by extending to renters at least one tax benefit of homeownership.[7]

DISCUSSION. This policy creates an indirect subsidy by reducing federal tax revenues. Landlords now count tenants' rents as gross income and deduct property taxes as expenses. If tenants explicitly paid property taxes, landlords would no longer deduct them. But landlords' gross incomes would be lower too, since the tenants' funds they formerly used to pay property taxes would go directly from the tenants to local governments (even if the landlords acted as collecting agents). Thus landlords would report the same amount of taxable net income, but tenants would report less because they could deduct property taxes. This policy would also be difficult to administer. Local governments would have many more problems collecting taxes from highly mobile tenants than from landlords anchored by their properties. Problems of allocating taxes among specific units, including vacant ones, would also arise. Moreover, deductions always disproportionately benefit taxpayers in high brackets per dollar deducted (although that could be avoided by using a tax credit).

NET EVALUATION. The disadvantages and difficulties of this policy outweigh its benefits.

4. Create a comprehensive housing voucher program.

NATURE AND PURPOSE. This policy would modify the Section 8 subsidy and expand it into a housing allowance available to all low-income renters willing to occupy decent units. It is the most comprehensive policy considered in this analysis. It could aid as many as 7.2 million households at a total cost of $10.7 billion a year in 1980 dollars.[8]

Every household with income below a certain level would be eligible to receive the difference between the "standard" minimum cost of a "decent" housing unit in its area and a certain fraction of its income (25 to 30 percent). This subsidy would continue as long as the household's income remained below the eligibility level and the household was living

7. This policy is advocated in Marshall M. Holleb, "A Modest Proposal for Tenants' Equality," *Real Estate Review*, vol. 6 (Winter 1977), pp. 67–71.

8. Estimates from the Department of Housing and Urban Development. Also see Garland E. Allen, Jerry J. Fitts, and Evelyn S. Glatt, "The Experimental Housing Allowance Program," in Katharine L. Bradbury and Anthony Downs, eds., *Do Housing Allowances Work?* (Brookings Institution, 1981), pp. 29–30.

POSSIBLE FEDERAL POLICIES

in a unit that met minimum quality standards. Each household would arrange its own rental agreement in the market, and there would be no ceilings on the rents recipients could pay. Households could move and retain their subsidies, as long as they had appropriate income and the new units they occupied also met the quality standards.[9]

Housing vouchers would greatly increase the ability of poor households to pay rent, thereby helping maintain the rental inventory in good condition. This could have a huge beneficial effect on the rental housing supply in the long run.

This program could also be implemented on a smaller scale by providing vouchers only to some eligible households, although that would require inequitable rationing by some other criteria. All past U.S. housing subsidy programs have been similarly rationed to keep their costs down.

DISCUSSION. The experimental housing allowance program showed that only about half of all eligible households would participate in a national housing voucher program. Moreover, those not participating would include many of the poorest households living in the worst units. Hence a housing voucher program would not achieve as much equity as might be supposed. Even so, housing vouchers would aid many more households for each dollar of subsidy than any other type of direct housing assistance, especially subsidies for new construction.

In nearly all housing voucher programs, most of the funds are used for purposes other than improving housing quality. Poor renters typically pay a high fraction of their income for rent; they use voucher payments to reduce that fraction, treating them mainly as added income. Thus a housing voucher program may be considered to be a direct income maintenance program. Its main virtue is helping low-income households pay the high costs of living in decent housing units—including those they occupy already. However, the minimum-quality requirement would generate more housing improvements than unconstrained income payments.

Nevertheless, why not use the same funds for direct income mainte-

---

9. The 1983 budget proposed by the Reagan administration in February 1982 recommended administrative changes in the Section 8 program quite similar to those described here. These included abolishing rent ceilings, paying recipients directly instead of landlords, allowing recipients to strike any bargains they wished as long as they occupied "decent-quality" units, and restricting aid to five-year, fixed-payment contracts with recipient households. However, there was no suggested expansion of the program to serve all eligible households. See Department of Housing and Urban Development, *Fiscal Year 1983 Budget: Summary* (GPO, February 1982), pp. H-1–H-7.

nance without reference to housing? This would make the recipient households better off because none would be compelled to spend more on housing than it desired. Furthermore, about twice as large a fraction of eligible households would participate.[10] Though this would not improve rental housing as much as housing vouchers, it would still help landlords by raising the income of their poor tenants.

NET EVALUATION. Most economists believe adopting one comprehensive income maintenance program with an adequate minimum support level would be the best way to aid the poor. But Congress has consistently refused to do this. A reasonable second-best approach is adopting different earmarked aid programs which, taken together, achieve results similar to one comprehensive income maintenance program. Congress has been much more willing to adopt this approach, as shown by its funding of many specific aids to the poor. Health care assistance and food stamps could be two key elements in such a combination, and housing vouchers another. Housing vouchers also have the advantage of being able to take account of the large differences in costs of living across the nation.[11] However, a housing voucher program would greatly increase housing subsidy outlays for at least several years and perhaps permanently. Yet this is the best subsidy to use if the nation can afford to expand any housing subsidy.

Even if expansion of housing vouchers into a full-scale entitlement program is not financially feasible, *some expansion* of the existing Section 8 program, administratively revised as suggested above, would be desirable. Such a partial approach was recommended by the President's Housing Commission in 1982.[12]

5. *Expand Section 8 new construction subsidies.*

NATURE AND PURPOSE. This program induces developers to create new rental units for the poor by guaranteeing them rental payments for up to twenty years. Local public housing authorities then provide eligible tenants with access to these new units. This program was the main source of new directly subsidized rental units in the late 1970s and early 1980s.

DISCUSSION. A major problem of new construction under Section 8 is its high annual subsidy for each household—more than triple the average

10. Ibid., pp. 122, 130–31.
11. Raymond J. Struyk and Jill Khadduri pointed out this advantage in *Housing Vouchers: From Here to Entitlement?* (Urban Institute, 1980).
12. President's Commission on Housing, press release, April 29, 1982.

annual subsidy for existing structures under Section 8. Hence expanding this program would be vastly more expensive than providing housing vouchers to the same number of households. Moreover, new Section 8 units are much more visible to the community than existing units occupied by voucher recipients, so the former would rouse much more neighborhood resistance. Nonetheless, new Section 8 units add to the total housing supply. They can also provide new investments in deteriorating areas that need visible evidence of public concern.

NET EVALUATION. This subsidy program should not be expanded, even if some of its funds were used to build new rental units in deteriorating areas. In fact, the program could be scaled back, with current funds better used as housing vouchers.[13]

6. Create a mortgage subsidy for middle-income rental housing.

NATURE AND PURPOSE. This program was proposed by the Department of Housing and Urban Development (HUD) during the Carter administration as a means of producing more new rental units than the Section 8 new construction program provided for each dollar of subsidy. It was also proposed by Senator Richard Lugar of Indiana in the 1981–82 Congress. It would provide a "shallow" subsidy (low cost for each household) by reducing mortgage interest rates for new rental units. In some versions, any household could occupy these units; other versions require 20 percent occupancy by poor households receiving Section 8 funds for existing units.

DISCUSSION. Providing such subsidies to the nonpoor is justified by the assertion that acute shortages of rental housing exist in many markets, but construction of new units is not feasible without subsidies. New units are expensive, and subsidizing them for the poor requires "deep" subsidies (high cost for each household). But deep subsidies produce far fewer added units than shallow subsidies for the same cost. In fact, this program, with a 20 percent Section 8 subsidy requirement on existing units, would aid more poor households than a Section 8 new construction program using the same subsidy, while producing five times as many added new units.

The validity of this argument depends greatly on whether acute rental

13. In its proposed 1983 budget, the Reagan administration suggested eliminating new construction subsidies for all but 10,000 units a year, with those going only to elderly and handicapped households. Department of Housing and Urban Development, *Fiscal Year 1983 Budget*.

shortages actually exist. As indicated earlier, few areas now have severe shortages, although some may appear later in the 1980s. Moreover, such shallow subsidies for new units would be both costlier and less focused on poor households than housing vouchers.

NET EVALUATION. This program focuses new subsidies on nonpoor households when subsidies for the truly needy are being slashed; hence it should not be adopted.

7. Build more public housing.

NATURE AND PURPOSE. Public housing is one of the two largest rental subsidy programs serving the poor. One way to expand the supply of low-rent units would be to build more public housing.

DISCUSSION. Because community resistance to all public housing except that for the elderly is strong nearly everywhere, it would be difficult to find new public housing sites acceptable to nearby residents. This difficulty would be lessened if the new units were built only in small, scattered clusters. New large public housing units would be the only available housing adequate for many large poor families who cannot afford unsubsidized units and are not welcomed by private landlords. There are thousands of such families in U.S. urban areas, including many on waiting lists for public housing.

This policy involves a higher cost than housing vouchers for each household subsidized. A new public housing unit—especially one for a large family—costs far more than the current value of the units occupied by many unsubsidized taxpayers. Hence this program would be both less equitable and less efficient than helping poor households occupy existing housing. Yet there may be no other source of very big units adequate for large poor families.

Building public housing for the elderly might be socially efficient if many older households would move into it from large single-family homes. New units for the elderly can be small enough to cost less than the average unsubsidized unit. Moreover, if such new units attracted elderly persons out of large existing homes, those homes could be occupied by unsubsidized low- and moderate-income families.

NET EVALUATION. This policy is too costly to serve as a major source of added low-income housing. But it might be followed on a selective basis to create (1) some big units for large low-income families in cities containing many such families now badly housed and (2) units for the elderly in cities where surveys reveal that many elderly tenants would move from large single-family homes.

8. Provide grants or low-interest loans for rehabilitation.

NATURE AND PURPOSE. Many owners of deteriorating rental units have difficulty obtaining the credit needed for repairs or modernization. A federal program of grants or low-interest loans could help them. It could involve either direct grants, interest-rate subsidies on private loans, or direct federal loans at below-market interest rates. To affect rental units occupied by poor households, such loans would have to have very low interest rates.

DISCUSSION. From 1964 to 1981 the federal government made direct low-interest rehabilitation loans under Section 312. Loans were for a maximum of $27,000 over no more than twenty years at 3 percent interest. Eligible units had to be located in restricted areas, such as those with homesteading, urban renewal, or community development block grant programs. By 1976 about 47,500 such loans had helped renovate 75,000 units, an average of only 6,800 units a year (over eleven years). Since 80 percent went to owner-occupants, fewer than 1,400 rental units a year benefited from such loans in that period.[14] Intermittent funding of this program over the years is one reason it has been so small.

The Carter administration planned to expand the Section 312 program, but the Reagan administration has proposed replacing it with direct grants of up to $5,000 a unit to help owners of multifamily units rehabilitate them. This proposed new program would eventually assist 30,000 rental units a year—over twenty times as many as were aided annually under the Section 312 program from 1964 to 1976.[15] However, grants would have a much smaller limit for each unit than a Section 312 loan. That change may have occurred because the full amount of each grant or loan is a budgeted outlay when made. This big first-year budgetary impact could be reduced by retaining a loan program, but converting it to an interest-rate subsidy with private lenders supplying the capital and making the loans. The proposed huge expansion of rental rehabilitation aid will be hindered by the difficulty of keeping any program offering

14. Data from Raymond J. Struyk and Beth J. Soldo, *Improving the Elderly's Housing* (Ballinger, 1980), pp. 208–9.
15. See *The Budget of the United States Government, Fiscal Year 1983*, pp. 5-95, 5-96.

each recipient such small amounts of aid relatively free from fraud and waste.

NET EVALUATION. A rehabilitation aid program for rental units should be part of the federal government's rental housing strategy and should receive far more emphasis than in the past, in terms of both funding and promotion.

9. *Develop a voucher program to help renters purchase units converted to condominiums.*

NATURE AND PURPOSE. As condominium conversions increase, more renters unable to buy the units they live in will be displaced. Their displacement could be reduced, and homeownership promoted, if some could receive federal housing vouchers to help them buy converted units. This aid could be restricted to persons with low income (no more than 80 percent of the area's median income).

DISCUSSION. The experimental housing allowance program proved that housing vouchers could be effectively used by homeowners. Hence such aid could be offered to poor renters about to be displaced by condominium conversion to help them buy their units.

But why should such aid be restricted only to this narrowly defined class of homeowners? Inequities would result because other homeowners with the same income and other similar traits would be denied housing vouchers. The number of low-income households residing in converted rental units will be very small compared with all poor homeowners, and it would be politically difficult to discriminate against the latter. So this policy makes sense only as part of a broader extension of housing vouchers to all poor homeowners.

Low-income renters are more needy than low-income homeowners, however. The percentage of substandard housing units is somewhat higher among low-income renters than among low-income homeowners.[16] Homeowners also have more assets (including their homes) than renters, on the average, and homeowners already benefit from extensive indirect subsidies in the form of tax advantages. Therefore, any housing voucher

16. This was true of households enrolled in the supply experiment of the experimental housing allowance program taken as a group. However, among Green Bay area households, the initial inspection failure rate was slightly higher among owners than renters. See Francis J. Cronin and David W. Rasmussen, "Mobility," in Raymond J. Struyk and Marc Bendick, Jr., ed., *Housing Vouchers for the Poor: Lessons from a National Experiment* (Urban Institute, 1981), p. 110.

POSSIBLE FEDERAL POLICIES

program should give higher priority to aiding poor renters than poor homeowners.

NET EVALUATION. In view of the scarcity of federal subsidy funds, extending housing vouchers to all low-income homeowners is undesirable until after low-income renters have received such aid. Yet, because it would also be undesirable to aid only those low-income homeowners purchasing converted units, this program should not be adopted.

10. Expand use of tax-exempt bonds to provide low-interest mortgages for rental housing.

NATURE AND PURPOSE. Many states and some cities have floated bond issues exempt from federal income taxes and used the funds to provide mortgages for their citizens. Tax-exempt bonds usually have lower interest rates than conventional sources of mortgage funds. Hence this tactic permitted making mortgages with lower-than-normal rates. Rents in the new units so financed were often further reduced by other federal housing subsidies under the Section 8 program for existing units. When conventional mortgage rates soared in the 1970s, billions of dollars' worth of such bonds were issued.

This policy strongly appeals to state and local government officials. It adds to their popularity at no cost to them because the subsidy involved is paid by federal taxpayers as a whole. State and local governments do not even assume liability for the bonds.

Congress recently blocked further issuance of such bonds except under restricted conditions, such as income limits on occupants. This policy would remove that limitation on rental housing or increase emphasis on the use of such bonds within the prescribed limits.

DISCUSSION. Congress limited issuance of mortgage-backed tax-exempt bonds because (1) those bonds were unfairly competing with conventional mortgage lenders, (2) the federal subsidies involved were benefiting many nonpoor households, and (3) large-scale flotation of those bonds was driving up interest costs for other state and local government financing. Furthermore, interest rates rose so high in mid-1981 that construction of rental housing was not feasible even at tax-exempt rates. Before 1980, state housing agencies had long been using tax-exempt bonds to finance rental housing for low- and moderate-income households. This was considered inefficient by economists, since U.S. Treasury tax losses were much larger than reductions in rent caused by lower interest rates. Paying direct subsidies to rental housing developers would be more efficient. But that would require specific acts of Congress, whereas tax-exempt mortgage bonds could be issued by state and local governments without congressional approval.

Such approval seems even more remote in 1983. Moreover, direct federal subsidies are less easily available to help produce rents that low-income households can afford. Yet major unmet needs for more rental units available to low-income households are likely to emerge in the 1980s. Where existing housing inventories contain many vacant or underused units, meeting these needs will not require new construction. But in fast-growing regions without such inventories, more new construction may be desirable.

NET EVALUATION. State and local housing agencies should be permitted to use tax-exempt financing for new rental housing where three conditions exist: (1) local rental housing shortages for the poor have become pressing, (2) the tax-exempt interest differential makes such housing feasible, and (3) the units so financed are occupied primarily by low-income households. In spite of the inefficiency of this subsidy, it is superior to direct federal subsidies for new units because most new units it creates are less encumbered by cost-raising regulations. However, as long as tax-exempt interest rates remain high and direct subsidies are not available to help lower rents, meeting these three conditions will be extremely difficult.

11. Convert public housing subsidies to vouchers for tenants.

NATURE AND PURPOSE. One approach to making local public housing authorities more accountable to their tenants would be converting present public housing subsidies to vouchers paid to those tenants.[17] These vouchers could be used for either public or private units. Then each public housing authority would be competing in the general housing market. It would even be able to sell its units or convert them to higher-rent units.

DISCUSSION. This policy presumes that public housing authorities could become competent managers and entrepreneurs in a competitive market. Yet there is little evidence for that presumption in view of the managerial difficulties so many have experienced. This policy also assumes

---

17. For an analysis of public housing problems, see Raymond J. Struyk, *A New System for Public Housing: Salvaging a National Resource* (Urban Institute, 1980).

society would be willing to shift a significant share of the nation's 1.3 million public housing units to occupancy by nonpoor households. That could happen if public housing agencies needed higher-rent tenants to meet expenses and therefore started catering to nonpoor households. Or if many existing tenants move out, there might not be enough other local poor households receiving subsidies to fill the authority's units, especially if no comprehensive housing voucher program is adopted. The public housing authority might then become bankrupt and be forced to evict its remaining tenants. If this occurred in many communities, the total supply of rental units available to poor households could fall.

In fact, it is hard to see how this policy could increase that supply. One possible source of increase is the many vandalized public housing units that are now vacant because authorities cannot afford repairs. If those authorities could borrow money against potentially higher rents from nonpoor tenants, they might be able to rehabilitate these units. But such loans would be too risky for private lenders without government guarantees. Even if this approach worked, it would expand the rental supply for nonpoor households, not poor ones. Renting parts of some large public housing projects to nonpoor households might reduce the projects' blighting influence on surrounding neighborhoods—*if* any nonpoor households could be induced to live there. But that would also reduce the number of rental units set aside for the poor. Hence it would be sensible only where plenty of private housing was available to low-income households at rents they could afford with housing vouchers.

NET EVALUATION. Because of this policy's many uncertainties, it should not be widely adopted until small demonstration projects have been tried. They should be undertaken only in communities with (1) large public housing projects that contain many vacant units and are blighting surrounding areas and (2) enough private housing available to accommodate displaced households.

12. *Sell public housing units to occupants or investors.*

NATURE AND PURPOSE. This policy seeks to transform present public housing tenants from renters into homeowners or to shift public housing units from the low-income market into higher-income markets. If local authorities sold their units to tenants, the tenants would need financial assistance to buy them. Hence this policy presupposes a housing voucher program such as that in policy 11, with tenants eligible to continue receiving vouchers after they become homeowners. This policy would create the same kinds of inequities as policy 9. Many of the issues raised by policy 11 are relevant to this policy, too.

NET EVALUATION. This policy should be tried initially on a small scale under the conditions specified in the discussion of policy 11.

13. *Sell surplus FHA or other federal units to local housing authorities.*

NATURE AND PURPOSE. In some big cities, the Federal Housing Administration (FHA) has repossessed many single-family homes with defaulted mortgages. These homes now stand vacant; they are often vandalized, blighting their neighborhoods. Yet local public housing authorities have long waiting lists of large households unable to find adequate but affordable units. Why not sell these vacant FHA units to public housing authorities at low cost to accommodate such households?

DISCUSSION. This policy has been successful in Baltimore on a small scale. But Baltimore received demonstration funds from HUD to renovate the units involved. Without similar aid, most housing authorities could not afford such renovations. In fact, many are unable to repair vacant units in their existing projects, nor can they afford to pay the FHA the full mortgage amount to buy its homes. Hence the FHA would have to absorb a capital write-down if it transferred these units to local authorities at low prices. This is no loss of real resources where such units cannot be sold privately at higher prices. However, it increases *apparent* federal spending without giving FHA officials any organizational rewards; hence it may not be feasible.

NET EVALUATION. This policy would be highly desirable in a few cities where FHA-owned units are a serious blight. It should be adopted selectively, but not considered a universal federal tactic.

APPENDIX C

Possible Local Policies on Rental Housing

THIS APPENDIX analyzes the effectiveness of fifteen possible local policies in achieving the objectives in chapter 8. Policies already discussed in detail in chapter 8 are not included here, nor are policies likely to be highly ineffective. Table C-1 summarizes the evaluations.

1. Prohibit or restrict conversion of rental units to condominiums.

NATURE AND PURPOSE. Conversion of rental units to condominiums has notably reduced the rental supply in certain areas. From 1970 to 1979 about 1.3 percent of all 1970 rental units were converted, according to a study by the Department of Housing and Urban Development (HUD).[1] But in Chicago, Denver, and Washington, D.C., more than 5 percent of 1970 rental units had been converted by 1979. The highest fraction converted was 9.3 percent in Chicago's suburbs.

Conversion sometimes displaces households that do not want to purchase their units or cannot afford to do so. Moreover, it sometimes involves inadequate notice to affected households, high-pressure sales tactics, and other undesirable behavior. In reaction, some groups have urged cities to ban conversions or halt them for long periods. Others advocate ordinances limiting the conversion process, including laws that prohibit conversions unless a certain percentage of tenants approve. These laws confer limited ownership rights on the tenants.

1. U.S. Department of Housing and Urban Development, *The Conversion of Rental Housing to Condominiums and Cooperatives* (U.S. Government Printing Office, 1980), p. IV-7.

Table C-1. Evaluation of Possible Local Policies on Rental Housing

		Relationship of policy to objective				
			Encouraging good maintenance and			
Policy number	Policy	Stimulating new rental construction	conversion of non-new structures	Helping low-income renters	Encouraging home-ownership	Evaluation
	General regulatory policies					
1	Prohibit or restrict conversion of rental units to condominiums.	...	−	+	−	Reasonable regulations are desirable, but conversions should be encouraged.
	Tax policies					
2	Provide tax abatements for conversion of nonresidential properties to rental housing.	...	++	...	...	Desirable but low priority.
3	Postpone property tax increases on rehabilitated properties.	...	++	+	+	Desirable in cities with much older property.
4	Award property tax abatements to new rental housing.	++	...	...	...	Undesirable on a large scale; useful only in special situations.
5	Lower assessment ratios on rental housing.	++	+	+	...	Desirable, but applicable in only a few places.
	Subsidy policies					
6	Create low-interest loans for rehabilitating rental housing.	...	++	+	...	High priority for community development block grant funds.

7	Use FHA and other federal surplus units for public housing.	...	+	...	Low priority unless federal funding for rehabilitating FHA units is available.
	Zoning policies				
8	Allow conversion of large single-family units to multifamily use.	...	++	+	Very desirable; should have high priority.
9	Expand areas zoned for multi-family housing.	+	...	...	Desirability varies widely in different communities.
10	Raise allowable densities in areas zoned for multifamily housing.	++	...	...	Desirable but unpopular; should be combined with careful aesthetic planning of higher-density projects.
11	Reduce the length and complexity of permission processes.	++	+	...	Desirable in every city.
12	Make surplus schools and public land available for rental housing.	+	+	...	Desirable where surplus school properties are available.
	Code enforcement policies				
13	Differentiate code enforcement by neighborhood.	...	++	+	Highly desirable in all but very new cities.
14	Require rental units to pass code inspections before rental or sale.	...	++	...	Desirable in cities with no very deteriorated areas.
	Other policy				
15	Encourage owner residence in rental buildings.	...	++	+	Extremely desirable; should have highest priority.

Source. Author.
Key: ++ Policy is very effective.
 + Policy is somewhat effective.
 − Policy has negative effect.
 ... not applicable.

DISCUSSION. Reasonable government regulation of condominium conversion is certainly appropriate. It could require adequate notice, full disclosure of building condition, protection from undue harassment, tenants' right of first refusal on purchase, and some compensation to displaced tenants. Such compensation is most appropriate for low-income tenants who have lived in one place for a long time and cannot easily find other housing nearby.

However, condominium conversion should be regarded by local governments as basically desirable because it increases possibilities for homeownership among local residents. On the average, homeowners maintain their properties better than renters and take greater interest in community affairs.

Moreover, most conversions have involved relatively high-rent units; inhibiting the process will not protect the poor. In addition, prolonged moratoriums on conversions or prohibition of conversions without prior consent from some fraction of tenants seem undue abridgements of rental property owners' rights.

NET EVALUATION. Regulation should try to create reasonable conditions for conversion to condominiums, not to halt or severely inhibit it.

2. *Provide tax abatements for conversion of nonresidential properties to rental housing.*

NATURE AND PURPOSE. In New York City, nonresidential properties can be converted to residential use or replaced with new housing without any increase in property taxes for a certain period, even if the properties have much higher market values afterward than before. This tax abatement encourages replacement of "surplus" or deteriorated nonresidential property with additional housing units.

DISCUSSION. This policy can be effective only if a city contains well-located nonresidential property with low property taxes. Such property is often found in older fringes of downtown areas or close to expressways. Property taxes form a large share of rental housing operating costs, so keeping them low increases the feasibility of such housing. This policy does not involve any losses of existing tax revenues, since it abates only potential increases. But it will not evoke much added rental supply unless interest rates fall, too.

NET EVALUATION. This policy is relatively costless fiscally, but will probably not produce much added rental housing. Hence it is desirable but should have low priority.

POSSIBLE LOCAL POLICIES

3. Postpone property tax increases on rehabilitated properties.

NATURE AND PURPOSE. Whenever an owner renovates a property, its market value increases—so its assessed value should rise, too. But the owner will then have to pay higher property taxes. This discourages renovation, rehabilitation, and even proper maintenance. To reduce this disincentive, city governments can postpone reassessment or collection of higher taxes on renovated properties for some initial period. This period could last until the property changes owners or for some set time, such as five years. Or the appropriate tax increase could be phased in gradually.

DISCUSSION. Owners of many deteriorated older properties have limited resources for improving them. Possible immediate increases in property taxes can deter their making such investments. This policy therefore encourages maximum use of the existing inventory. It also creates administrative difficulties, since properties with the same current market values must be treated differently, depending on whether they got those values through renovation. But computerized systems can handle such complexities.

Ultimately, all property improvements should result in higher taxes to avoid great tax inequities. But initial postponement of such increases should be part of every city's incentives for property renovation.

NET EVALUATION. This is a desirable policy for all cities containing much older property.

4. Award property tax abatements to new rental housing.

NATURE AND PURPOSE. To encourage housing creation, New York City abates property taxes on new units for ten years. Under Section 421 of the Real Property Tax Law, during construction and for two years after completion, any eligible property is fully exempt from taxes. In the next two years, it is 80 percent exempt; every two years thereafter, the exemption is decreased by 20 percent. The property becomes fully taxable in the eleventh year.[2] With property taxes often equaling 15 to 25 percent of total rents, such abatement can make an enormous difference to a project's economic feasibility. However, this policy may require reductions in existing city revenues. In 1978 New York City gave $44 million

2. Matthew Drennan and Georgia Nanopoulos-Stergiou, "The Local Economy and Local Revenues," in Raymond D. Horton and Charles Brecher, eds., *Setting Municipal Priorities, 1980* (Allenheld, Osmun and Co., 1979), p. 31, n. 6.

in exemptions and $9 million in abatements through its Section 421 and J-51 programs. About 10 percent of all new housing units built in New York City in 1971–77 received tax abatements.[3]

DISCUSSION. Most new privately financed housing built under New York's tax abatement programs serves middle- and upper-income households. Hence this subsidy can be justified in fiscally strapped cities only if it helps generate housing easily accessible to downtown and needed to retain white-collar jobs. But few cities have shortages of such housing.

NET EVALUATION. Large-scale tax abatements for new housing are undesirable in most cities. They reduce local tax revenues without aiding low-income households. Hence such abatements should be used only as special incentives to stimulate redevelopment of blighted areas.

5. Lower assessment ratios on rental housing.

NATURE AND PURPOSE. In some cities, various types of properties are assessed at different ratios to actual market values. Single-family homes are normally assessed at the lowest ratio, and industrial and commercial properties at the highest. In some areas this practice is legal, but it is often carried out implicitly even though statutes require identical treatment for all properties. Where rental housing has a higher assessment ratio than single-family housing, tax burdens on rental properties can be decreased by reducing their ratio. In the early 1970s, for example, Cook County, Illinois, assessed single-family homes at 22 percent of market value but rental apartments at 30 percent. Reducing the rental ratio to 22 percent would have cut taxes on rental units by over 25 percent, substantially improving their profitability.

DISCUSSION. This policy applies to only a few areas. Moreover, if a community contains much rental housing, reducing its assessment ratios will either cut local government tax revenues or force up taxes on other properties. Nevertheless, taxing rental housing more heavily than owner-occupied housing is both economically inefficient and inequitable.

NET EVALUATION. Equalizing assessment ratios on all housing is desirable.

3. From 1971 to 1977, 138,500 new housing units were built in New York City. Of these, 10.3 percent were public housing, 54.0 percent were publicly aided, and 35.7 percent were private—including private ones with tax exemptions. About 29 percent of the private units, or 10.3 percent of all new units, were aided by partial tax exemptions. See Elizabeth Roistacher and Emanuel Tobier, "Housing Policy," in Horton and Brecher, eds., *Setting Municipal Priorities*, 1981, p. 147.

6. Create low-interest loans for rehabilitating rental housing.

NATURE AND PURPOSE. Many local governments make low-interest rehabilitation loans for the same reasons that the federal government created the Section 312 program (discussed under policy 8 in appendix B). Most such local programs employ federal community development block grant (CDBG) funds. In the first year of the CDBG program 21 percent of the money was used for housing (mostly for rehabilitation); by the sixth year 39 percent was so used.[4]

DISCUSSION. Helping owners rehabilitate housing should be part of each local government's neighborhood strategy. Most such aid aims at single-family homes, but multifamily rental units also qualify under some programs. In many big cities, large absentee-owned apartment buildings are the greatest blighting factors. Those cities have much to gain from successful housing rehabilitation programs.

The justification for subsidizing private rehabilitation is the low profitability of rental properties and the consequent difficulty owners have obtaining credit. The private market alone cannot remedy this situation where low profitability results from tenant poverty and high interest rates. If such properties are ever to be renovated, their owners must obtain credit at below market cost. Local governments in areas containing such housing should therefore regard themselves as lenders of last resort.

Rehabilitation loan programs are hard to administer because of too much red tape and not enough sophistication among property owners. Moreover, many absentee apartment owners have no strong incentives to participate.

NET EVALUATION. In spite of their problems, low-interest rehabilitation loans for rental housing are a desirable use of CDBG funds.

7. Use FHA and other federal surplus units for public housing.

NATURE AND PURPOSE. This policy was described in appendix B as policy 13.

---

4. Paul R. Dommel and others, *Targeting Community Development* (GPO, 1980), pp. 120–22; Paul R. Dommel and others, *Implementing Community Development*, draft report to the Department of Housing and Urban Development (Brookings Institution, 1981), p. 4-3. The sample of cities on which these data are based covers about 22 percent of all CDBG expenditures, but is somewhat biased toward larger cities.

DISCUSSION. Some cities contain single-family and multifamily units that the Federal Housing Administration (FHA) has foreclosed but has been unable to return to private use. These cities would benefit from adding some FHA units to their public housing inventories—if they had the funds to purchase, renovate, and operate those units. Single-family units would be especially desirable because they could help large families blend in with nearby unsubsidized households. But few public housing authorities can afford to take on such units without federal aid. Thus the feasibility of this policy depends on the availability of added federal funds. Yet, as noted in appendix B, this is probably a low-priority federal policy.

Most local governments will not use their scarce community improvement funds for this purpose; they regard helping to renovate privately owned housing as more efficient. Such renovation can aid households not as poor as those in public housing; therefore, it requires less subsidy per household. Moreover, it is easier to leverage public funds with added private capital when renovating existing privately owned units. Also, private investors do not always hire union-rate workers or meet as costly renovation standards as public agencies.

NET EVALUATION. Without specific federal aid, this policy is too costly for most cities. Moreover, it should have lower priority for city funds than rehabilitating privately owned rental units, which can generate more output for each dollar of public funding.

8. Allow conversion of large single-family units to multifamily use.

NATURE AND PURPOSE. Many large older single-family homes occupied by small households, often elderly, contain space that could be rented to other households, benefiting both owners and tenants. But such homes are often located in areas zoned only for single-family occupancy. So renting rooms in them, or renovating them into multiunit structures, is illegal. Nevertheless, thousands of owners are already doing this surreptitiously. This policy recognizes the social benefits of creating added rental housing units from present single-family homes under reasonable regulations.

DISCUSSION. In 1979, 15.9 million single-family owner-occupied homes across the nation contained seven or more rooms; of these, 9.6 million

POSSIBLE LOCAL POLICIES

had four or more bedrooms.[5] If just 10 percent of these large homes were subdivided into two or more units, they could provide 1.6 million added rental units. This would generate triple benefits for owners (who would get added income), tenants (who would get well-located units), and society (which would make better use of the existing inventory to meet rental housing needs).

However, some neighbors of to-be-converted dwellings claim that subdivision of single-family homes would make their neighborhoods much less desirable. They cite earlier experiences where large, older homes were divided into rooming houses, and subsequently entire neighborhoods declined from high-quality areas into slums. They also claim that rising local population density, accompanied by greater traffic and demands for more on-street parking, would reduce the quality of their environment.

These objections correctly point out harmful consequences that might accompany completely unregulated conversion of large older homes into multiunit dwellings. However, local governments could prevent these undesirable results by creating reasonable regulations governing conversion and rigorously enforcing them. These regulations should require subdivided units to be of adequate size and quality and to contain separate plumbing, entrances, and amenities. Off-street parking could be required, depending on how crowded local streets were already. The total amount of such conversion allowed in any one area should be limited so low-density neighborhoods are not suddenly transformed into high-density ones.

Permitting such conversions under reasonable regulations, rather than prohibiting them, is also a sensible response to the higher real cost of capital in the 1980s. That higher cost puts pressure on everyone to use space more efficiently, hence more densely. Society should respond by allowing more people to live in large homes originally designed for much bigger households than those now occupying them.

NET EVALUATION. This policy should have high priority for most cities and suburbs containing older housing. It would cost their governments almost nothing, yet provide net benefits for nearly everyone concerned if neighborhood effects were carefully regulated. In fact, by raising the market values of some existing dwellings, it should increase local tax

5. Data from Department of Housing and Urban Development and U.S. Bureau of the Census, *Annual Housing Survey, 1979, Part C* (GPO, 1981), p. 3.

revenues. However, it must be accompanied by more vigorous code enforcement than now occurs in most neighborhoods.

9. *Expand areas zoned for multifamily housing.*

NATURE AND PURPOSE. A major constraint on building of new rental housing is lack of land zoned for multifamily units, particularly in suburbs. Where very little land is so zoned, its price is increased by such artificial scarcity. This reduces the feasibility of developing new units with rents affordable by low- or even middle-income households. High land cost is not the only factor making new rental units infeasible, so zoning more land for multifamily use would not cause an immediate surge of new building. But it would reduce the price of such land even where the added land so zoned is now occupied by other structures, such as old single-family homes. Changing zoning from single-family to multifamily usually raises land prices on the specific sites involved. But it should reduce the areawide average price of multifamily land, compared with what it would otherwise be.

DISCUSSION. Application of this policy will vary greatly among communities, depending on how fully the land in each is developed, how much multifamily land it already contains, and so forth. The policy will be most useful in suburbs containing large amounts of vacant land zoned single-family at low densities and very little land zoned multifamily. Because of local diversity, no generalizations can be made about this policy's desirability.

10. *Raise allowable densities in areas zoned for multifamily housing.*

NATURE AND PURPOSE. The feasibility of rental housing partly depends on its density. The more units on each acre, the less the average land cost for each unit, other things being equal. Landowners try to capture the added profits from higher density by raising land prices, but they rarely succeed in obtaining all of it. Moreover, if allowable densities are increased on enough multifamily-zoned land, rental savings can be passed on to tenants.

DISCUSSION. In most cities, raising allowable densities on land already zoned multifamily could expand the rental housing supply more than zoning additional land for such use. Higher densities are more likely to make building additional rental housing feasible. However, such "up-

POSSIBLE LOCAL POLICIES 191

zoning" reverses the widespread recent trend toward "down-zoning" residential land. Some residents oppose even moderate densities, fearing either greater congestion or lower single-family land values. Hence they often pressure local governments into reducing allowable densities.

Increased multifamily density need not imply high-rise structures. Up to twenty-five units on each acre can be achieved in structures no more than three stories high. Even at that density, well-designed rental projects will not appear to be cramming too many units onto their sites.

NET EVALUATION. Every city contains some areas where this policy would greatly increase the feasibility of new rental housing without damaging the neighborhood environment. Hence this policy is often appropriate, but it is usually very unpopular. Yet it can achieve local support if promoted in connection with aesthetically pleasing projects designed in consultation with neighborhood residents.

11. Reduce the length and complexity of permission processes.

NATURE AND PURPOSE. Recent local government regulations have greatly increased the time and expense required to develop or renovate rental housing. These regulations require filing plans, receiving approvals from various agencies, participating in public hearings, and obtaining city council or zoning board approvals. Although these rules were initially adopted to protect the public interest, they have gone beyond what is necessary for that purpose because (1) many communities deliberately use such rules to raise housing costs and thus exclude low-income households, (2) local officials want to increase their power, and (3) such officials bear no costs from making rules more costly or time-consuming to follow.[6]

When developers have made large initial investments, as they must in buying land, the mere passage of time is extremely expensive, especially at high interest rates. Moreover, costly inputs of labor, professional skills, and even materials are needed to get through the permission process. These added costs decrease the feasibility of all new housing, but especially rental housing, since its feasibility is tenuous for many other reasons. Greatly reducing the initial time and money required to complete the permission process would help make new rental housing development more likely.

6. For an analysis of these points see Anthony Downs, *Neighborhoods and Urban Development* (Brookings Institution, 1981), chap. 4.

DISCUSSION. The National Association of Home Builders estimates that "excessive" costs imposed by local regulations add as much as 20 percent to new single-family home prices. No comparable estimate has been made for rental housing, but the percentage of added costs would probably be at least as great. Moreover, in many areas, getting the permissions necessary to build new multifamily housing is so frustrating, time-consuming, and uncertain that most competent developers who could build apartments refuse to try. Reducing the complexity of this process would thus both cut the costs of development and induce more people to engage in it. Hence every city should streamline its real estate permission process.

NET EVALUATION. This is a desirable policy in every city.

12. *Make surplus schools and public land available for rental housing.*

NATURE AND PURPOSE. Recent declines in the number of school-aged children have resulted in surplus public school buildings and sites in many cities. These properties are often located in residential areas with strong demands for additional rental housing. Many school buildings are physically suitable for conversion to rental housing. New rental units built on vacant schoolyards would have adequate off-street parking and open space. This policy would make such properties available to rental housing developers.

DISCUSSION. No community has enough surplus school properties to greatly expand its total housing supply. However, such properties are often ideally located for added rental housing. So this policy represents a relatively costless, perhaps profitable way for local governments to create more rental housing and to use their existing resources more efficiently.

One caution is that local school-aged populations may expand again in the future. More babies will be born in the United States during the 1980s than were born in the 1970s. In addition, some cities are experiencing large in-flows of immigrants likely to have many children, especially newcomers from Latin America. So local officials should be sure their surplus schools will not be needed again for education before converting them to housing.

NET EVALUATION. This is a useful policy where surplus properties controlled by the local government are available.

POSSIBLE LOCAL POLICIES   193

13. Differentiate code enforcement by neighborhood.

NATURE AND PURPOSE. In theory housing and building codes are supposed to be enforced with equal rigor in every neighborhood, regardless of its physical condition or its residents' incomes. But in reality nearly every big city government enforces codes differentially by neighborhood. It upholds higher physical standards in high- and middle-income areas and areas where all structures are in excellent condition than in low-income areas and areas where many structures are somewhat or greatly deteriorated.

This selective code enforcement does not result from any conspiracy among inspectors and property owners (although corruption of building inspectors sometimes exists). Rather, it occurs where low-income households cannot afford to maintain their dwellings in full compliance with local housing codes. Many poor owner-occupants cannot keep their own homes in such compliance, and many poor tenants cannot pay high enough rents to permit their landlords to do so. Rigorous enforcement of codes in all low-income, deteriorating areas would pressure owners to make big investments bringing their properties "up to code." But some of those properties are not very profitable and could not earn enough added income to justify further investments. Many owners would abandon such properties before they would invest large additional sums in them. If local officials then evicted all the occupants because the properties were violating codes, where would those people go? In most big cities no alternative supply of dwellings in full compliance is available. Consequently, some toleration of housing code violations is nearly universal.

Why not pass housing codes that focus solely on serious hazards rather than cosmetic features? Such codes could be rigorously enforced everywhere without causing the undesirable results mentioned above. But this strategy has two serious drawbacks. Nearly every building characteristic covered by housing codes can become a serious hazard if deterioration gets bad enough. For example, violation of the requirement for well-finished walls is cosmetic if they have just a few cracks. But it can be a serious hazard if the walls are in danger of collapse or are covered with peeling, lead-based paint. Hence it is hard to design a code that focuses on truly hazardous conditions. Homeowners in affluent neighborhoods want codes that contain cosmetic elements because they want their areas maintained at very high standards.

Selective code enforcement recognizes these realities and accommodates them in a systematic, constructive way. This policy should involve the following ingredients.

—Rigorously requiring repair or demolition of all structures that are serious hazards to health or safety. This means the city should pressure owners to act as quickly as the courts will allow and take action if owners delay unduly. This is best done through an "early warning system" that spots potentially hazardous structures and follows them up closely.

—Recognizing differential quality levels as targets for code enforcement concerning nonhazardous aspects of structures. High quality should be maintained in areas where it is already well established, but lower quality permitted in other areas commensurate with prevailing conditions.

—Making the primary goal of code enforcement (other than immediate removal of hazards) the encouragement of owners to maintain their properties as well as they can, not their punishment for failing to do so. Enforcement should therefore be viewed mainly as a process of informing, persuading, and assisting owners.

—Closely linking code enforcement to counseling owners on how to maintain their properties, where to obtain financing, how to find good contractors and skilled workers, and so forth. Code enforcement should also be closely tied in with city programs, such as rehabilitation loans and homesteading. These aids should be just as readily available to owners of rental units as to owner-occupants.

DISCUSSION. Code enforcement is the most important regulatory measure available to any city government to help maintain its housing in good condition. It will work best if building inspectors have been trained to adopt a positive, persuasive attitude and have access to services that will assist owners.

In most big cities, housing inspection staffs are too small to inspect every unit periodically. Often they cannot even respond to all complaints swiftly. It may therefore seem impractical to urge them to help owners maintain their properties better and to refer those owners to appropriate sources of advice, skill, and money. Nevertheless, this basic strategy should underlie code enforcement in every city, no matter how small its staff. To make this strategy work well, the staff should be large enough to visit all heavily deteriorated areas periodically and to respond quickly to urgent complaints.

NET EVALUATION. Nearly every city containing neighborhoods in differing physical condition should practice selective code enforcement.

POSSIBLE LOCAL POLICIES 195

Doing so effectively requires strong leadership of housing inspection personnel so that they will act primarily as advocates of good maintenance.

14. Require rental units to pass code inspections before rental or sale.

NATURE AND PURPOSE. A few cities require landlords to obtain certificates of compliance with housing codes whenever they rent to new tenants or sell their units. Each owner applying for such a certificate pays a fee that covers part of the costs of the inspection then made to check compliance. Such programs are designed (1) to pressure all owners to maintain their properties well and (2) to raise each owner's confidence in the future viability of his or her neighborhood by increasing the likelihood that other owners nearby will also maintain their properties well. This higher confidence will presumably prevent each owner from failing to improve his or her property through fear of its depreciation because of surrounding deterioration.

DISCUSSION. This policy can only be carried out in communities with (1) no large deteriorated neighborhoods, (2) building department staffs big enough to conduct immediate inspections, (3) close cooperation from the police (who spot night move-ins), and (4) close cooperation from neighborhood groups (who spot other move-ins not reported by owners). If a city contains badly deteriorated neighborhoods, rigorous code enforcement there might generate as much abandonment as rehabilitation, as noted in discussing policy 13. Hence this policy is usually appropriate only in middle-sized or small cities (often suburbs) where deterioration is just starting. There the policy can be quite effective at maintaining the existing inventory in good condition. University City, Missouri—a St. Louis suburb containing about 50,000 people—started such a program in the late 1960s to help maintain housing quality during rapid racial transition. The program is still in effect and appears quite successful.[7] This policy is even more effective at maintaining single-family homes than rental units because single-family home sales are easier to monitor than changes in rental tenancy.

---

7. The program is described briefly in Department of Housing and Urban Development, Office of Policy Development and Research, *Neighborhood Preservation: A Catalog of Local Programs* (GPO, 1975), pp. 23–25.

NET EVALUATION. This policy can be used in both large cities and smaller communities that have no major deteriorated areas.

15. *Encourage owner residence in rental buildings.*

NATURE AND PURPOSE. Multifamily rental buildings in which the owners are resident are typically far better maintained than buildings owned by absentee landlords. Resident owners can respond faster to maintenance needs and tenant complaints. The owners' continual presence inhibits vandalism and inspires tenants to treat these properties better because, presumably, they know the owners can observe them mistreating it. Resident owners also have stronger incentives to keep their properties in good condition, since those properties are their home environments. Moreover, they take keener interest in what is happening throughout their neighborhoods, often by participating in community organizations. Therefore, local governments should encourage rental property owners to live in their own buildings.

DISCUSSION. Few local governments have any policies designed to encourage owners to live on their rental premises. They could offer a partial property tax exemption or tax credit for units occupied by resident landlords in structures with more than some minimal number of rental units, say, six. They could also award resident landlords better access to low-interest rehabilitation loans. Although it might be hard to determine whether owners were actually residing on their premises, concrete incentives would be far more effective in getting them to do so than mere exhortation. Moreover, the potential gains in the quality of maintenance from resident ownership over absentee ownership are huge; it would be worthwhile for a city to sacrifice considerable tax revenue to obtain them. No other local government policy is likely to have as much impact on the physical condition of a city's rental housing as persuading many more owners to live on their premises.

NET EVALUATION. This policy is hard to carry out because most incentives are not likely to change the behavior of owners. However, its potential is so great that cities should experiment much more in developing effective incentives. HUD should therefore develop some demonstration grants to help local governments pursue that goal.[8]

---

8. Since HUD funds would then be involved, this could also be considered a federal policy.

Index

Aaron, Henry, 144n, 146n
Abandonment, 195
Age distribution, 96
Allen, Garland E., 170n
American Council of Life Insurance, 101n
Anderson, Arthur, 48n
Annual Housing Survey, 2n, 29, 34, 42n, 52n, 73, 80, 103
Apartment syndicators, 5, 112
Apgar, William C., Jr., 62n
Appreciation: anticipated, 109, 110–11; condominiums and, 5; price, 129; slower, 113–14; value, 108
Assessment, 33; lowering, 186; reassessment and, 148

Baltimore, 180
Bendick, Marc, Jr., 176n
Birch, David, 88n
Boeckh, E. H., 28
Bonds: profitability model and, 111–12; state housing agencies and, 9; tax-exempt, 146, 177
Borrowing, 45–48, 137, 162. See also Capital; Loans; Mortgages
Bradbury, Katharine L., 19n, 144n, 170n
Brecher, Charles, 185n, 186n
Builder (NAHB magazine), 38
Building codes, 140; enforcing by neighborhood, 193–95; rental units and, 195–96
Bureau of the Census, 64, 153–56, 159
Bureau of Labor Statistics (BLS), 27, 29, 30
Butcher, Preston, 96n

Cain and Scott, Inc., 97n, 107n, 108
California, 138
Capital, 12, 138; borrowing terms in 1970s and, 45–78; effects of higher real costs of, 58–61; expectation of inflation and, 45; flow into housing, 43–45, 136; household savings in 1970s and, 51–54; housing versus alternative investment and, 48–49; real estate finance changes and, 54–58; rental property's disadvantages in attracting, 49–51
Capital costs: future effects of, 58–61; rent gap and, 5–6
Carter administration, 173, 175
Cash flow, 102, 110, 111, 114
Charles Shaw Company, 96n
Chicago, 42, 181
Cities. *See* Urban sector
Community development block grant (CDBG), 187
Condominiums, 83, 95, 121, 129; anticipated appreciation and, 5; conversion rate of, 40–41; interim rentals and, 51; local regulations and, 181–84; new construction and, 75–76; profitability and, 133; rental inventory and, 79–80; restricting, 149; voucher program and, 176
Congressional Budget Office (CBO), 144, 168
Connecticut, 139
Construction, 3, 6, 7–8, 14, 32, 42n, 44, 60, 61, 97, 116; housing inventory changes, 74–78, 80, 81–82, 83, 86; multifamily, 37; normative approach and, 85; public policy and, 9–10; removal of old, 40; Section 8, 172–73; shortfalls and, 117–26; supply objectives and, 133; tax abatement for, 185–86; tax shelters and, 165; withdrawals and, 17
Construction costs, 3–4, 40
Consumer price index (CPI), 3, 104, 133n; measuring rents and, 27–31
Consumption, 54; of housing space, 8
Conversions, 7, 95; banning condominium,

197

181–84; interim rentals and, 51; non-new creations and, 125, 126–27, 128, 133; of nonresidential structures, 7, 78, 184; rate for condominium, 40–41, 129; rental inventory and, 78, 79–80; of single-family homes, 188–90
Cook County, Illinois, 33, 186
Cooperative units, 75, 76, 79
Costs: of first-year occupancy, 46; housing, 7, 65; local regulations and, 191–92; for poor tenants, 10–12; rent gap and, 3–6; for users, 50. *See also* Capital costs; Construction costs; Operating costs; Rents
Cream skimming, 5, 112
Cronin, Francis J., 176n
Cullingworth, J. B., 37n
Current Population Survey, 64

Debt service, 32, 39, 46; profitability model and, 101, 114; refinancing and, 98–99, 100
de Leeuw, Frank, 62n
Demand for rental housing, 7, 35, 38, 60, 84, 115; conversion and, 41; forecasting overall, 69–70; methodology for forecasting, 62–63; need versus demand in future, 63–64; population growth and, 64–69; reduced vacancy and, 37; shift in, 33–34; shortfalls and forecasting, 119–26; withdrawals and, 17
Denver, 181
Department of Commerce, 75, 76
Department of Housing and Urban Development (HUD), 1, 19–20, 41, 51, 76, 79, 173, 181, 196
Depreciation, 61, 96n; accelerated, 165n; cost, 50; profitability model and, 102, 103, 110, 112
deSalvo, Joseph S., 36n
Developers, 3, 40, 76n, 133, 145, 146, 191
Diamond, Douglas B., 46n
Displacement, 184
Dommel, Paul R., 187n
Down payment, 109; capital costs and, 58–59; profitability model and, 102, 107; refinancing and, 97
Downs, Anthony, 19n, 47n, 93n, 138n, 140n, 144n, 170n, 191n
Drennan, Matthew, 185n

Economic Recovery Tax Act of *1981*, 48, 57, 61, 96, 102n, 117, 137, 146, 168n
Elderly, 174, 175
Equity: debt service and, 101; profitability model and, 110, 111, 114; rental housing investment and, 4, 38, 40, 45; savings and, 51, 52–53
Europe, 151
Evans, Owen, 54n

Federal Housing Administration, 146, 180, 187–88
Federal policies: adjustments for households and, 12; credit and, 136–39; desirable, 142–46; existing housing inventory and, 10; future of rental, 149–51; to help poor renters, 9, 10–12; homeownership and, 168–69; housing market and, 140–41, 143–45; importance of, 135–41; interest rates and, 135–36; limitations of, 141–42; low-interest mortgages and, 177–78; new construction and, 9–10; overview of, 131–33; public housing and, 146, 174–75, 179–80; rate ceilings and, 57; rehabilitation and, 146, 175–76; rent control and, 145–46; subsidies and, 1–2, 139, 172–74; supply and demand objectives and, 132, 133–35; tax benefit for tenants and, 169–70; taxes and, 136–39, 165–68, 168–69; tax-exempt bonds and, 146; voucher program and, 170–72, 176–77, 178–79
Feldstein, Martin, 48n
Finance. *See* Capital; Financial institutions; Refinance
Financial institutions: borrowing terms and, 45–48; debt service and, 101; expectation of inflation and, 45; real estate finance changes and, 54–58; thrift, 51, 54–55, 57, 136–38
Fitts, Jerry J., 170n
Frieden, Bernard, 96n

Giliberto, Michael, 47, 93n
Glatt, Evelyn S., 170n
Grants, 10, 175, 196
Great Britain, 12, 37, 149

Haveman, Robert H., 143n
Hendershott, Patric H., 46n, 50
Holleb, Marshall M., 170n
Homeowners: income of, 21–22; renting or owning and, 5, 12; rent raising and, 115; savings and, 52–53; size of household and, 22; units of, 7
Homeownership, 38, 49, 115, 118, 137, 164; belief in, 2–3; federal tax policy and, 168–69; husband-and-wife households and, 7, 161–163; investment in, 137–39; leveraging, 46; profitability and,

INDEX 199

58–59; rise in income and, 21; rise in rents and, 33–34; tax benefit, 11
Horton, Raymond D., 185n, 186n
Household formation, 96, 128, 156–58
Households: adjustments to help, 12; Census Bureau's projections of, 153–56; female-headed, 22n, 25, 160, 163–64; homeownership and, 2–3; male-headed, 25, 160, 163–64; projecting tenure of, 161–64; projecting types of, 158–61; renters and types of, 25; younger, 53–54, 128. *See also* Husband-and-wife households; Poor households
Household savings. *See* Savings
Household size: *1980* census and, 153, 154–56; renters and, 22–23; turnover rate and, 26
Housing allowance program, 35, 176
Housing codes, 10, 148; enforcing by neighborhood, 193–95; rental units and, 195–96
Housing construction. *See* Construction
Housing inspection staffs, 194, 195
Housing units. See Owner-occupied housing; Rental housing
Housing vouchers, 10–11, 144–45, 146, 150, 170–72, 174, 176–77, 179
HUD. *See* Department of Housing and Urban Development
Hughes, James W., 33n, 158
Hu, Joseph C., 157
Husband-and-wife households: homeownership and, 25; increase in, 21n; projections and, 160; renting decline and, 68, 70, 124, 130; switching from renting to ownership and, 7; tenure of households and, 161–63. *See also* Households

Immigrants, 148, 155, 192
Incentives: federally funded, 142, 145; owner residence and, 196
Income, 55, 60, 66; housing and, 12; inflation and, 46, 48; investors and taxable, 144n; physically inadequate units and, 19n; poor household, 20, 31, 38, 143n, 144; renter, 21–22; rents and, 27–28; Section 8 subsidies and, 131n; sheltering, 96. *See also* Rental income
Income maintenance program, 171–72
Inflation, 50, 52, 56, 57, 93, 107, 111, 112, 114, 135, 137; carrying costs and, 46; interest rates and fear of, 5; investments and, 48, 49; lenders and, 45; leveraging during, 95; real estate finance and, 54, 55; rent control and, 36; rents and, 38–39

Interest rates, 9, 59, 66, 92, 95, 109, 118, 139, 144, 165, 168, 169n; adverse effects of, 5; contract, 28; federal policies and, 135–36; inflation and, 5, 94–95, 137; low nominal, 45, 55; market expectations and, 93–94; mortgages and, 177–78; profitability model and, 101–02, 103, 106, 112, 113; real estate finance changes and, 56–58; real and nominal, 47–48; refinancing and, 97, 98, 99, 100; rehabilitation and, 175–76, 187; rental units and, 8; rent gap and, 4
Investment: gap, 99; housing, 33, 137–39, 145; in housing versus alternative sectors, 48–49; initial cash, 39; permission process and, 191; reinvestment and, 169. *See also* Capital
Investors, 3, 61, 76; income taxes and, 144n; leveraging and small, 38–39; profitability and, 109–113; sale of public housing to, 179–80; tax shelters and, 38. *See also* Small-scale investors

Jaffee, Dwight, 156n, 157
Johnson, M. Bruce, 96n
Jones, Mary S., 44n

Kain, John, 62n
Khadduri, Jill, 20, 139n, 144n, 172n
Kullberg, Duane R., 48n

Landlords, 8, 94, 172; absentee, 196; fear of rent control and, 36–37; poor tenants and, 31–32; in residence, 196; tax benefits and, 169–70
Land use, 141–42, 147, 149
Leveraging, 109, 110; borrowing and, 45–46; homeownership and, 46, 59; inflation and, 95; initial equity, 114; lenders and, 6; operating income and, 4
Lincoln Properties, 61, 96n, 112
Loans, 47, 137; apartment property, 28; low-interest, 10, 45, 175–76; Section 312, 175, 187. *See also* Borrowing; Mortgages
Local housing agencies, 180
Local policies, 94; assessment, 186; code enforcement and, 193–95; condominium regulations and, 181–84; existing inventory and, 10; local ordinances and, 147–49; multifamily housing densities and, 10; overview, 131–33; owner-occupied housing tax and, 33; owner residence and, 196; permission process and, 191–92; schools for rental housing and, 192; single-family unit conversion and, 188–

90; supply and demand objectives and, 133–35; surplus federal housing and, 187–88; tax abatement, 184–86
Low-income households. *See* Poor households
Lowry, Ira S., 4n, 23n, 27n, 28n, 30, 31, 35, 36n, 102–07
Lugar, Richard, 173
Lynn, Laurence E., 143n

McGough, Duane T., 16, 127n
Maintenance, 3, 19; income payments and, 171–72; owner residence and, 196
Management, 40, 95
Market adjustment, shortfalls and, 127–30
Market value, 40; forecasting, 114–16; influences on, 92–95; model for profitability and, 100–09; rent gap and, 4; vacancy and, 37
Masnick, George, 156n
Methodology (demand forecasting), 62–63, 87n
Migration, 6
Mobile homes, 7, 18, 75, 81, 86
Model for profitability and market value, 100–09. *See also* Market value; Profitability
Money market certificates, 55
Mortgages, 12, 49, 55, 56, 144, 162, 168, 169n; capital costs and, 59–60; capital flow and, 43–44; fixed rate, 38–39, 46; interest rate policy and, 135; low-interest, 177–78; profitability model and, 101–02, 103, 113; refinancing and, 97–100; subsidy for, 173–74; thrifts and, 136–39
Moving. *See* Turnover
Multifamily housing: conversion from single-family units, 188–90; densities and, 10, 190–91; forecasting, 118; new construction and, 37, 74, 76, 81; owner residence in, 196; replacement and, 87; zoning and, 190

Nanopoulos-Stergiou, Georgia, 185n
National Association of Home Builders, 192
Neighborhoods: code enforcement and, 193–95; consultation with residents in, 191; cooperation with, 195; rental housing shortages in urban, 42
New York, 139
New York City, 42; rent control in, 36, 134–35, 150; tax abatements in, 184, 185–86
Non-new housing units. *See* Conversions

Nonresidential structures. *See* Conversions

Occupancy: first-year costs and, 46; high-turnover, 61; of small housing units, 6
Operating costs, 39, 46; profitability model and, 101, 102, 104, 106, 107, 109; raising rents and, 36n; refinancing and, 98–99; rent gap and, 4, 5, 28, 40
Out-migration, 6
Owner-occupied housing, 43n, 145, 148, 188; conversion and, 74n; expansion of, 14; household size and, 22, 23; inventory, 80–83, 87; local tax and, 33; multifamily units and, 76; price appreciation and, 129; rent controls and, 141; shortfalls, 119–22; tax policies and, 136; turnover rate and, 26; user cost and, 50; value of, 52n. *See also* Homeowners; Homeownership; Single-family housing
Ownership housing. *See* Owner-occupied housing
Ozanne, Larry, 28n, 29, 30n

Palmer, John L., 143n
Physical inadequacy, 19, 63, 88
Pitkin, John, 156n
Plotnick, Robert D., 143n
Policy. *See* Federal policies; Local policies; State policies
Political pressure, 36
Poor households: defined, 20; income and, 31; inflation and, 38; owners and, 31–32; physically inadequate units and, 63; policies to help, 9, 10–12; public housing and, 174–75; rent and, 34; rent escalation and, 133; subsidies and, 131n, 139, 143–45, 151, 178; use of older units and, 148; voucher program and, 170–72, 176; zoning and, 140, 141, 191. *See also* Households
Population, 153, 155
Population growth, 64–69
Poverty. *See* Poor households
Poverty level, 131n, 143
Premiums on interest rates, 56–57. *See also* Interest rates
Prices, 108; home, 5–6; land, 190; profitability and, 111; rental housing, 4
Private rental markets. *See* Rental housing; Unsubsidized housing
Profitability, 32, 190; capital costs and, 58, 59; forecasting, 114–16; importance of, 3; inflation and, 38; influences on, 95–96; interest rates and, 135; market value and, 92–95; model for, 100–09; refinancing and, 97–100, 103; rent decline and

INDEX

investment profit increase and, 109–13; slower appreciation and, 113–114; supply and demand and, 133; vacancy and, 37

Property taxes. See Taxes, property

Public housing, 146, 174–75, 179; selling to occupants, 179–80; surplus federal housing and, 187–88. See also Poor households; Federal policies; Local policies

Public policy. See Federal policies; Local policies

Quality of housing, 128, 140

Rand Corporation, 36
Rasmussen, David W., 176n
Rates of return, 3, 110; down payment, 59; household savings and, 51–52; inflation and, 39
Reagan administration, 1, 131, 145, 171n, 173n, 175
Real estate finance changes, 54–58
Refinance, 32; profitability and, 97–100, 103; shift to, 44
Regulation: condominiums and local, 181–84; conversions and, 189; costs and local, 191–92; deposits in thrifts and, 55, 57; of housing, 140
Rehabilitation, 90, 146, 195, 196; low-interest loans for, 175–76, 187. See also Renovation
Removed units. See Withdrawals
Renovation, 32, 180, 188. See also Rehabilitation
Rental housing: capital flow into, 43–45; characteristics of, 13–20; current trends in, 2–3; demand for, 7; demand forecasting and, 62–70; disadvantages of attracting capital to, 49–51; equity gain and, 52–53; in Europe, 151; future supply of, 7–8; high costs of capital and, 58–61; investments in other sectors and, 48–49; physically inadequate, 19, 63, 88; real estate finance changes and, 54–58; rent gap and, 3–6, 8, 11, 40–42, 115, 150; renter traits and, 21–26; schools as, 192; surplus FHA units as, 146. See also Federal policies; Local policies
Rental housing inventory, 13; changes in, 14–18, 73–79; conditions in, 18–19; conversions and, 77–78; growth rate and, 73–74; net replacement rates and, 84–89; new construction and, 74–78, 80, 81–82, 83, 86; non-new units and, 17, 18, 78; owner-occupied housing and, 80–83; rent and, 33–34; subsidized, 19–20; use of existing, 10; withdrawals and, 77–78

Rental housing shortfalls: forecasting demand and, 119–21; future construction compared with future demand and, 121–26; market adjustment and, 127–30; need vs. demand, 63–64; projected new construction and, 117–19; severity of, 1; urban, 42; withdrawals and non-new units and, 126–27

Rental income: inflation and, 39; rent gap and, 3–6; vacancy and, 35. See also Income

Rental units. See Rental housing; Rental housing inventory

Rent controls, 6, 8, 9, 39, 95, 116; landlord fear of, 36–37; local policies and, 149–51; market intervention and, 140–41; in New York City, 36, 134–35, 150; prohibition of, 145–46; rental supply and, 11–12

Renters. See Tenants

Rent gap, 3–6, 8, 11, 40–42, 115, 150

Rents, 60; consumer price index and measuring, 27–31; increases in, 133, 146; inflation and, 38–39; investment profit increase and decline in, 109–13; poor tenants and, 10–12, 31–32; profitability model and, 103–07; reason for slow rise in, 32–38; rent gap and, 3–6, 8, 11, 40–42, 115, 150; required increases in, 95, 103–07; residential, 115; shortfalls and, 128; turnover and increasing, 61

Replacement, 63, 84–91, 125–26, 130

Roistacher, Elizabeth A., 1n, 186n

Rosen, Kenneth, 62n, 156n, 157

Rydell, C. Peter, 37n

Santa Monica, 134
Savings, 51–54, 55, 137–38
Sawhill, Isabel V., 143n
Schools as rental housing, 192
Seattle, 4
Shortages. See Owner-occupied housing; Rental housing shortfalls
Simon, Lawerence, 1n
Single-family housing, 9, 15, 138, 175, 191, 195; assessment and, 186; decline in sale of, 57–58; into multifamily units, 188–90; new construction and, 74, 76, 81; profitability model and, 113–14; replacement and, 86; small-scale investors and, 50–51; zoning and, 190. See also Owner-occupied housing

201

Skidmore, Felicity, 143n
Small-scale investors: dominance of, 34–35; profitability model and, 114, rents and, 34–35, 40; single-family units and, 50–51; tax shelter and, 38; vacancy and, 35. *See also* Investors
Smith, Laurence B., 37n
Soldo, Beth J., 175n
State policies: overview, 131–33; supply and demand objectives and, 133–35; tax exempt bonds and, 9
Sternlieb, George, 33, 158
Stocks, 48; profitability model and, 111–12
Storey, James R., 143n
Struyk, Raymond J., 20n, 62n, 139n, 144n, 172n, 175n, 176n, 178n
Subdivision ordinances, 140, 148, 188–90
Subsidies, 9, 10, 64, 85, 134, 138, 149, 170, 171, 186; direct, 178; housing inventory characteristics and, 19–20; mortgage, 173–74; new housing for poor, 148; to poor renters, 139, 143–45, 151; rehabilitation, 187; Section 8, 20, 131n, 172–73; Section 236, 20; tax shelter policy and, 165; for tenants, 178–79; unsubsidized housing versus, 1–2. *See also* Unsubsidized housing
Suburban sector: conversion of older housing in, 189; exclusionary zoning and, 140, 141; multifamily zoning and, 190
Summers, Lawrence, 48n
Supply of rental housing, 7–8, 35, 85, 150; rent control and, 11–12. *See also* Rental housing inventory
Surrey, Stanley S., 48n
Syndicators, 5, 112

Taxes, 110; abatements for conversion and, 184; abatements for new rental housing and, 185–86; affluent and, 139; benefits, 11, 38, 102, 169–70; bracket creep and, 48; capital gains, 109–10, 168; federal policy and, 168–69; interest deductibility and, 103; mortgage interest and, 144–45; property, 10, 39, 141, 144, 165, 170, 185–86; rehabilitated property and, 10
Tax-exempt bonds, 9, 146, 177
Tax shelter, 39, 61, 109, 110; advantages of, 38; federal policy and, 165–68; high-bracket investors and, 4; profitability and, 95–96, 114
Tenants, 94, 95, 190; household size and, 22–23; household tenure and, 163–64; household types and, 25; income of, 21–22; increase in unit for, 42n; owners and poor, 31–32; rent increases and, 133; rise in rents and poor, 34; selling public housing to, 179–80; subsidies for, 178–79; tax benefits for, 169–70; turnover rates and, 25–26
Thibodeau, Thomas, 29, 30n
Tobier, Emanuel, 186n
Tomlinson, Peter, 37n
Transfer payments, 143n
Turnover, 61, 95, 112; investors in housing and, 34–35; renters and, 25–26

Uncertainty: forecasting, 90; future values and, 120; inflation and, 56
Units. *See* Owner-occupied housing; Rental housing; Single-family housing
University City, Missouri, 195
Unsubsidized housing, 39, 60, 133, 188; construction of new, 7–8; slowdown in, 40, 42; subsidized housing versus, 1–2. *See also* Subsidies
Urban sector, 42, 142, 189, 191

Vacancy, 70; demand and, 37; recessions and, 115; shortfall forecasts and, 121–26; slow rise in rents and, 37; small-scale owners and, 35; tenant subsidies and, 179
Villani, Kevin E., 1n, 2n
Voucher entitlements. *See* Housing vouchers

Washington, D.C., 181
Weicher, John C., 1n, 44n
West Germany, 12
Withdrawals, 15; condominium conversions and, 41; housing inventory changes and, 77–78, 82–83; permanent, 17; replacement and, 84; shortfalls and, 126–27, 128–29; slower building of new units and, 40; temporary, 16–17
Woodfill, Barbara M., 36n

Yap, Lorene, 44n
Yezer, Anthony M., 19n, 29n
Yield. *See* Rates of return

Zoning, 10, 188; densities for multifamily housing and, 10, 190–91; exclusionary, 140, 141, 191; local (land use), 147; multifamily, 190; permission process and, 191–92